International Views

Other readers featured in the "Longman Topics" series include:

A Longman Topics Reader

International Views

America and the Rest of the World

KEITH GUMERY
Temple University

PEARSON
Longman

New York   San Francisco   Boston
London   Toronto   Sydney   Tokyo   Singapore   Madrid
Mexico City   Munich   Paris   Cape Town   Hong Kong   Montreal

Senior Sponsoring Editor: Virginia L. Blanford
Marketing Manager: Sandra McGuire
Production Manager: Donna DeBenedictis
Project Coordination and Electronic Page Makeup: Integra Software
    Services Private Limited
Cover Design Manager: John Callahan
Cover Designer: Kay Petronio
Cover Photo: Courtesy of Corbis, Inc.
Manufacturing Manager: Lucy Hebard
Printer and Binder: Courier Corporation/Westford
Cover Printer: The Lehigh Press, Inc.

Library of Congress Control Number: 2006013738

Please visit us at www.ablongman.com

ISBN 0-321-38881-X

1 2 3 4 5 6 7 8 9 10—CRW—09 08 07 06

This book is dedicated to

Ray and Edith Gumery
with love as always

and to

Richard Shortt
because I promised

CONTENTS

This book is an anthology of readings from different perspectives designed for college writing students. The readings have been chosen to offer differing points of view, suggest areas for research and argumentation, and widen our understanding of how the United States sees the world and how the world, in turn, sees the United States and its influence. The articles have been collected from a variety of sources and disciplines and include work by writers who are U.S. based and writers who are spokespeople for the Rest of the World. I felt that it was important to keep the focus of this collection current, and so many of the incidents and key figures referred to in the collection are specific as well as being part of a wider picture and subject to wider issues.

While I was working on this book I turned on the television and found myself watching an ice-skating tournament. The contest? The United States versus the Rest of the World. It seemed to me that this is so often the dichotomy that is set up in many fields, not just sport, and yet in this culture that is so focused on the idea of athletic competition it was a way into the kind of thinking I want to address here. In the field of sports, the United States will often realign national competition and recast it as international or global. In football, for example, the national champion is crowned world champion; the baseball championship is called the World Series; and the winner of the NBA title is named as the champion of the world. None of these sports comes close to the international reach of, for example, soccer or rugby; sports that are played globally and in which U.S. teams compete but with limited success. Olympic coverage over the years has illustrated the myopic approach that is foisted onto us by the networks as an assumption of what we viewers want to see. Heats of events are shown only if there is an American competitor involved. Coverage is interspersed with the hard-luck stories of American athletes who have overcome great odds. Are their hardships really greater than an athlete from Ethiopia, Sudan, or a state with an oppressive and discriminatory government? Is the American public being done a disservice by the judicial presentation of a localized and limited view? Such coverage simply sets up the idea that the United States is competing against the bulk known as the Rest of the World, instead of competition seen as being multi-faceted, with other nations competing against each other as well as against the United States. When U.S. sports figures travel overseas, it is true that they are given great attention by fans from other countries. Often this is due to the exposure that they have received through commercial endorsements or guest appearances on entertainment shows that have been marketed internationally.

Sometimes, it is true, that the appeal of U.S. athletes is often unrelated to their sporting ability: Shaquille O'Neal, for example, is an attraction for some overseas fans simply because of his enormous size rather than his playing ability. Interestingly enough, one of the few successful imports into the American culture of advertising and endorsement has been Yao Ming, the seven-foot, five-inch basketball player for the Houston Rockets. His size has been his fortune, providing an identifiable figure to promote products such as Apple computers, Visa cards, and Nike. However, this is synergy that rarely works both ways. The use of athletes to market products, and the salaries they command, is not particular to the American market, yet it is on a greater scale than elsewhere in the world. Perhaps this is why the expectations of American success in the world arena are so much greater than elsewhere: for example, an American swimmer who had recorded a personal best and won an Olympic silver medal was asked by the interviewer, "What went wrong?"

For many people around the world knowledge of the United States comes from popular culture as well as from sport. I grew up in the United Kingdom, and my view of the United States was formed before I ever came here. Walking around New York was like being on a film set: Smoking manholes covers were a big thrill for me because they MEANT New York. I knew them from television shows and movies. A steaming manhole cover was as much an establishing shot as one of the Empire State building. It came as no surprise to me to see film crews working on the streets of New York City. In a sense, also, it came as no surprise that the cataclysm of a September morning in 2001 also happened there. It is New York after all that is the target for alien attacks in cinematic blockbusters such as *Independence Day*. So many comments about the attack on the World Trade Center echoed this, likening the images of the planes hitting the towers as being "just like a movie." New York is also often the cinematic target of natural disasters, from *The Day After Tomorrow* to *Armageddon*. When the great natural disaster of our times did hit, the tsunami of December 2004, it was not New York but the coastlines of south Asia that took the brunt of the force. The movies of the tsunami from shaky video cameras may not have the scale of the American blockbusters, but the devastation was greater and the loss of life real and not digitally rendered.[1]

Iconic images, like the Hollywood sign in Los Angeles, carry power for those who have grown up understanding that the center of cultural power lies in the film industry of the United States. How easy it is for us to forget (or never to find out) that the Indian film industry challenges the U.S. output in terms of viewers, revenues, and star power and that the output of the Chinese film industry, for example, reaches as many people as American movies (the majority being within China's own borders). But while these markets can also carry American films, the American market rarely makes room for overseas movies. Instead, we are more likely to see American studios remaking overseas movies in an American image. *The Vanishing*, *The Ring*, *The Grudge*, *The Good Thief*, *The Birdcage*, *The Magnificent Seven*, *City of Angels*, *Vanilla Sky*, and *Insomnia*[2] were all American-funded remakes of films from overseas—rarely bettering the originals and often (as in the case of *The Vanishing*) removing elements that made the originals seminal. These are only a few examples. There are many more.

The purpose of this collection of readings, then, is to examine both the reach of American influence and power and how those outside the United States feel about it and react to it. Clearly recent events have caused a seismic shift in the U.S. relationship with many countries and governments around the world—traditional allies as well as those with whom it has had long ideological disagreements. For many of these countries, U.S. military involvement in various theaters has compounded the problems that led to primary resistance to American power—Iraq has seen a wave of insurgency; the Taliban in Afghanistan appears to be regrouping; and Al-Qaeda has claimed a series of attacks throughout the Arab world and beyond.

---

[1]The devastation of Hurricanes Katrina and Rita on the southern coast of the United States should not be underestimated, but the tsunami killed over 175,000 people, while the official U.S. death toll was just over 1000.

[2]These movies represent films originally from Holland, Japan, France, Germany, Spain, and Norway.

While the reach of American cultural and economic power is undoubted, another aspect that is becoming increasingly vital is how those outside of the United States feel about this influence—how they see it and moves they are making to struggle against it. This discussion has become important and unavoidable since the events of 2001, and how the United States has reacted to actions that were, in their own way, a reaction will determine much about the way the world situation develops for some time to come. The reach of American power and influence has been unnoticed or uncommented upon for many years, and yet it has been globally pervasive. For many, this has been positive, but for others American involvement in their lives has come to be troubling and disruptive.

There is no doubt that the influence of the United States in the world is tremendous. Economically and culturally, the United States exercises influence that reaches far beyond its borders and appears in the daily lives of millions around the globe. It might be in the employment that people have, working for American companies in their home land. It could be in the influence of American music, fashion, movies, or the kind of food that they are eating.

American political influence in the world is often seen by other countries as being condescending and controlling, challenging the autonomy of sovereign nations. The United States has the economic power to advance its wishes, and if that does not work there is military power of mammoth proportions to back it up. In the last few decades we have seen American economic and military might used to advance agendas in countries around the world, from the continuing embargo on Cuba to the invasion of Iraq. The divisions between the United States and the United Nations have highlighted a gulf that exists between the world's mightiest power and the other constituents of the planet. The unilateral decision to pursue military deployment in Iraq has caused a sense of unease internationally that will be hard to defuse. When one country has the ability to go-it-alone against the declared wishes of a sizeable coalition, there is an imbalance that nullifies international cooperation and increases the very resentment and opposition that such military action was supposed to eliminate. In international treaties the United States will often stand away from an agreement that relies on its agreement, becoming—in a sense—a majority of one. The U.S. refusal to back the Kyoto agreement on the reduction of greenhouse gas emissions is an example of this. Another would be the United States opposing the creation of a nuclear arsenal by other nations while it continues to maintain its own. This may be seen as a question of trust. The United States trusts itself to be responsible with the power of nuclear weapons, but it does not trust other nations to act in the same way. On the other hand, many nations around the world do not trust the U.S. administration to be responsible. After all, the United States is the only nation to ever deploy nuclear weapons during a conflict.

Many nations around the world, then, often see the United States as an imperial power imposing its might and ideological underpinnings on smaller and weaker states. Even in areas where economic investment or military intervention has been to the improvement of vast numbers of people, there can still be resentment. We might think that capitalism and a free-market economy is the best way to operate, but other countries would disagree with us and may feel that imposing such a system on them would lead to more hardship than good. Sometimes this can be the case. Why would anyone oppose progress and new technology, we might ask? Well, it might be that such change would compromise traditions and ways of operating that have been successful for hundreds of years. Such implementation could lead to massive upheaval, a loss of national identity, the destruction of a heritage, and a feeling of being occupied—if not physically, then through the imposition of ideals. Think, for example, of how you might feel if China decided that the American government was letting down its people because it didn't offer universal state-supported health care, launching an ideological and military mission to force such change. If the government didn't comply, then the Chinese government would feel obligated to move in and force the change for the general good. Many would benefit from this, but national resentment about such interference would be high, because so many other factors would come into play: national identity; political autonomy; democratic governmental ideals; outside "tampering."

There is a general assumption within the United States that reaching out into the rest of the world and imposing the U.S. will is a good thing for the world in general. From the perspective of the rest of the world this is rarely true. Some aspects of American influence may be welcomed—clothing styles, movies, music—but other elements of American influence are seen as much more problematic. Military action, pollution caused by American companies operating overseas, and (increasingly in recent years) a perception of a divine right given by a Judeo-Christian God to make decisions for people of all faiths will all lead to resistance and resentment.

How you react to these articles and the points of view that they put forward is for you to gauge. Some may make you angry, while others may enlighten you. It is important to remember that these are real voices, coming from people with real experience in the world beyond the borders of the United States. Your feelings, thoughts, and opinions will define whether you leave this book feeling that it is the United States *versus* the Rest of the World or whether there is a way for the United States *and* the Rest of the World to find a balance that works for all.

KEITH GUMERY

ACKNOWLEDGMENTS

I would like to thank the authors included in this book for their thoughtful and important work. I extend my personal gratitude to those who kindly waived their own fees because they supported the scope and purpose of this project. This includes both American authors and those from around the world—ideological differences were set aside for the purpose of education, and I thank you.

I am grateful to the reviewers of this manuscript, whose comments informed its development, including Russel Durst, University of Cincinnati; Kathleen Hohenleitner, University of Central Florida; Rick Iadonisi, Grand Valley State University; Kevin Mahoney, Kutztown University; and Richard Zumkhawala-Cook, Shippensburg University.

I appreciate the input and perspective offered by family and friends while I was working on this project as well as the support of my colleagues and peers at Temple University in Philadelphia.

K. G.

What the World Thinks of America

In 2004 Andrew Marr, the BBC's political editor, presented a unique BBC-led global television debate about the place of the United States in the world. Here he explores the links and divisions between the United Kingdom and America, while a journalist from Jordan and one from Brazil reflect on the feelings towards the United States from within their own countries. In these commentaries we get a view of America from Europe, the Middle East, and South America. These views and opinions were posted onto the BBC website, and they are a good place for us to begin to recognize a multiplicity of international voices and opinions.

UNITED KINGDOM

Once upon a time the Americans were the British lost on the narrow lip of a distant continent, clutching their faith, songs, customs and memories. They were 17th Century space travellers, cut off from Planet Europe with its corruptions and tyrannies. Today, the British sometimes seem more like strayed Americans, islanders who speak American, watch American, eat American, and increasingly think American too. Looking at us, a visiting anthropologist from Mars might conclude that we must be a tribe of migrants from Pennsylvania who ended up, for obscure reasons, squatting off France. Almost all countries in the world are touched, in some way, by American power—Hollywood reaches deep into Asia and Russians eat Big Macs—but the British are more intensely soaked in U.S. culture than anyone else, except the Canadians. This is about language, first and foremost;

though France, for instance, is heavily Americanised, the French language acts as a formidable buffer, as does German.

Multi-Ethnicity

The second reason for the similarity is that Britain, like the U.S., is a fully multi-ethnic country. British multi-ethnicity is different in history and tempo. It is not about a fresh slate but an old empire. As British Asians sometimes put it: "We're only over here because you were over there." But the effect is to make the UK as open to cultural mingling and change as coastal America. London has more language communities and international business headquarters than New York. Manchester has even more Sikh taxi-drivers than Boston. Third, of course, there is history. The U.S. constitution is an idealised and codified reworking of British constitutional thinking. American business practice grew from the commercial laws, property rights and trading customs of 18th Century London and Bristol. For all these reasons, and lesser ones, modern Britain has been more open, more porous, to contemporary American power than rivals.

Class Divide

Modern Britain is *The Simpsons*, *24*, *Friends*, Starbucks, Amazon, Gap, the White Stripes and Michael Moore, along with the Commons, the Queen and Martin Amis. There are class elements to this, since the posher British are likelier to feel themselves European, with their Italian holiday homes and raggedly idiomatic French, while the poorer, because they watch more telly, absorb more American programming and American food. Where are the evangelical churches gaining ground in Britain? Among the poorer blacks and whites of the inner cities. But British-Americanism transcends class too. The high-income political obsessives of Westminster hoover up the latest books on Clinton and Bush, watch *The West Wing* and speculate about Ari Fleischer's future. Writers I know who cross the Atlantic like frantic petrels wryly describe themselves as "Nylons" (New Yorker-Londoners) or, more poetically, Atlanticans. Dig below the surface similarities, and you find deeper ones—the shared interest in global policing, the more-similar-than-not business cultures, the high level of internet usage, the populations that will continue to grow as those of France, Germany and Italy fall.

Vive la Difference?

But if British-Americanism is intense, it also offers an interesting lesson for the rest of the world: for the corollary seems to be an equally intense desire to assert a different identity too. You find it in humour; in sport; in the monarchy (far stronger than most people would have predicted a decade ago). You will see it in Britain's newspaper culture; in soap operas and the tone of British television news; in the mere existence of Radio 4, which is perhaps the most un-American act carried out daily in English; and in the generally far less religious atmosphere of modern Britain, a secular, indeed Godless place by American standards. When British culture stands up to, or against, American culture, it is persistent and dogged. Baseball has made no inroads. President Bush's born-again Methodism is met with blank disbelief, or amazed distaste. In Britain, there is no issue deader than the death penalty. And what patriotism is to middle America, knowing self-deprecation is to middle Britain. It is as if there is a complex, winding internal border in the mind of every British adult. On the one side there is a shared American culture which enriches our lives. When, after September 11, the "Star-Spangled Banner" was played outside Buckingham Palace, or at the last night of the Proms, it was a family tribute. But on the other side of that mental border is an untouched other, a way of feeling that is beyond the reach of Drs Kissinger or Seuss.

For the British it is impossible not to be American and intolerable to be only American. It is a condition of self-division that may become universal. This double-ness can be held in any head without pain, and indeed with great pleasure. The trick is understanding that, in a world which has America, any form of local purity is an impossible mirage.

• • •

JORDAN

Al Jazeera's Lamees Al Hadidi examines Jordan's position in the Arab world and its relationship with the United States.

Trapped between the Palestinian-Israeli conflict and the Iraqi-Gulf conflict, Jordanian relations with the U.S. have been subject to extreme changes. Throughout much of its history, Jordan has been a pro-Western, modernising country that has adopted moderate policies on most regional issues. Its small size and lack of major economic resources have made it dependent on aid from Western and neighbouring Arab countries, which presents a dilemma: whether to adopt American policies or look out for Arab interests.

Jordan's geographic position—wedged between Israel, Syria, Iraq and Saudi Arabia—has made it vulnerable to the strategic designs of its more powerful neighbours, but has also given Jordan an important role as a buffer between these potential adversaries. This, and other reasons, led the U.S. to depend on Jordan and on its late King Hussain, then his son King Abdulla, to help sustain its policies in the Middle East.

Rift over Iraq

The 1990s, however, saw a brief rift in American-Jordanian relations. Jordan had close economic ties with Iraq, which allowed it to import cheap oil. Initially, King Hussain expressed an unwillingness to join the allied coalition against Iraq after its invasion of Kuwait, which disrupted relations between the U.S. and the Gulf States. However, that did not last long. The same King Hussain changed course by getting more involved in the Arab-Israeli peace process in late 1991 by tightening the enforcement of UN economic sanctions against Iraq, allowing an Iraqi opposition group to establish an office in Jordan and permitting U.S. fighter aircrafts in Jordan to help enforce the no-fly zone in southern Iraq. Jordan, nevertheless, managed to maintain long-standing economic ties with Baghdad and the popular sympathy many Jordanians have with the Iraqi people; at least 400,000 Iraqis live in Jordan. Jordan's role in the peace process was another milestone in its relations with the U.S. In October 1994, Jordan and Israel signed a fully-fledged peace treaty at a ceremony on the Jordanian-Israeli border attended by former U.S. President Bill Clinton.

U.S. Aid

The history of American aid to Jordan goes back to 1951. Total aid given until 1997 is estimated at $3.9bn including $2.1bn in economic assistance and $1.8bn in military aid. Levels of American aid have fluctuated, increasing in response to threats faced by Jordan and decreasing during periods of political tension. In 1991, due to Jordan's sympathy for Iraq during the Gulf crisis, the U.S. Congress suspended aid to Jordan. But the president exercised a waiver later that year to maintain informal funds. After signing a peace treaty with Israel, stipulation on aid to Jordan was removed. As part of a 5-year Middle East peace and stability fund announced by the Clinton administration in 1997, both Egypt and Israel agreed to the diversion of $50m from each of their respective aid programmes in 1997 and 1998 to augment economic aid funds available to Jordan. That brought U.S. economic aid to Jordan to $112m in 1997 and $150m in 1998, and total aid for Jordan for those years to $152m and $228m respectively (including military aid). Since then U.S. aid stabilised at $150m in economic assistance, $75m in foreign military financing and $1.6m in international military education and training. In 2003, however, the Bush administration sought to double the U.S. aid to Jordan in view of its support for the "War on Terror." In October 2000, Jordan and the U.S. signed a free trade agreement, the third for the U.S. and its first with an Arab state, which eliminates duties and commercial barriers to bilateral trade in goods and services originating in the two countries.

Jordanian "Anger"

Great political and economic ties between Jordan and the U.S., however, do not reflect the mood in the Jordanian street. Because of American support for Israel—perhaps half the Jordanian population originates from Palestine—and the anger at what happened in Iraq, the Jordanians find themselves filled with deep anger at American policies. That anger was reflected in several violent acts against U.S. diplomats and local police. Though the Jordanian Government has described them as "isolated incidents," these were signs of resentment of U.S. policies in the region, and this anger cannot be mended by free trade agreements or direct economic assistance. Whether that will change with more American involvement in implementing the road map, and exhorting more pressure on Israel, remains to be seen.

• • •

BRAZIL

TV Globo's Renato Machado reflects on the love-hate relationship his country has with the United States.

Brazilians' feelings towards the United States have turned bitter, to say the least. There has always been a stream of anti-Americanism running through Brazil's intelligentsia. A double-sided sort of mistrust was fed through populist politics by the nationalist dictatorships which ruled most of Latin America through the 1980s.

But together with political malaise, an unabashed admiration of the American way of life also ran deep in people's minds. Movies, jeans, music, comics and heroes formed a solid cultural block which eventually became a model for art and business. The critical view of the U.S., shared by other nations, tends to confound the American Government and the American people, who in the end carry the blame for the Bush administration's foreign policy simplifications.

American Empire?

Many think Americans agree with the Pentagon's view of the world. Or George W Bush's view, for that matter. The "You are either with us or against us" syndrome has made things worse. In other words, the war against Iraq deepened the perception of the United States as an empire which simply dictates its overwhelming economic and strategic interests, defying any diplomatic considerations, even if it meant running over the UN, as it did. Few journalists and commentators stressed the international importance of getting rid of a ruthless dictator such as Saddam Hussein. The existence of many cumbersome dictatorships on the United States' side, like Saudi Arabia and Egypt, to name a few, has made the argument pointless. To say nothing of the fact that the reason for the war—weapons of mass destruction illegally possessed by Saddam Hussein's regime—is now little more than a cynical excuse. Still, the cult of American values such as freedom and cultural glamour persist. One wonders if consumer goods and Gwyneth Paltrow's charm at the Oscar extravaganza can by themselves turn the page on a damaged record.

CHAPTER 1

Globalization or Americanization?

As technology has allowed communication and trade to bypass the physical world and inhabit the digital realm, it has become possible for countries all over the world to compete and contribute to the global marketplace and international culture. The United States, with its financial and physical advantages, has obviously been in a position of great influence, reaching out to shape other nations, often in its own image. The opening of a global market has been seen by some, chiefly the influential and affluent Western nations, as something positive. The countries that come under such Western influence, however, may not see this effect as completely constructive. While the lives of some may be improved immeasurably, the lives and cultures of others may be the price paid by Western-influenced "progress."

This is why the concept of globalization is sometimes seen by those affected as nothing more than Americanization. This process can lead to political and militaristic resistance as well as ideological outrage.

The essays in this chapter reflect different points of view on this issue and clarify many of the terms involved in such a discussion. The writers consider the benefits and shortcomings of globalization, the influence of the United States in forming the ideology of the global marketplace, and possible elements of resistance. Economists, political analysts, journalists, and cultural critics try to make sense of the power paradigm of global influence. Thomas L. Friedman examines our acceptance of the balance of power and questions whether the United States can and will retain the preeminent position in a free market that it has so often encouraged.

Americanization

ROGER DE LA GAARDE

In his essay, Roger de la Gaarde is examining the cultural outreach and influence of American materials and ideas. He begins with an example of how American culture and an older, more traditional culture interact and how a Canadian news program reported it. From there, de la Gaarde examines what he calls "cultural imperialism" and its insidious effect. His point lies in the assertion that the main effect of American influence lies in the use of American goods and cultural influence, rather than in the actual supply of such materials. This essay is taken from the archive of the Museum of Broadcast Communications in Chicago, Illinois.

———————————— ✦ ————————————

During a nightly newscast of *CBC (Canadian Broadcasting Corporation) Prime Time News*, the anchorman, in the last news item before the public affairs portion of the program, presented words to this effect: How would you like to have a house that would cost next to nothing to build and to maintain, no electrical, and no heating bills? Viewers were then shown four young Inuit adults building an igloo. They were born in the Arctic region, said the spokeswoman of the group, but had not learned the ancestral skills of carving (literally) a human shelter out of this harsh environment (−35 Celsius at night). It was a broad hint that the spin on this story would be "Young Aboriginals in search of their past." The real twist, however, was that their instructors, a middle aged man and woman, were Caucasian and that the man was born in Detroit. The American had studied something which sounded like environmental architecture and was teaching this particular technique to the young Inuits.

When asked if they were embarrassed by this arrangement, the spokeswoman answered, "No. If he teaches us what we need to know then that's all right." When asked if he found the situation a bit strange, the Detroit born man also answered in the negative: "I was born in Detroit but I do not know how to build a car." In fact it was one of the Inuit hunters who had taught him how to repair his snowmobile. So why shouldn't he teach young Inuits to build igloos? In the last scene the igloo builders lay out their seal rugs and light a small fire using seal oil, enabling the heat to ice the inside walls, thus insulating the dwelling from the outside cold and creating warmth within. A final shot shows the lighted igloos against the black night sky.

Many things can be read into this short narrative. First, the typical, white, Canadian anchorman, by referring to concerns of Southern Canadians (low building and maintenance costs, no taxes, clear air and quiet neighborhoods), trivializes a technology which, over thousands of years, has allowed populations to survive and create specific societies and cultures in this particular environment. Secondly, we are made aware of the benefits of international trade: an Inuit teaches a Detroit born American how to repair a motor vehicle and, in return learns how to build an igloo. Thirdly, we are led to understand that what the students expect from the teacher is basic working skills.

The temptation to build a case denouncing cultural imperialism, bemoaning the alienation of aboriginal cultures and the shredding of their social fabric, is strong here. On the basis of this one example, however, the argument would at best be flawed, at worst biased. But for students of popular culture, national identity, and cultural industries this is but one of the many thousand daily occurrences which exemplify the dynamic complexity of the concept of "americanization."

Embedded within it are at least two notions; the American presence and the presence of an American. In this news story, both notions are at work. On the one hand, the viewer is made aware of the American presence, the influence of American technology on this remote society, through the reference to the snowmobile. (Although the inventor lived and worked in Quebec, Canada, the fact that the Detroit born American puts the snowmobile on the same footing as the automobile implicitly makes it an American invention.) On the other hand, the viewer sees and hears the American instructor.

It is the first form of presence that usually defines the concept of americanization. It usually refers to the presence of American products and technology and it is against this presence that most critics argue. Surprisingly, few argue against the presence of Americans. As individuals, Americans are well liked and friendly; it is the presence of their way of life, of their culture, that makes americanization such an ugly word. Others like them but do not want to be like them; this is the basic attitude in opposition to americanization.

One is led to believe that s/he will become an American, will be americanized, not by interacting with citizens of the United States but by using American products, eating American (fast) food, and enjoying American cultural artifacts. One can go so far as to live and work in the United States while remaining staunchly Canadian or Australian or British, as many artists who have succeeded in the American music and film industries remind us. The danger of becoming americanized seems greater, however, if one stays in the comfort of home enjoying American cultural products such as magazines, novels, movies, music, comics, television shows and news, or computer software and games.

While these two embedded notions, the presence of Americans and the American presence, make for a fascinating debate, the concept of americanization conceals the parallel dual notion of "the host." Hosting the American presence seems to be more prevalent and more americanizing than hosting Americans themselves. To be a host is to make the visitor feel welcome, to make the visitor seem familiar, non-threatening, at home. In this case, to be a host is to be a consumer, to be a friendly user. To become americanized it is presumed not only that one consumes a steady diet of readily accessible made-in-the-U.S. products, but also consumes these cultural products with ease, i.e. as would any American.

American products are distributed internationally but are not made for international markets: they are made for the U.S. market, by, for, and about Americans. Thus, one can conclude, to enjoy these easily accessible products one must be or become American and the more one consumes, the more one becomes American, thereby enabling increasing pleasure and ease in this consumption. Americanization is a case in point of a basic process of acculturation. It results in sounding the alarms of cultural imperialism and cultural alienation: you become what you consume, because in order to consume you must become the targeted consumer. This is the equivalent of saying: because Science (as we believe we know it) is a product of Western European civilization, then to become a scientist one must become westernized, i.e. adopt Western mores, values, and ways of thinking.

In most host countries in the world there is an overwhelming presence of American products. The pull and pressure of those products must not be underestimated. Still, the news story of the Inuit mechanic and the Detroit igloo builder serves as a reminder that culture, or at least certain types of culture, are less bound by the economics of their technological environment and modes of production than was once assumed and theorized.

The fact that the Inuit travel on snowmobiles, live in suburban dwellings, watch a great deal of television, and have forgotten

how to build igloos does not necessarily make them more americanized when compared with the Detroit born teacher, who is
made no less American by his ability to build an igloo. Skills,
products, and ideas take root in historically given contexts: they
bear witness to their times. When they travel, they bring with
them elements of their place of origin. To use these ideas and
products, one must have an understanding of their historical
background or context, of their original intent and of their mode
of operation. If the invention and the corresponding mode of production of goods and ideas are context bound, so too are their
uses and in many cases these have an impact on the very nature of
products and ideas. This perspective leads to a better understanding of americanization.

Undoubtedly American composers, playwrights, and various
other artists have affected the popular arts of the world. With the
same degree of certitude, one can proclaim that American entrepreneurs and American entrepreneurship have affected the cultural
industries the world over. But perhaps the most profound impact of
this particular historical culture and its modes of production is
found in the social uses American society has made of these cultural
products. If one wishes to speak of americanization in the realm of
popular (or mass) culture, one must focus on the social uses of
industrially produced and commercially distributed sounds and
images. To show American-made movies in local theaters, to watch
American sitcoms on the television set, to listen to American music
on the radio—or to use copycat versions of any of these materials—
is not, necessarily, to become americanized. To build into the local
social fabric a permanent presence of these sounds and images, is to
become americanized but not necessarily American.

To have a *permanent* background of American images and
sounds (for example, television sets turned on all day, ads over-
flowing in print, on buses, on T-shirts, talk radio, Walkmans, etc.)
means to live and work and play in a permanent kaleidoscope
world plugged into a never ending soundtrack. *This*, it can be
argued, is to become americanized.

The *Dallas* imperialism syndrome, and its legitimate heir, the
O.J. Simpson Trial, are good illustrations of this. The debate surrounding *Dallas* rekindles the debate which greeted the American
penny press and Hollywood cinema. Its central question: is communication technology a threat to basic (Western) values, local
cultures, and the human psyche? *Dallas* symbolized this ongoing
debate, a debate central to Western culture. But *Dallas* also
symbolized a social evolution which has not received the attention

it deserves. The worldwide popularity of *Dallas* revived the paradigm of the "magic bullet" theory of direct media effects, a theory suggesting that media content and style can be "injected" into the cultural life system, infecting and contaminating the "healthy" cultural body. It also revived discussions of cultural imperialism, but in a more sophisticated fashion and on a much grander scale. And it also raised the counter paradigm of the uses and gratifications model in communication studies.

Many researchers were eager to publish their claims that *Dallas* did not magically turn all its viewers into Americans, but that the program signified many things to many viewers. Moreover, they pointed out that, on the whole, national cultural products (including television programs) still outsold imported American ones. And if they did not, they certainly enjoyed more popular support and provided more enjoyment.

Forgotten in this foray was the fact that *Dallas* symbolized the popularization and the banalization of television viewing, its normal integration within the activities of everyday life, its quiet nestling in the central foyer of the household environment. Television viewing, a remarkable new social practice in many locations, quickly and quietly became, inside and outside academia, a major source of everyday conversation, the measuring stick of many moral debates, the epitome of modern living. In so doing television viewing displaced the boundaries of centuries-old institutions such as family, work, school and religion. The *Dallas* syndrome symbolized the fact that in a large number of host countries, communication technology had become a permanent part of the everyday social environment, that its messages had become a permanent part of the social fabric and that its spokespersons had joined the public club of opinion makers.

While one can debate the pros and cons of this social fact, one can also speculate that television is not the revolution that many of its critics as well as admirers had hoped or feared. It did not destroy a sacred treasure of Western values based on the technology of the written word. Rather it revealed a blind spot among many social thinkers: the constructed centrality of the spoken word in modern societies. Television possibly revealed to the most industrialized society of the postwar era, the United States, that it was and still is, by and large, an oral society.

Communication technology did not trigger a revolution, social, moral, or sexual; it became part of the establishment in every way, shape, and form. And just as U.S. cultural industries have become an American institution, a part of the social order and a sustainer of culture in American society, so too have cultural industries in many other societies. In this sense, other societies have become americanized. Americanization is not to be found in the consumption of American cultural products. It lies in the establishment of a particular social formation. This formation is, to be sure, defined in part by the use of the products of national cultural industries. But it is also defined by alterations in patterns of everyday life and by the emergence of "new" voices that take their place among existing relations and structures of power. The uses of television throughout the world are both cause and effect within these cultural and social shifts.

Thus americanization is neither a boon nor a threat—it is a cultural and economic fact of life in most (Western) countries. The debate then, is not over whether to stop or to hasten the consumption of American cultural products. It should instead be centered on the impact of specific social uses of industrially mass-produced cultural products, whether foreign or national. For better or worse, the socialization of sounds and images, and socialization through sounds and images, have made more visible, and more mainstream, the oral traditions and the tradition of orality not only in American society but also in all (Western) americanized societies.

It matters little whether television and other technologically based cultural industries were invented by the Americans or not. What they invented was a particular social use of these technologies: the massification of production, distribution, and consumption and the commodification of industrially produced cultural products. In return, this particular social use revealed to American society, and to other industrialized societies which followed suit, the forgotten presence of traditional, non-national, oral cultures. Cultural industries, and television in particular, revealed that print technology (the written word) had not subverted oral technology (the spoken word); it had only partially silenced it by making it less "visible." Television made words and sound once again "visible" and "audible" to the eyes and ears of the mind. In doing so it also revealed to the heavily industrialized, print oriented, Western societies that they were blinded by their most popular visual aid, television.

Questions for Discussion and Writing

1. The author talks about acculturation (paragraph 10). What is acculturation and how does it work in the examples that de la Gaarde offers?
2. The author makes the point that people from other countries can come into the United States and maintain their national identities, yet those who stay home

will be more affected by the reach of "americanization." Why might this be? Do you agree with him? How does this fit with the insistence of groups calling themselves Italian-Americans, Polish-Americans, Mexican-Americans, etc.?

3. There is a very conscious decision not to capitalize the term "americanization" in this essay. Why do you think that is? Does it bother you that the lowercase is used? What point might the author be making?

4. This essay refers to the *Dallas* effect and to international coverage of the O. J. Simpson trial. Use international sources to investigate differences between how the series *Dallas* was viewed in the United States compared to how it was seen in other parts of the world. What did the O. J. Simpson trial mean to international viewers who may not have been aware of Simpson as a football player?

Globalization

ANTHONY GIDDENS

Anthony Giddens was the director of the London School of Economics from 1997 to 2003. He was born in London in 1938 and was educated at the University of Hull, LSE, and Cambridge University. His work has helped to form what is known as the "third way" in politics, something that has influenced a number of world leaders, including Prime Minister Tony Blair of the United Kingdom and President Bill Clinton of the United States. The Reith Lectures are delivered each year by a chosen speaker and are funded by a legacy from Lord Reith, the first Director General of the British Broadcasting Corporation. Professor Giddens was the speaker in 1999. In this, his first lecture of the series, he explores what globalization is and how it affects nation-states, the economic environment, and established institutions. In the course of the lecture he also assesses America's role as the sole superpower with the new system of globalization.

◆

A friend of mine studies village life in central Africa. A few years ago, she paid her first visit to a remote area where she was to carry out her fieldwork. The evening she got there, she was invited to a local home for an evening's entertainment. She expected to find out about the traditional pastimes of this isolated community. Instead, the evening turned out to be a viewing of *Basic*

Instinct on video. The film at that point hadn't even reached the cinemas in London.

Such vignettes reveal something about our world. And what they reveal isn't trivial. It isn't just a matter of people adding modern paraphernalia—videos, TVs, personal computers and so forth—to their traditional ways of life. We live in a world of transformations, affecting almost every aspect of what we do. For better or worse, we are being propelled into a global order that no one fully understands, but which is making its effects felt upon all of us.

Globalization is the main theme of my lecture tonight and of the lectures as a whole. The term may not be—it isn't—a particularly attractive or elegant one. But absolutely no-one who wants to understand our prospects and possibilities at century's end can ignore it. I travel a lot to speak abroad. I haven't been to a single country recently where globalization isn't being intensively discussed. In France, the word is *mondialisation*. In Spain and Latin America, it is *globalizacion*. The Germans say *globalisierung*.

The global spread of the term is evidence of the very developments to which it refers. Every business guru talks about it. No political speech is complete without reference to it. Yet as little as ten years ago the term was hardly used, either in the academic literature or in everyday language. It has come from nowhere to be almost everywhere. Given its sudden popularity, we shouldn't be surprised that the meaning of the notion isn't always clear, or that an intellectual reaction has set in against it. Globalization has something to do with the thesis that we now all live in one world—but in what ways exactly, and is the idea really valid?

Different thinkers have taken almost completely opposite views about globalization in debates that have sprung up over the past few years. Some dispute the whole thing. I'll call them the skeptics. According to the skeptics all the talk about globalization is only that—just talk. Whatever its benefits, its trials and tribulations, the global economy isn't especially different from that which existed at previous periods. The world carries on much the same as it has done for many years.

Most countries, the skeptics argue, only gain a small amount of their income from external trade. Moreover, a good deal of economic exchange is between regions, rather than being truly world-wide. The countries of the European Union, for example, mostly trade among themselves. The same is true of the other main trading blocs, such as those of the Asia Pacific or North America.

Others, however, take a very different position. I'll label them the radicals. The radicals argue that not only is globalization very real, but that its consequences can be felt everywhere. The global marketplace, they say, is much more developed than even two or three decades ago, and is indifferent to national borders. Nations have lost most of the sovereignty they once had, and politicians have lost most of their capability to influence events. It isn't surprising that no one respects political leaders any more, or has much interest in what they have to say. The era of the nation state is over. Nations, as the Japanese business writer Keniche Ohmae puts it, have become mere "fictions." Authors like Ohmae see the economic difficulties of last year and this as demonstrating the reality of globalization, albeit seen from its disruptive side.

The skeptics tend to be on the political left, especially the old left. For if all of this is essentially a myth, governments can still intervene in economic life and the welfare state remain intact. The notion of globalization, according to the skeptics, is an ideology put about by free-marketeers who wish to dismantle welfare systems and cut back on state expenditures. What has happened is at most a reversion to how the world was a century ago. In the late 19th Century there was already an open global economy, with a great deal of trade, including trade in currencies.

Well, who is right in this debate? I think it is the radicals. The level of world trade today is much higher than it ever was before, and involves a much wider range of goods and services. But the biggest difference is in the level of finance and capital flows. Geared as it is to electronic money—money that exists only as digits in computers—the current world economy has no parallels in earlier times. In the new global electronic economy, fund managers, banks, corporations, as well as millions of individual investors, can transfer vast amounts of capital from one side of the world to another at the click of a mouse. As they do so, they can destabilize what might have seemed rock-solid economies—as happened in East Asia.

The volume of world financial transactions is usually measured in U.S. dollars. A million dollars is a lot of money for most people. Measured as a stack of thousand dollar notes, it would be eight inches high. A billion dollars—in other words, a million million—would be over 120 miles high, 20 times higher than Mount Everest. Yet far more than a trillion dollars is now turned over each day on global currency markets, a massive increase from only ten years ago, let alone the more distant past. The value of whatever money we may have in our pockets, or our bank accounts, shifts from moment to moment according to fluctuations in such markets. I would have no hesitation, therefore, in saying that globalization, as we are experiencing it, is in many respects not only new, but revolutionary.

However, I don't believe either the skeptics or the radicals have properly understood either what it is or its implications for us. Both groups see the phenomenon almost solely in economic terms. This is a mistake. Globalization is political, technological and cultural, as well as economic. It has been influenced above all by developments in systems of communication, dating back only to the late 1960's. In the mid-19th Century, a Massachusetts portrait painter, Samuel Morse, transmitted the first message, "What hath god wrought?" by electric telegraph. In so doing, he initiated a new phase in world history. Never before could a message be sent without someone going somewhere to carry it. Yet the advent of satellite communications marks every bit as dramatic a break with the past. The first communications satellite was launched only just over thirty years ago. Now there are more than two hundred such satellites above the earth, each carrying a vast range of information. For the first time ever, instantaneous communication is possible from one side of the world to the other. Other types of electronic communication, more and more integrated with satellite transmission, have also accelerated over the past few years. No dedicated transatlantic or transpacific cables existed at all until the late 1950s. The first held less than one hundred voice paths. Those of today carry more than a million.

On the first of February 1999, about one hundred and fifty years after Morse invented his system of dots and dashes, Morse code finally disappeared from the world stage, discontinued as a means of communication for the sea. In its place has come a system using satellite technology, whereby any ship in distress can be pinpointed immediately. Most countries prepared for the transition some while before. The French, for example, stopped using Morse as a distress code in their local waters two years ago, signing off with a Gallic flourish: "Calling all. This is our last cry before our eternal silence."

Instantaneous electronic communication isn't just a way in which news or information is conveyed more quickly. Its existence alters the very texture of our lives, rich and poor alike. When the image of Nelson Mandela maybe is more familiar to us than the face of our next door neighbor, something has changed in the nature of our everyday experience.

Nelson Mandela is a global celebrity, and celebrity itself is largely a product of new communications technology. The reach of media technologies is growing with each wave of innovation. It took forty years for radio in the United States to gain an audience of fifty million. The same number were using personal computers only fifteen years after the PC was introduced. It needed a mere four years, after it was made available for fifty million Americans to be regularly using the Internet.

It is wrong to think of globalization as just concerning the big systems, like the world financial order. Globalization isn't only about what is "out there," remote and far away from the individual. It is an "in here" phenomenon too, influencing intimate and personal aspects of our lives. The debate about family values, for example, that is going on in many countries might seem far removed from globalizing influences. It isn't. Traditional family systems are becoming transformed, or are under strain, in many parts of the world, particularly as women stake claim to greater equality. There has never before been a society, so far as we know from the historical record, in which women have been even approximately equal to men. This is a truly global revolution in everyday life, whose consequences are being felt around the world in spheres from work to politics.

Globalization thus is a complex set of processes, not a single one. And these operate in a contradictory or oppositional fashion. Most people think of it as simply "pulling away" power or influence from local communities and nations into the global arena. And indeed this is one of its consequences. Nations do lose some of the economic power they once had. However, it also has an opposite effect. Globalization not only pulls upwards, it pushes downwards, creating new pressures for local autonomy. The American sociologist Daniel Bell expresses this very well when he says that the nation becomes too small to solve the big problems, but also too large to solve the small ones.

Globalization is the reason for the revival of local cultural identities in different parts of the world. If one asks, for example, why the Scots want more independence in the UK, or why there is a strong separatist movement in Quebec, the answer is not to be found only in their cultural history. Local nationalisms spring up as a response to globalizing tendencies, as the hold of older nation-states weakens.

Globalization also squeezes sideways. It creates new economic and cultural zones within and across nations. Examples are the Hong Kong region, northern Italy, or Silicon Valley in California. The area around Barcelona in northern Spain extends over into France. Catalonia, where Barcelona is located, is closely integrated into the European Union. It is part of Spain, yet also looks outwards.

The changes are being propelled by a range of factors, some structural, others more specific and historical. Economic influences are certainly among the driving forces, especially the global financial system. Yet they aren't like forces of nature. They have been shaped by technology, and cultural diffusion, as well as by the decisions of governments to liberalize and deregulate their national economies.

The collapse of Soviet communism has added further weight to such developments, since no significant group of countries any longer stands outside. That collapse wasn't just something that happened to occur. Globalization explains both why and how Soviet communism met its end. The Soviet Union and the East European countries were comparable to the West in terms of growth rates until somewhere around the early 1970s. After that point, they fell rapidly behind. Soviet communism, with its emphasis upon state-run enterprise and heavy industry, could not compete in the global electronic economy. The ideological and cultural control upon which communist political authority was based similarly could not survive in an era of global media.

The Soviet and the East European regimes were unable to prevent the reception of western radio and TV broadcasts. Television played a direct role in the 1989 revolutions, which have rightly been called the first "television revolutions." Street protests taking place in one country were watched by the audiences in others, large numbers of whom then took to the streets themselves.

Globalization, of course, isn't developing in an even-handed way, and is by no means wholly benign in its consequences. To many living outside Europe and North America, it looks uncomfortably like Westernization—or, perhaps, Americanization, since the U.S. is now the sole superpower, with a dominant economic, cultural and military position in the global order. Many of the most visible cultural expressions of globalization are American—Coca-Cola, McDonald's.

Most of giant multinational companies are based in the U.S. too. Those that aren't all come from the rich countries, not the poorer areas of the world. A pessimistic view of globalization would consider it largely an affair of the industrial North, in which the developing societies of the South play little or no active part. It would see it as destroying local cultures, widening world inequalities and worsening the lot of the impoverished. Globalization, some argue, creates a world of winners and losers, a few on the fast track to prosperity, the majority condemned to a life of misery and despair.

And indeed the statistics are daunting. The share of the poorest fifth of the world's population in global income has dropped from 2.3% to 1.4% over the past 10 years. The proportion taken by the richest fifth, on the other hand, has risen from 70% to 85%. In Sub-Saharan Africa, twenty countries have lower incomes per head in real terms than they did two decades ago. In many less developed countries, safety and environmental regulations are low or virtually non-existent. Some transnational companies sell goods there that are controlled or banned in the industrial countries—poor quality medical drugs, destructive pesticides or high tar and nicotine content cigarettes. As one writer put it recently, rather than a global village, this is more like global pillage.

Along with ecological risk, to which it is related, expanding inequality is the most serious problem facing world society. It will not do, however, merely to blame it on the wealthy. It is fundamental to my argument that globalization today is only partly Westernization. Of course the western nations, and more generally the industrial countries, still have far more influence over world affairs than do the poorer states. But globalization is becoming increasingly de-centered—not under the control of any group of nations, and still less of the large corporations. Its effects are felt just as much in the western countries as elsewhere.

This is true of the global financial system, communications and media, and of changes affecting the nature of government itself. Examples of "reverse colonization" are becoming more and more common. Reverse colonization means that non-western countries influence developments in the west. Examples abound—such as the Latinizing of Los Angeles, the emergence of a globally-oriented high-tech sector in India, or the selling of Brazilian TV programs to Portugal.

Is globalization a force promoting the general good? The question can't be answered in simple way, given the complexity of the phenomenon. People who ask it, and who blame globalization for deepening world inequalities, usually have in mind economic globalization, and within that, free trade. Now it is surely obvious that free trade is not an unalloyed benefit. This is especially so as concerns the less developed countries. Opening up a country, or regions within it, to free trade can undermine a local subsistence economy. An area that becomes dependent upon a few products sold on world markets is very vulnerable to shifts in prices as well as to technological change.

Trade always needs a framework of institutions, as do other forms of economic development. Markets cannot be created by purely economic means, and how far a given economy should be exposed to the world marketplace must depend upon a range of criteria. Yet to oppose economic globalization, and to opt for economic protectionism, would be a misplaced tactic for rich and poor nations alike. Protectionism may be a necessary strategy at some times and in some countries. In my view, for example, Malaysia was correct to introduce controls in 1998, to stem the flood of capital from the country. But more permanent forms of protectionism will not help the development of the poor countries, and among the rich would lead to warring trade blocs.

The debates about globalization I mentioned at the beginning have concentrated mainly upon its implications for the nation-state. Are nation-states, and hence national political leaders, still powerful, or are they becoming largely irrelevant to the forces shaping the world? Nation-states are indeed still powerful and political leaders have a large role to play in the world. Yet at the same time the nation-state is being reshaped before our eyes. National economic policy can't be as effective as it once was. More importantly, nations have to rethink their identities now the older forms of geopolitics are becoming obsolete. Although this is a contentious point, I would say that, following the dissolving of the cold war, nations no longer have enemies. Who are the enemies of Britain, or France, or Japan? Nations today face risks and dangers rather than enemies, a massive shift in their very nature.

It isn't only of the nation that such comments could be made.

Everywhere we look, we see institutions that appear the same as they used to be from the outside, and carry the same names, but inside have become quite different. We continue to talk of the nation, the family, work, tradition, nature, as if they were all the same as in the past. They are not. The outer shell remains, but inside all is different—and this is happening not only in the U.S., Britain, or France, but almost everywhere. They are what I call shell institutions . . . They are institutions that have become inadequate to the tasks they are called upon to perform.

As the changes I have described in this lecture gather weight, they are creating something that has never existed before, a global cosmopolitan society. We are the first generation to live in this society, whose contours we can as yet only dimly see. It is shaking up our existing ways of life, no matter where we happen to be. This is not—at least at the moment—a global order driven by collective human will. Instead, it is emerging in an anarchic, haphazard, fashion, carried along by a mixture of economic, technological and cultural imperatives.

It is not settled or secure, but fraught with anxieties, as well as scarred by deep divisions. Many of us feel in the grip of forces over which we have no control. Can we re-impose our will upon them? I believe we can. The powerlessness we experience is not a sign of personal failings, but reflects the incapacities of our institutions. We need to reconstruct those we have, or create new ones, in ways appropriate to the global age. We should and we can look to achieve greater control over our runaway world. We shan't be able to do so if we shirk the challenges, or pretend that all can go on as before. For globalization is not incidental to our lives today. It is a shift in our very life circumstances. It is the way we now live.

Questions for Discussion and Writing

1. Professor Giddens states that "Instantaneous electronic communication isn't just a way in which news or information is conveyed more quickly. Its existence alters the very texture of our lives, rich and poor alike." Do you agree? How do you think your lives are different, for example, from those of your parents, who grew up in a different era? Which aspects of electronic communication do you use every day?

2. Giddens claims that many of the most successful companies that benefit from globalization are based in the United States. Does this undercut a sense of global reach and turn it to Americanization? Could globalization simply be a cover for American influence and control?

3. What do you think about Giddens' idea that globalization leads to a growth of nationalism and a redefinition of a native cultural identity?

4. What is the World Trade Organization? Why are protests frequently held against what the WTO represents? Research websites and publications that support and dispute the aims of the WTO and explain the role and purpose of the organization for a general reader.

5. Find out what percentage of American households have a personal computer. Compare this to countries in South America, Africa, and Asia. How does this access to technology affect the daily lives of world citizenry?

We Are All Americans
VICENTE VERDÚ

This article is taken from the newspaper El País, *published in Madrid, Spain, on April 27, 2002. Vicente Verdú was born in Elche, Spain, in 1942. He was educated at the Sorbonne in Paris and is a member of the Nieman Foundation of Harvard University. For* El País *he has been Opinion Editor and Cultural Editor. He has written books about the relationships between couples and about the rituals of soccer. He is a best-selling author in his home country. Verdú and his family lived in Haverford, Pennsylvania, from 1993 to 1995. In this article the author is responding to a school shooting in Efurt, Germany. An expelled pupil walked into his school carrying a pump-action shotgun and a pistol and killed 14 teachers, 2 girls, a policeman, and then himself. The incident at Nanterre, France, referred to in this essay cost the lives of 8 people when a gunman opened fire at a local council meeting. Verdú argues that such actions are influenced by American culture but that there are many more things resulting from American society that should be seen as positive. He sees a time when national borders will be immaterial, because everyone in the world will be, for good or ill, American.*

---------------- ✦ ----------------

Years ago, we believed that the Americanization of the world was due to cultural influence. Now we know that it is because of a gene. The final phase of capitalism, of which the United States is decidedly in charge, has ceased to be a system of material production. It has become a civilization, and sooner or later all of us will be caught up in it, for better or worse.

The most recent massacre by a young man in a small city in Germany is a repeat of what happened in April, three years ago, in another small city, this one in Colorado, called Littleton. The shooting then also took place at a school, and in exactly the same way: The victims were students and teachers. And the attacker killed himself afterward.

The American model of life repeats itself like a fractal in the many different aspects of everyday existence, be it community life, sex, art, or money. There is an international prototype, which coincides with the American model, to be found in painting, architecture, and even in cyberspace. So why shouldn't there be an international mass killing with its own "Made in America" label?

Until recently, the image of the serial killer who burst into a McDonald's, pulled out a machine gun, and shot down everyone eating their Big Macs was something distinctively American. But now this is a worldwide brand, and it can be found in 116 countries, with over 40,000 franchises in all. How could one not expect that in these identical settings, we would not find identical events, given that values, formations, and arms trafficking have become global?

American influence is not, in and of itself, harmful, despite what the French say. And after all, on March 27, the French themselves witnessed a similar massacre in Nanterre. American influence consists of a whole bundle of things, of varying degrees of goodness and toxicity. Thanks to the example of the United States, a large part of the world takes democracy as a natural value. Almost no nation for many years now has dared to declare itself anything except a democracy, and in doing that, subscribe to an entire list of human rights—regardless of whether or not it continues to violate them.

Equally, no one doubts the Puritan mandate for transparency, although it may exclude such murky incidents as Enron and others. The American way has become the global paradigm, and the world follows its example, follows its orders and those of its representatives at the International Monetary Fund or the World Bank.

Thanks to the Americans, we have ecology, although the United States did not sign the Kyoto Accord, and thanks to the Americans we have hard-line feminism, militant gays, nontraditional couples, equity within couples, and acceptance of multiculturalism.

The United States is like a unit of currency that magnifies the role of the dollar, fast food, and English to encyclopedic dimensions. It has been costly to accept it, but it seems as if contemporary American life will continue to become our own, and will be adopted with increasingly shorter delay.

To give itself some local color, McDonald's in France serves salade niçoise along with hamburgers; in Greece, it serves feta cheese; and in Singapore, it serves fried chicken. In Norway, McDonald's uses salmon instead of beef, and in India, they call the Big Mac a Maharaja Mac and make it out of lamb rather than beef in accordance with Hindu beliefs. But it is still McDonald's. And, as is well-known by now, since 1986 Big Mac has been the term used by *The Economist* to express the varying values of the world's currencies.

Is this Americanization sufficiently appreciated? Probably not, because how can it be distinguished from globalization? And how can we distinguish it from ourselves? This article will be one of the last texts written to separate what is American from what is not. Soon, we will not be able to compare what happened at the school in Erfurt with previous events at American schools. We will all be part of the same institution, the same psychiatric hospital, the same dreams, and the same destiny.

Questions for Discussion and Writing

1. How do you think would your understanding of American culture might change if you lived in another country?
2. What kinds of things would you miss about America if you lived in another country? What different cultures would you like to experience and why?

The World Gets in Touch with Its Inner American

G. PASCAL ZACHARY

G. Pascal Zachary was a senior journalist with the Wall Street Journal *for 13 years before moving to Time Inc.'s magazine* Business 2.0. *He also lectures at Stanford University. He has contributed articles to* The New York Times, The San Francisco Chronicle, *and* The New Republic. *This essay, written in 1999, looks ahead to the twenty-first century and examines whether the world will have a choice about whether or not to be Americanized. Zachary draws his examples from countries as different as Germany, France, Borneo, and Thailand.*

———————————— ✦ ————————————

The woman sitting across from me in Bangkok's swank Dusit Thani hotel is one of Thailand's best and brightest. Educated in the U.S., she's a computer whiz at a prominent local company. She wears a basic business suit and impresses me with talk of "TCP/IP" and other Internet protocols. But when our conversation comes around to her romantic life, her fiancé—a New Yorker seated next to her—squirms. She admits it's a little odd not to be marrying a Thai. Still, she says in a low, conspiratorial voice, "Many Thai women dream of having an American's baby."

My jaw drops. I expect her to give her boyfriend, who works for a U.S. corporation here, a reassuring smile, as if to say that she isn't one of them. But she goes right on talking. "Thai people think these babies are more beautiful, better endowed," she says. "They're all the rage."

The Thai passion for Americana doesn't stop with babies. Thai consumers learned the concept of "nutritional value" labeling from Frito-Lay packages, the first in the nation to carry an analysis of potato chip ingredients. The government's response to its financial collapse, which triggered the Asian economic meltdown, "draws from the United States" handling of its S&L crisis in the 1980s. Thailand's largest private employer, Seagate Technology, is a U.S. high-tech company. And the country's new constitution retreats from Asian communalism by emphasizing a core American value: individual rights. Others countries are following Thailand's lead. A few days before arriving in Bangkok, I listen to Ella Fitzgerald piped over a stereo system in a restaurant in Kuala Lumpur's trendy Bangsar district. I am eating a bowl of *laksa*, a traditional stew. My lunch companion is Karim Raslan, a lawyer and leading Malaysian social critic. Notoriously prickly about their own culture, Malaysians have criticized Americans for our unbridled individualism. Yet in the face of the country's economic contraction, the unthinkable suddenly makes sense. "Can we develop beyond this point without importing American ideas about the conception of the individual?" Raslan asks. "Probably not." Fascinated by what he calls "the imagined communities of the American West," he believes Malaysians can reinvent themselves in much the way Americans do: by asserting a new identity that works.

Two months before, halfway around the globe in Provence, France, I meet another enthusiast of all things American, Marc Lassus. He is the chief of Gemplus, a manufacturer of "smart cards," which can be used as electronic money to purchase telephone time or to store information such as medical records. It's nearly midnight, and I watch him exhort his factory workers to act more American. The typical French executive treats manual laborers with veiled contempt, but Lassus revels in them, working the factory floor like a politician. He betrays his nationality only when it comes to greeting the female machine operators: He kisses them lustily.

Lassus fights the impulse to be, in his words, "too Frenchie." Incredibly, he often speaks English on the job and encourages his co-workers to do the same. The company's marketing materials are expressly written in American English, by writers imported from California's Silicon Valley. Lassus has hired an American number-cruncher to push the idea that the bottom line matters as much in France as it does in the States. Because the French are famously chauvinistic, I am astonished by Lassus' frank admiration of American ways. His e-mail handle says it all: John Wayne.

Thailand, Malaysia, and France aren't unique in their emulation of the United States. "Americanization" is a more apt term than "globalization" for the increasing concentration of U.S.-based multinational companies operating worldwide. Pundits glibly assert that different societies in the world are becoming more alike as if all were influencing and being influenced in equal measure, creating a kind of global melting pot. I don't see it that way. In the 1990s, the world has Americanized at an unprecedented rate, reaching as far as Borneo.

Of course, Levi's, Nike, and Hollywood have long held international sway. But American influence goes deeper than pop culture. Technology—especially computers, software, and the Internet—is seen as quintessentially American. And the way we do business is now also admired worldwide. Once believed to be in permanent decline, the strongest U.S. companies again dominate global markets. Their stress on profits, efficiency, innovation, and "shareholder value" is the envy of capitalists from Tokyo to Buenos Aires.

The notion of "pay for performance," once rare outside of the U.S., is also catching on. Throughout the world, a growing number of companies are adopting the concept of merit, rewarding employees with a slice of the company's total earnings, given as bonuses rather than wages. Risk-taking and even failure, once cast as pure negatives in Asia and Europe, now are viewed increasingly as preludes to success. Office dress is more casual, corridor talk less formal. The old-boy networks, based on what schools people graduated from (Europe) or which family and personal connections they could draw from (Asia), are slowly breaking down.

"Within five to 10 years, these practices won't [just] be American anymore; they will be everywhere," says Roel Pieper, a senior executive at Philips, the Dutch electronics multinational. American social and political ideas are also taking hold. At a time when Japan—hugely influential in the 1980s—is stagnant, the American willingness to improvise is trumping the virtues of traditionalism. Countries such as Japan and Germany, where the concept of nationality is rooted in the racially based idea of bloodlines, are starting to accept that a polyglot country such as the United States has fundamental advantages.

Scholars throughout Europe now vie to publish their articles in American journals. In Berlin, worried parents recently convinced educators to begin teaching English in the first grade rather than waiting until the third. And in Penang, Malaysia, primary schools stage storytelling competitions—in English.

For all its seductiveness, however, Americanization has a dark side, an underbelly that perhaps we know better than anyone else. And as Americans, who can blame us for asking whether the relentless spread of our values is worth the price?

It is a warm September evening in Washington, D.C., and I am sitting on an outdoor patio at a fashionable restaurant, the Tabard Inn. My companion is Andrea Durbin, director of international programs for Friends of the Earth. She is part of a broad movement that opposed NAFTA (unsuccessfully), helped kill fast-track (Clinton's effort to gain a free hand in negotiating trade pacts), and is now trying to bring the International Monetary Fund to heel. The IMF recently won an $18 billion commitment from Congress to replenish reserves exhausted by the fund's successive bailouts of Thailand, South Korea, Indonesia, and Russia. An unusual alliance of conservatives and radicals forced the fund, as a condition of this new cash infusion, to provide more information about its inner workings, which may make it easier for critics to track how the IMF protects U.S. investors and promotes an American capitalism.

The IMF generally opposes trade barriers, low interest rates, and deficit spending. These policies, Durbin points out, have led the IMF to mishandle the global capitalist crisis that began with a whimper in July 1997 when the Thai baht collapsed. Using a formula wholeheartedly endorsed by the U.S. Department of the Treasury, the IMF drove Thai interest rates sky-high in a bid to protect the baht, strangling liquidity in a banking system rife with cronyism. At the same time, the fund and the U.S. insisted on new bankruptcy laws—leading to a fire sale of sorts and freeing the way for foreign companies, including American ones, to snap up assets, such as Thai car companies, on the cheap.

The story is the same elsewhere in the world. The result is that world capitalism is in shambles. In Brazil and Mexico, living standards are falling and stock markets are in disarray even though governments have curtailed spending on social services and privatized essential public monopolies. In Indonesia, a quarter century of rising living standards was reversed during the Asian financial crisis, while an IMF "rescue" program succeeded only in helping to bankrupt the country. In Russia, after the IMF's "help," the ruble collapsed. The dollar is now king; it greases so much commerce that some argue that the greenback should be the official currency . . . All over the world, meanwhile, the moneyed classes are converting local currencies into dollars and shipping them to the United States. According to the Federal Reserve Board, about two-thirds of all U.S. currency (the bills themselves) circulate abroad—an estimated $300 billion. The dollarization of the world economy is just one aspect of the Pyrrhic victory of the worldwide spread of American values. Durbin ticks off her own list of the worst aspects of Americanization:

Inequality The American economic model has led to increasing disparities of wealth and income. Both stock options and pay for performance are becoming popular in Europe, where, in a number of countries, inequality is rising even faster than in the U.S., according to the Luxembourg Income Study, the leading source on the subject. "The U.S. still has the most inequality based on income," says Timothy Smeeding, an economist at Syracuse University. But, incredibly, even Denmark and Sweden have seen income gaps widen more rapidly than in the U.S. That's partly because, as in most other countries, Scandinavians are paying much higher wages to skilled workers and squeezing labor costs at the bottom.

Consumerism U.S. per capita consumption is up to 20 times greater than in the developing world. "If even half the world's people achieve the American way of life," says Durbin, "we'll have an environmental disaster on our hands." This is a critical point: According to the World Resources Institute, the U.S. consumes a quarter of the world's oil, a third of its paper, and 40 percent of its beef and veal. If such patterns are replicated—say in China alone—the effect on world resources will be dramatic.

Cultural monotony When . . . Kobe Bryant merits giant billboards in
Paris, the mania for U.S. culture has gone too far. "Our culture is
such a strong one it tends to dominate and erode other cultures,"
Durbin says. "They have a lot to contribute to the international
dialogue, but we're losing them."

Imitators of the U.S. rightfully worry about the price of
American cultural domination. Consider Germany. One sunny
Saturday morning, I am drinking a café au lait on Munich's main
square, watching as a *glockenspiel* strikes noon and sends a small,
mechanical army parading around the old tower, attracting
tourists. Just off the square, though, German shoppers are pouring into a Disney store, packed with Pocahontas purses, Mickey
Mouse towels, and Winnie-the-Pooh dresses. Germans at least
have a sense of irony about iconic American brands. It's more dis-
tressing to visit some of the most remote river villages of Borneo,
as I did a year ago, and find evidence of a bizarre love affair with
Americana.

One steamy afternoon, I take a high-speed riverboat to
Marudi, a logging town that serves as the hub for various jungle
tribes, many of whose members still live in longhouses and
follow traditional customs. Seated across from me is an old
Orang Ulu woman. Her body is covered with brightly colored tattoos, and her ears are elongated, the result of attaching heavy
weights to her lobes. Once the boat hits its cruising speed, the
captain puts a video into the ship's TV. It shows professional
wrestlers from the United States. Two big white guys with long
hair toss each other around the ring. The Orang Ulu woman
howls with laughter, her face brightening each time a big hulk
falls to the canvas. Hers is no isolated affection. I spend that
evening with a militant anti-logging activist in Marudi—a Kayan
tribe member considered so dangerous by the government that
it had seized his passport. After dinner, he invites me into his
house and, with geckos running up and down his walls, plays
a traditional Kayan guitar for me. When I tell him about the
woman, he confesses that he, too, loves watching American
wrestling. So does everyone in the longhouses.

Environmentalists enjoy painting these native people as idyllic
traditionalists, but the truth is that they want a piece of America
too—but on their own terms. Their resistance to resource exploitation is certainly authentic, and their logging blockades deserve the
wholehearted support of outsiders. Yet for these tribespeople,
the biggest symbol of progress is American-made: the Johnson

outboard motor. Once these river tribes used long poles to push their boats up the region's shallow rivers. How much happier many of them are now with a craft powered by a small motor. Far from looking bucolic, they resemble edgy Long Islanders, speeding back and forth on the water, their ungainly poles snugly on the bottom of their thin, low boats.

Americanization seems unstoppable. Resistance is rising, however. The governments of France and Germany are taking steps to address the inequities fostered by their own embrace of the American model. Both are raising taxes on wealthy people and corporations and, in France's case, paying people the same amount for working fewer hours. In September, Malaysia, long a haven for U.S. investment, slapped controls on its currency, making it harder on foreign investors. Even cultural rebellions are taking place: The Israeli government announced in November that it may require its radio stations to devote half their airtime to songs sung in Hebrew in order to slow down Israel's cultural shift toward Americanization.

The pervasiveness of Americanization, in other words, doesn't mean the world will end up full of Clint Eastwoods. Many foreigners drawn to U.S. values and practices are nonetheless disturbed that the U.S. often exports its pathologies. Consider the attitude of Simon Tay, a lawyer and Member of Parliament in Singapore. In a country where Western values are relentlessly criticized, Tay's admiration for American society stands out. He has a degree from Harvard University and has published a book about his travels in the United States. Yet as we sip cold drinks on a patio outside a mammoth high-rise this spring, he tells me, "Sometimes I feel you're exporting the worst of America." He mentions the traits that many people in Singapore equate with the American Way: violence, workaholism, disrespect for authority, an endless obsession with instant gratification. Tay realizes that this image of the U.S., gleaned from American movies and television, is something of a caricature. "In your movies and your materialism, we don't see the real America," he admits.

Like many in Asia, he hungers for a more freewheeling society, one that can respect tradition while breaking free from it when necessary. He fears that the so-called Asian miracle came undone partly because rigid Asian societies can hamper American-style creativity. In Singapore, however, the drive to acquire the more eccentric aspects of American life borders on parody. Many years ago, the government banned street performers, considering them beggars. When Tay returned from his stay in the U.S., the sterility of Singapore's streets—all orderly and clean, with no one present without a purpose—weighed on him. In 1997 the government permitted street performers for the first time, but then the government drew a line, requiring performers to audition before a national board. Not only that, whatever money they collected had to be donated to charity. "This is crazy," says Tay. "It's a good example of the tension between wanting a livelier Singapore and maintaining control." (Later, following criticism from Tay and others, the government relaxed the conditions.)

Clearly, says Tay, foreigners may imitate Americans, but that doesn't mean they automatically become like them. This, he concludes, may help preserve Singapore's own cultural traditions as it integrates American ones. "If American values aren't imposed on us, but come in a softer way, I'd welcome that," he says.

But that isn't likely. The global capitalist crisis paradoxically reinforces the power of the United States. Foreign assets are cheaper than they've been in decades. Before the crisis runs its course—and it may take years—U.S. investors may own a much bigger chunk of the developing world: from factories to mines to forests to auto loans, all picked up for a song.

• • •

U.S. power stands at a new pinnacle, only this time victory isn't measured in the defeat of an ideological foe but in the influence gained over the world's wealth, culture, and individual identity. If the bulk of the 20th century was defined by American military might, its last decade may be summed up by this maxim: "We are all Americans now, like it or not."

Questions for Discussion and Writing

1. How would you characterize American practices of business as described in this essay? Do you think this a fair description?
2. How are countries responding to the Americanization of their processes? Do you see this as a justified resistance? Can you understand why this resistance might be happening?
3. What is the IMF? How does it function? What role does the United States play in the way it is administrated?
4. What is NAFTA? What was it designed to do? What are the points that support such an agreement and what criticisms are leveled at it?

It's a Flat World, After All

THOMAS L. FRIEDMAN

Thomas L. Friedman is a regular columnist for The New York
Times *and the author of influential books on international affairs,
such as* The Lexus and the Olive Tree *(2000). He has won three
Pulitzer Prizes—two for foreign reporting and one for commentary.
Friedman was born in Minneapolis, Minnesota, in 1953 and was
educated at Brandeis University and Oxford University in the
United Kingdom. His latest book,* The World Is Flat: A Brief
History of the Twenty-First Century, *was published in April 2005
by Farrar, Straus & Giroux and it is from this book that this article
is adapted. It appeared in* The New York Times Magazine *on April
3, 2005. In his essay Friedman argues that globalization has flattened the playing field of economics and commerce, making the
small and emerging nations true competitors to the United States.
Instead of international barriers being erected, as they were during
the Cold War period of the 1950s, they are being pulled down as the
twenty-first century dawns. This offers a new challenge to U.S.
dominance, and Friedman writes about new considerations as
the United States faces new and hungry competitors in the free
marketplace.*

◆

In 1492 Christopher Columbus set sail for India, going west. He
had the Nina, the Pinta and the Santa Maria. He never did find
India, but he called the people he met "Indians" and came home
and reported to his king and queen: "The world is round." I set off
for India 512 years later. I knew just which direction I was going.
I went east. I had Lufthansa business class, and I came home and
reported only to my wife and only in a whisper: "The world is flat."

And therein lies a tale of technology and geoeconomics that is
fundamentally reshaping our lives—much, much more quickly
than many people realize. It all happened while we were sleeping,
or rather while we were focused on 9/11, the dot-com bust and
Enron—which even prompted some to wonder whether globalization was over. Actually, just the opposite was true, which is why
it's time to wake up and prepare ourselves for this flat world,
because others already are, and there is no time to waste.

I wish I could say I saw it all coming. Alas, I encountered the flattening of the world quite by accident. It was in late February of last year, and I was visiting the Indian high-tech capital, Bangalore, working on a documentary for the Discovery Times channel about outsourcing. In short order, I interviewed Indian entrepreneurs who wanted to prepare my taxes from Bangalore, read my X-rays from Bangalore, trace my lost luggage from Bangalore and write my new software from Bangalore. The longer I was there, the more upset I became—upset at the realization that while I had been off covering the 9/11 wars, globalization had entered a whole new phase, and I had missed it. I guess the eureka moment came on a visit to the campus of Infosys Technologies, one of the crown jewels of the Indian outsourcing and software industry. Nandan Nilekani, the Infosys C.E.O., was showing me his global video-conference room, pointing with pride to a wall-size flat-screen TV, which he said was the biggest in Asia. Infosys, he explained, could hold a virtual meeting of the key players from its entire global supply chain for any project at any time on that supersize screen. So its American designers could be on the screen speaking with their Indian software writers and their Asian manufacturers all at once. That's what globalization is all about today, Nilekani said. Above the screen there were eight clocks that pretty well summed up the Infosys workday: 24/7/365. The clocks were labeled U.S. West, U.S. East, G.M.T., India, Singapore, Hong Kong, Japan, Australia.

"Outsourcing is just one dimension of a much more fundamental thing happening today in the world," Nilekani explained. "What happened over the last years is that there was a massive investment in technology, especially in the bubble era, when hundreds of millions of dollars were invested in putting broadband connectivity around the world, undersea cables, all those things." At the same time, he added, computers became cheaper and dispersed all over the world, and there was an explosion of e-mail software, search engines like Google and proprietary software that can chop up any piece of work and send one part to Boston, one part to Bangalore and one part to Beijing, making it easy for anyone to do remote development. When all of these things suddenly came together around 2000, Nilekani said, they "created a platform where intellectual work, intellectual capital, could be delivered from anywhere. It could be disaggregated, delivered, distributed, produced and put back together again—and this gave a whole new degree of freedom to the way we do work, especially work of an intellectual nature. And what you are seeing in

Bangalore today is really the culmination of all these things coming together."

At one point, summing up the implications of all this, Nilekani uttered a phrase that rang in my ear. He said to me, "Tom, the playing field is being leveled." He meant that countries like India were now able to compete equally for global knowledge work as never before—and that America had better get ready for this. As I left the Infosys campus that evening and bounced along the potholed road back to Bangalore, I kept chewing on that phrase: "The playing field is being leveled."

"What Nandan is saying," I thought, "is that the playing field is being flattened. Flattened? Flattened? My God, he's telling me the world is flat!"

Here I was in Bangalore—more than 500 years after Columbus sailed over the horizon, looking for a shorter route to India using the rudimentary navigational technologies of his day, and returned safely to prove definitively that the world was round—and one of India's smartest engineers, trained at his country's top technical institute and backed by the most modern technologies of his day, was telling me that the world was flat, as flat as that screen on which he can host a meeting of his whole global supply chain. Even more interesting, he was citing this development as a new milestone in human progress and a great opportunity for India and the world—the fact that we had made our world flat!

This has been building for a long time. Globalization 1.0 (1492 to 1800) shrank the world from a size large to a size medium, and the dynamic force in that era was countries globalizing for resources and imperial conquest. Globalization 2.0 (1800 to 2000) shrank the world from a size medium to a size small, and it was spearheaded by companies globalizing for markets and labor. Globalization 3.0 (which started around 2000) is shrinking the world from a size small to a size tiny and flattening the playing field at the same time. And while the dynamic force in Globalization 1.0 was countries globalizing and the dynamic force in Globalization 2.0 was companies globalizing, the dynamic force in Globalization 3.0—the thing that gives it its unique character—is individuals and small groups globalizing. Individuals must, and can, now ask: where do I fit into the global competition and opportunities of the day, and how can I, on my own, collaborate with others globally? But Globalization 3.0 not only differs from the previous eras in how it is shrinking and flattening the world and in how it is empowering individuals. It is also different in that Globalization 1.0 and 2.0 were driven primarily by European and American companies and countries. But going forward, this will be less and less true. Globalization 3.0 is not only going to be driven more by individuals but also by a much more diverse—non-Western, nonwhite—group of individuals. In Globalization 3.0, you are going to see every color of the human rainbow take part.

"Today, the most profound thing to me is the fact that a 14-year-old in Romania or Bangalore or the Soviet Union or Vietnam has all the information, all the tools, all the software easily available to apply knowledge however they want," said Marc Andreessen, a co-founder of Netscape and creator of the first commercial Internet browser. "That is why I am sure the next Napster is going to come out of left field. As bioscience becomes more computational and less about wet labs and as all the genomic data becomes easily available on the Internet, at some point you will be able to design vaccines on your laptop."

Andreessen is touching on the most exciting part of Globalization 3.0 and the flattening of the world: the fact that we are now in the process of connecting all the knowledge pools in the world together. We've tasted some of the downsides of that in the way that Osama bin Laden has connected terrorist knowledge pools together through his Qaeda network, not to mention the work of teenage hackers spinning off more and more lethal computer viruses that affect us all. But the upside is that by connecting all these knowledge pools we are on the cusp of an incredible new era of innovation, an era that will be driven from left field and right field, from West and East and from North and South. Only 30 years ago, if you had a choice of being born a B student in Boston or a genius in Bangalore or Beijing, you probably would have chosen Boston, because a genius in Beijing or Bangalore could not really take advantage of his or her talent. They could not plug and play globally. Not anymore. Not when the world is flat, and anyone with smarts, access to Google and a cheap wireless laptop can join the innovation fray.

When the world is flat, you can innovate without having to emigrate. This is going to get interesting. We are about to see creative destruction on steroids.

How did the world get flattened, and how did it happen so fast?

It was a result of 10 events and forces that all came together during the 1990's and converged right around the year 2000. Let me go through them briefly. The first event was 11/9. That's right—not 9/11, but 11/9. Nov. 9, 1989, is the day the Berlin Wall came down, which was critically important because it allowed us to think of the world as a single space. "The Berlin Wall was not only a symbol of keeping people inside Germany; it was a way of preventing a kind of global view of our future," the Nobel Prize-winning economist Amartya Sen said. And the wall went down just as the windows went up—the breakthrough Microsoft Windows 3.0 operating system, which helped to flatten the playing field even more by creating a global computer interface, shipped six months after the wall fell.

The second key date was 8/9. Aug. 9, 1995, is the day Netscape went public, which did two important things. First, it brought the Internet alive by giving us the browser to display images and data stored on Web sites. Second, the Netscape stock offering triggered the dot-com boom, which triggered the dot-com bubble, which triggered the massive overinvestment of billions of dollars in fiber-optic telecommunications cable. That overinvestment, by companies like Global Crossing, resulted in the willy-nilly creation of a global undersea-underground fiber network, which in turn drove down the cost of transmitting voices, data and images to practically zero, which in turn accidentally made Boston, Bangalore and Beijing next-door neighbors overnight. In sum, what the Netscape revolution did was bring people-to-people connectivity to a whole new level. Suddenly more people could connect with more other people from more different places in more different ways than ever before.

No country accidentally benefited more from the Netscape moment than India. "India had no resources and no infrastructure," said Dinakar Singh, one of the most respected hedge-fund managers on Wall Street, whose parents earned doctoral degrees in biochemistry from the University of Delhi before emigrating to America. "It produced people with quality and by quantity. But many of them rotted on the docks of India like vegetables. Only a relative few could get on ships and get out. Not anymore, because we built this ocean crosser, called fiber-optic cable. For decades you had to leave India to be a professional. Now you can plug into the world from India. You don't have to go to Yale and go to work for Goldman Sachs." India could never have afforded to pay for the bandwidth to connect brainy India with high-tech America, so American shareholders paid for it. Yes, crazy overinvestment can be good. The overinvestment in railroads turned out to be a great boon for the American economy. "But the railroad overinvestment was confined to your own country and so, too, were the benefits," Singh said. In the case of the digital railroads, "it was the foreigners who benefited." India got a free ride.

The first time this became apparent was when thousands of Indian engineers were enlisted to fix the Y2K—the year 2000—computer bugs for companies from all over the world. (Y2K should be a national holiday in India. Call it "Indian Interdependence Day," says Michael Mandelbaum, a foreign-policy analyst at Johns Hopkins.) The fact that the Y2K work could be outsourced to Indians was made possible by the first two flatteners, along with a third, which I call "workflow." Workflow is shorthand for all the software applications, standards and electronic transmission pipes, like middleware, that connected all those computers and fiber-optic cable. To put it another way, if the Netscape moment connected people to people like never before, what the workflow revolution did was connect applications to applications so that people all over the world could work together in manipulating and shaping words, data and images on computers like never before.

Indeed, this breakthrough in people-to-people and application-to-application connectivity produced, in short order, six more flatteners—six new ways in which individuals and companies could collaborate on work and share knowledge. One was "outsourcing." When my software applications could connect seamlessly with all of your applications, it meant that all kinds of work—from accounting to software-writing—could be digitized, disaggregated and shifted to any place in the world where it could be done better and cheaper. The second was "offshoring." I send my whole factory from Canton, Ohio, to Canton, China. The third was "open-sourcing." I write the next operating system, Linux, using engineers collaborating together online and working for free. The fourth was "insourcing." I let a company like UPS come inside my company and take over my whole logistics operation—everything from filling my orders online to delivering my goods to repairing them for customers when they break. (People have no idea what UPS really does today. You'd be amazed!). The fifth was "supply-chaining." This is Wal-Mart's specialty. I create a global supply chain down to the last atom of efficiency so that if I sell an item in Arkansas, another is immediately made in China. (If Wal-Mart were a country, it would be China's eighth-largest trading partner.) The last new form of collaboration I call "informing"—this is Google, Yahoo and MSN Search, which now allow anyone to collaborate with, and mine, unlimited data all by themselves.

So the first three flatteners created the new platform for collaboration, and the next six are the new forms of collaboration that flattened the world even more. The 10th flattener I call "the steroids," and these are wireless access and voice over Internet protocol (VoIP). What the steroids do is turbocharge all these new forms of collaboration, so you can now do any one of them, from anywhere, with any device.

The world got flat when all 10 of these flatteners converged around the year 2000. This created a global, Web-enabled playing field that allows for multiple forms of collaboration on research and work in real time, without regard to geography, distance or, in the near future, even language. "It is the creation of this platform, with these unique attributes, that is the truly important sustainable breakthrough that made what you call the flattening of the world possible," said Craig Mundie, the chief technical officer of Microsoft.

No, not everyone has access yet to this platform, but it is open now to more people in more places on more days in more ways than anything like it in history. Wherever you look today—whether it is the world of journalism, with bloggers bringing down Dan Rather; the world of software, with the Linux code writers working in online forums for free to challenge Microsoft; or the world of business, where Indian and Chinese innovators are competing against and working with some of the most advanced Western multinationals—hierarchies are being flattened and value is being created less and less within vertical silos and more and more through horizontal collaboration within companies, between companies and among individuals.

Do you recall "the IT revolution" that the business press has been pushing for the last 20 years? Sorry to tell you this, but that was just the prologue. The last 20 years were about forging, sharpening and distributing all the new tools to collaborate and connect. Now the real information revolution is about to begin as all the complementarities among these collaborative tools start to converge. One of those who first called this moment by its real name was Carly Fiorina, the former Hewlett-Packard C.E.O., who in 2004 began to declare in her public speeches that the dot-com boom and bust were just "the end of the beginning." The last 25 years in technology, Fiorina said, have just been "the warm-up act." Now we are going into the main event, she said, "and by the main event, I mean an era in which technology will truly transform every aspect of business, of government, of society, of life."

As if this flattening wasn't enough, another convergence coincidentally occurred during the 1990's that was equally important. Some three billion people who were out of the game walked, and often ran, onto the playing field. I am talking about the people of China, India, Russia, Eastern Europe, Latin America and Central

Asia. Their economies and political systems all opened up during the course of the 1990's so that their people were increasingly free to join the free market. And when did these three billion people converge with the new playing field and the new business processes? Right when it was being flattened, right when millions of them could compete and collaborate more equally, more horizontally and with cheaper and more readily available tools. Indeed, thanks to the flattening of the world, many of these new entrants didn't even have to leave home to participate. Thanks to the 10 flatteners, the playing field came to them!

It is this convergence—of new players, on a new playing field, developing new processes for horizontal collaboration—that I believe is the most important force shaping global economics and politics in the early 21st century. Sure, not all three billion can collaborate and compete. In fact, for most people the world is not yet flat at all. But even if we're talking about only 10 percent, that's 300 million people—about twice the size of the American work force. And be advised: the Indians and Chinese are not racing us to the bottom. They are racing us to the top. What China's leaders really want is that the next generation of underwear and airplane wings not just be "made in China" but also be "designed in China." And that is where things are heading. So in 30 years we will have gone from "sold in China" to "made in China" to "designed in China" to "dreamed up in China"—or from China as collaborator with the worldwide manufacturers on nothing to China as a low-cost, high-quality, hyperefficient collaborator with worldwide manufacturers on everything. Ditto India. Said Craig Barrett, the C.E.O. of Intel, "You don't bring three billion people into the world economy overnight without huge consequences, especially from three societies"—like India, China and Russia—"with rich educational heritages."

That is why there is nothing that guarantees that Americans or Western Europeans will continue leading the way. These new players are stepping onto the playing field legacy free, meaning that many of them were so far behind that they can leap right into the new technologies without having to worry about all the sunken costs of old systems. It means that they can move very fast to adopt new, state-of-the-art technologies, which is why there are already more cellphones in use in China today than there are people in America.

If you want to appreciate the sort of challenge we are facing, let me share with you two conversations. One was with some of the Microsoft officials who were involved in setting up Microsoft's research center in Beijing, Microsoft Research Asia, which opened in 1998—after Microsoft sent teams to Chinese universities to administer I.Q. tests in order to recruit the best brains from China's 1.3 billion people. Out of the 2,000 top Chinese engineering and science students tested, Microsoft hired 20. They have a saying at Microsoft about their Asia center, which captures the intensity of competition it takes to win a job there and explains why it is already the most productive research team at Microsoft: "Remember, in China, when you are one in a million, there are 1,300 other people just like you."

The other is a conversation I had with Rajesh Rao, a young Indian entrepreneur who started an electronic-game company from Bangalore, which today owns the rights to Charlie Chaplin's image for mobile computer games. "We can't relax," Rao said. "I think in the case of the United States that is what happened a bit. Please look at me: I am from India. We have been at a very different level before in terms of technology and business. But once we saw we had an infrastructure that made the world a small place, we promptly tried to make the best use of it. We saw there were so many things we could do. We went ahead, and today what we are seeing is a result of that. There is no time to rest. That is gone. There are dozens of people who are doing the same thing you are doing, and they are trying to do it better. It is like water in a tray: you shake it, and it will find the path of least resistance. That is what is going to happen to so many jobs—they will go to that corner of the world where there is the least resistance and the most opportunity. If there is a skilled person in Timbuktu, he will get work if he knows how to access the rest of the world, which is quite easy today. You can make a Web site and have an e-mail address and you are up and running. And if you are able to demonstrate your work, using the same infrastructure, and if people are comfortable giving work to you and if you are diligent and clean in your transactions, then you are in business."

Instead of complaining about outsourcing, Rao said, Americans and Western Europeans would "be better off thinking about how you can raise your bar and raise yourselves into doing something better. Americans have consistently led in innovation over the last century. Americans whining—we have never seen that before."

Rao is right. And it is time we got focused. As a person who grew up during the cold war, I'll always remember driving down the highway and listening to the radio, when suddenly the music would stop and a grim-voiced announcer would come on the air and say: "This is a test. This station is conducting a test of the Emergency Broadcast System." And then there would be a 20-second high-pitched siren sound. Fortunately, we never had to live through a moment in the cold war when the announcer came on and said, "This is a not a test."

That, however, is exactly what I want to say here: "This is not a test."

The long-term opportunities and challenges that the flattening of the world puts before the United States are profound. Therefore, our ability to get by doing things the way we've been doing them—which is to say not always enriching our secret sauce—will not suffice any more. "For a country as wealthy we are, it is amazing how little we are doing to enhance our natural competitiveness," says Dinakar Singh, the Indian-American hedge-fund manager. "We are in a world that has a system that now allows convergence among many billions of people, and we had better step back and figure out what it means. It would be a nice coincidence if all the things that were true before were still true now, but there are quite a few things you actually need to do differently. You need to have a much more thoughtful national discussion."

If this moment has any parallel in recent American history, it is the height of the cold war, around 1957, when the Soviet Union leapt ahead of America in the space race by putting up the Sputnik satellite. The main challenge then came from those who wanted to put up walls; the main challenge to America today comes from the fact that all the walls are being taken down and many other people can now compete and collaborate with us much more directly. The main challenge in that world was from those practicing extreme Communism, namely Russia, China and North Korea. The main challenge to America today is from those practicing extreme capitalism, namely China, India and South Korea. The main objective in that era was building a strong state, and the main objective in this era is building strong individuals.

Meeting the challenges of flatism requires as comprehensive, energetic and focused a response as did meeting the challenge of Communism. It requires a president who can summon the nation to work harder, get smarter, attract more young women and men to science and engineering and build the broadband infrastructure, portable pensions and health care that will help every American become more employable in an age in which no one can guarantee you lifetime employment.

We have been slow to rise to the challenge of flatism, in contrast to Communism, maybe because flatism doesn't involve ICBM missiles aimed at our cities. Indeed, the hot line, which used to connect the Kremlin with the White House, has been replaced by the help line, which connects everyone in America to call centers in Bangalore. While the other end of the hot line might have had Leonid Brezhnev threatening nuclear war, the other end of the help line just has a soft voice eager to help you sort out your AOL bill or collaborate with you on a new piece of software. No, that voice has none of the menace of Nikita Khrushchev pounding a shoe on the table at the United Nations, and it has none of the sinister snarl of the bad guys in "From Russia With Love." No, that voice on the help line just has a friendly Indian lilt that masks any sense of threat or challenge. It simply says: "Hello, my name is Rajiv. Can I help you?"

No, Rajiv, actually you can't. When it comes to responding to the challenges of the flat world, there is no help line we can call. We have to dig into ourselves. We in America have all the basic economic and educational tools to do that. But we have not been improving those tools as much as we should. That is why we are in what Shirley Ann Jackson, the 2004 president of the American Association for the Advancement of Science and president of Rensselaer Polytechnic Institute, calls a "quiet crisis"—one that is slowly eating away at America's scientific and engineering base.

"If left unchecked," said Jackson, the first African-American woman to earn a Ph.D. in physics from M.I.T., "this could challenge our pre-eminence and capacity to innovate." And it is our ability to constantly innovate new products, services and companies that has been the source of America's horn of plenty and steadily widening middle class for the last two centuries. This quiet crisis is a product of three gaps now plaguing American society. The first is an "ambition gap." Compared with the young, energetic Indians and Chinese, too many Americans have gotten too lazy. As David Rothkopf, a former official in the Clinton Commerce Department, puts it, "The real entitlement we need to get rid of is our sense of entitlement." Second, we have a serious numbers gap building. We are not producing enough engineers and scientists. We used to make up for that by importing them from India and China, but in a flat world, where people can now stay home and compete with us, and in a post-9/11 world, where we are insanely keeping out many of the first-round intellectual draft choices in the world for exaggerated security reasons, we can no longer cover the gap. That's a key reason companies are looking abroad. The numbers are not here. And finally we are developing an education gap. Here is the dirty little secret that no C.E.O. wants to tell you: they are not just outsourcing to save on salary. They are doing it because they can often get better-skilled and more productive people than their American workers.

These are some of the reasons that Bill Gates, the Microsoft chairman, warned the governors' conference in a Feb. 26 speech that American high-school education is "obsolete." As Gates put it: "When I compare our high schools to what I see when I'm traveling abroad, I am terrified for our work force of tomorrow. In math and science, our fourth graders are among the top students in the world. By eighth grade, they're in the middle of the pack. By 12th grade, U.S. students are scoring near the bottom of all industrialized nations. . . . The percentage of a population with a college degree is important, but so are sheer numbers. In 2001, India graduated almost a million more students from college than the United States did. China graduates twice as many students with bachelor's degrees as the U.S., and they have six times as many graduates majoring in engineering. In the international competition to have the biggest and best supply of knowledge workers, America is falling behind."

We need to get going immediately. It takes 15 years to train a good engineer, because, ladies and gentlemen, this really is rocket science. So parents, throw away the Game Boy, turn off the television and get your kids to work. There is no sugar-coating this: in a flat world, every individual is going to have to run a little faster if he or she wants to advance his or her standard of living. When I was growing up, my parents used to say to me, "Tom, finish your dinner—people in China are starving." But after sailing to the edges of the flat world for a year, I am now telling my own daughters, "Girls, finish your homework—people in China and India are starving for your jobs."

I repeat, this is not a test. This is the beginning of a crisis that won't remain quiet for long. And as the Stanford economist Paul Romer so rightly says, "A crisis is a terrible thing to waste."

Questions for Discussion and Writing

1. The work ethic has always been a part of American culture. Friedman implies that workers overseas are prepared to work harder than their American counterparts and that this will shift an economic balance in their favor. How do you feel about this? Do you agree?

2. Bill Gates has doubts about the efficiency of an American education in the face of overseas improvements. Do you think there should be changes made? How do you think the American educational system could be improved to keep the United States competitive in the economic field?
3. What do you see as the advantages and disadvantages of outsourcing to other countries?
4. What kinds of industries resort to outsourcing? Research some statistics about how many jobs have been shifted overseas from the American labor market in the last five years and discuss what the implications might be for American workers.
5. Research the history of the World Wide Web. How did it come about? Who invented it? How does it work? Write a brief history for a general reader.
6. How effectively do you think that Friedman makes his points here? What kinds of argumentative moves do you recognize? Are there points with which you could take issue? How would you convince someone of a viewpoint different from that taken by the author?

General Questions for Chapter One

1. Can globalization ever mean anything other than Americanization? What elements do the two concepts share? How is any other country or culture going to ever have the global influence achieved by the United States? Use the essays in this chapter as source material for the arguments you make.
2. What is the negative effect of one country having such global influence as that demonstrated by the United States? What is the positive effect of the same phenomenon? Which of the writers in this chapter fall on each side of the argument and how do they make their positions stronger?
3. Write definitions of the following terms using examples from the essays in this chapter to illustrate the meaning of each concept: globalization; Americanization; hegemony; outsourcing; consumerism.

CHAPTER 2

Reflections on
U.S. Influence

The relationship between America and the rest of the world has long been complex and continues to be so. Many nations rely on the United States to provide funding, technology, and support for their failing or poor economies. Other nations, however, see American involvement as detrimental on a cultural and humanitarian level, as traditional and comfortable ways are rejected by those who bring in outside influence—industrial, financial and military—because "they know better."

With the role of being the world's greatest—perhaps only—superpower comes great responsibility. Despite repeated Presidential claims over the past decades that the focus of each administration would be on domestic issues, the inevitable impact of global actions will draw the United States into some kind of engagement. This may take the form of facilitating peace negotiations, creating free-trade zones, or direct military actions, but it is impossible for the world to ignore the United States or for the United States to ignore the rest of the world.

Because of its geographical position, the United States has often found itself protected from direct action by those who would attack or antagonize it. The Oklahoma City attack of 1995 was seen as an aberration—an attack launched from within the borders of the United States by one of its own citizens. Intelligence had indicated that foreign cells of anti-U.S. operatives were at work within America, and the bombing of the World Trade Center in 1993 had been a warning that tactics and resources were becoming more sophisticated. No one, however, was prepared for the scale of the attack and destruction that we witnessed in 2001.

Response to that attack spread worldwide instantly. Nations rallied to the support of the United States, and except for pockets of militant anti-American feeling, it seemed that there was to be the dawn of a new era of cooperation and collusion to stand firm against the terrorist threat that had breached the borders of the United States. Such support evaporated very quickly as it became clear that the United States would take its own route to address what is now known as "the war on terror." The stance that any nation that did not support the United States in its actions (often decided unilaterally) would be seen as an opponent produced huge division. The relationship between the United States and the United Nations is at an all-time low, and there are huge levels of distrust in the international community. Instead of consolidating the position of the United States as a world leader, the actions since 2001 have led to many nations seeing the United States as a demagogue to be resisted. In May 2005 a conference of 34 South American and Arab nations met in Brasilia, Brazil, to consider how they could reduce their reliance on the United States as a way of moving out from under its ideological influence.

In Chapter One we looked at the definitions and effects of Americanization and globalization. We will now open up our lens and take a look at how people within the United States and around the world are thinking and writing about American influence. There are no simple answers here, and we have to be prepared to see the picture getting blurrier rather than clearer. As we hear voices from India, Hungary, Palestine, and Lebanon as well as from within the United States, we have to be willing to consider what they have to say, even if it makes us uncomfortable. Our choice is whether to know how the world perceives the United States or to maintain a narrow view that could leave us uncertain of the causes and effects of world events.

One thing seems sure: The world is shrinking. Technology and easier travel have changed the global landscape. In my own life I have seen a hundred-mile drive go from a major adventure to something I will do for an evening out. I have flown across the Atlantic Ocean more times than I remember and traveled widely in Europe and Africa. Many of my friends have been to China, Japan, and Australia. Technical and customer support often comes from overseas—an operator in Manila, Philippines, helped me to set up a wireless network when I called for help from my home in Philadelphia. So it is important to know what kinds of opinions and reactions we will get when we travel to other places or interact with people as representatives of the United States.

The writers in this chapter will help to open up that discussion and provide us with a useful variety of perspectives.

What We Think of America (1)
HANAN AL-SHAYKH

Born in Beirut, Lebanon, in 1945, Hanan al-Shaykh is a leading writer in the Arab world, renowned as a novelist, short-story writer, and playwright. Her work frequently focuses on the repression of women by men within Arabic society. Her first novel was published in 1970, but it was her third novel, Hikayat Zahrah (The Story of Zahrah), *published in 1980, that brought her to international attention. She left Lebanon in 1976 because of the civil war in her country, spending some time in Saudi Arabia before settling in London. Her subsequent novels have been translated into multiple languages, while being banned by many Middle Eastern countries because of their content and the perceived attack on traditional Arab culture. The following article relates a visit Hanan al-Shaykh paid to her sister who had relocated to the United States. It gives the writer an opportunity to compare her imagined U.S. experience with the real thing.*

✦

I am the one visiting America this time, but I still remember America coming into our neighbourhood, our house, when I was a child. I remember pushing aside all the heads bending eagerly over it and the hands trying to touch it until I was face to face with it: a red satin cushion with a statue of a good-hearted woman on it, wearing a crown on her head and holding a lamp, a torch. The cushion was accompanied by a greetings card of high buildings which looked like the wooden art deco column in our sitting room, whose glass middle I once saw lit up.

My cousin sent America to our home after he went there to study aeronautical engineering. When he returned, four years later, sheep were slaughtered in his honour and he became an overnight celebrity. Our house was the focus of attention, as if we were all famous.

Years later, I come to visit my sister in America, in a state full of palm trees. As soon as we arrive, I hear my mother sighing bitterly, and wonder why the sun isn't ashamed to shine. My mother sighs from the depths of her heart, as if she hopes this will find my sister and her three children a place to live. They are going to be made homeless the day after tomorrow. My mother has never been homeless in Beirut, despite the war and the violence. "It's as if we're born with our houses on our backs in our country, like tortoises," she says.

My nephews and niece try to collect all their things together, but what about their posters, and the walls which have echoed to their music and their voices? My sister goes round gathering up clothes and books as if she is harvesting wheat, parcelling up bale after bale, only to have new shoots sprouting before her eyes. I see a belt that used to be mine among the clothes and handbags. Instead of rejoicing in the memories it evokes of happy times in Beirut, I feel sad for it, because it too has no home now.

My nephews shout at my sister because she's throwing away papers, falling to bits with age, which they had put in a corner, ready to take with them. Their noise alarms my mother, and my sister threatens to call the police. All this does is remind everyone that it was the police who came to evict them in the first place, after the neighbours complained. It wasn't the first time. My sister's children can only relax when they listen to rap. Its rhythm restores their equilibrium. They are talented musicians who write their own lyrics and set them to music. If this were a different kind of area, this unsolicited music might be seen as nourishment for its audience's soul.

In the past my sister used to send me photos of my niece and nephews from time to time. Americans, except for their Arab eyes. Don't ask me what Arab eyes are like. They have a kind of wariness, perhaps, with a hint of mischief in it. I would smile as I pictured them leaping through a mist, carrying lunch boxes and baseball bats, munching popcorn in an aura of cookies and Kool-Aid—that distinctive smell of their school lockers—and their rooms at home like toy departments, and later like caves where as teenagers they would take refuge with their dreams and pimples.

But here in reality I see cautious expressions, eyes that are dull yet rebellious, and the children living in rooms which are almost like garages or temporary refuges, where the body can rest, but not the soul.

The clock ticks. Tick tock. Tick tock. My mother climbs on top of her seven big suitcases and covers them with sheets so she can forget they exist. She is regretting having bought presents for her neighbours, friends, relatives and the local baker in Beirut, all of them expecting something from America, even just a tin ashtray from McDonald's. Everyone wants something from America, non-disposable nappies among other things, as if the bowels won't do what they are supposed to do if they're exposed to the wrong kind of fabric. People want bedcovers, medicines, children's toys, nail varnish, nighties, shoes of all sizes. I picture my mother throwing everything into the middle of the sitting room on her return: "Go on. Try them on. Take them if they fit."

My mother puts a hand to her forehead as if trying to dig out a name to contact in America. In vain. People here are like silkworms wrapped in their cocoons. Why is America empty? Where are the people? I want to see the owner of the property. My mother urges my sister to talk to him: "He's a human being after all. You can beg him to be kind to you for your children's sake, and let you stay on here. We'll tell him how all this country meant to your husband was women's breasts, blonde hair and alcohol, from the moment he set foot on American soil. How he left you for one of them, so it's hard for you to raise your children. We can promise the landlord that the children won't play instruments or listen to music from now on. This is meant to be the land of freedom . . . shouldn't freedom extend into the homes and streets, like blood and oxygen flowing round the body?"

My mother is pleased with her analogy and keeps repeating it until my sister tells her to be quiet. She's ringing round, trying to find another flat. To no avail: my sister has become well known among letting agencies, moving her children from one place to another like a cat. After numerous attempts she slams the phone down.

"Collateral, collateral. That's all they want. That's what held me back before, and nothing's changed."

My sister used to picture herself disembarking from a passenger liner and being received by official welcomers, taken by the hand, patted on the shoulder, starting her new life in this model country warmed by their encouraging smiles. America was the land of dreams, stretching to infinity, resembling no other country on earth. It had no antiquated laws. Its constitution was founded on equality and justice. Now she finds herself like a fish trapped in a net if she can't come up with some collateral. But if she does find some, they'll drown her in debt. Debts will rain down on her from all sides, once she starts the ball rolling.

She's discovered that her hands are tied. Bureaucracy has injected her with a deadly substance, sapping her resolve. As an immigrant, she has to have ready cash, or she's dead. She who came to the land of dreams like Venus emerging from the sea, naked except for her long hair. She had no references allowing her to open a bank account, no permanent address, no acquaintances with influence or status or property, who could give her credit and support her until she found her feet, equip her to rent a flat, buy a car, open a bank account.

She had to find a job at once, and it was impossible. The competition for jobs was like a war, showing her what a harsh society she was living in. She pleaded for a little time to become acquainted with the surroundings, the new culture, the unfamiliar way of life. It all reinforced her sense of insecurity and stripped her of her self-confidence. She went through one interview after another.

Now the whole process is repeating itself in front of me and my mother. Finally one of the letting agencies responds positively and a few hours later an employee from the agency arrives to negotiate the contract. My mother and I feel pleased that this woman has come in person from the agency, but my sister takes it as a bad sign: "She must want to make sure that I'm not a vagrant."

The woman sits in the middle of the room, cradling her laptop, looking around her apprehensively. She refuses my mother's offer of coffee and asks my sister if she really has a job, as she has tried her office number and had no luck. My sister replies that she didn't go into work today. My mother interrupts. "Sick," she explains, pointing at her heart.

"If your mother's sick, does that mean she'll be living with you too?"

My sister answers that my mother is just visiting, and will be gone next week.

"But how do you know that? Perhaps your mother will change her mind and stay in the United States."

"Me?" interrupts my mother again. "Stay here? I'd rather die."

The woman doesn't understand what she means, and asks my sister to produce her driving licence. My sister replies awkwardly, "I don't have a car. I don't know how to drive."

"So how do you get to work then? You just told me you have a job!"

"I go by bus."

"What? By bus! Surely only old people take the bus!"

The woman casts her eyes round the empty room, unable to believe her ears, pleading with the few remaining objects and my mother's seven suitcases to tell her the truth. Then she asks my sister again, or rather interrogates her: "Is it possible that you don't have a car?"

"Did you hear the joke about the man who was given a ticket by the police because they caught him walking?"

The woman doesn't smile. She asks my sister to give her the names of the people she works with. My sister flushes and turns as red as a pomegranate, especially when the woman refuses to accept two months' rent and demands four months, in advance because she doesn't have collateral.

After the woman has left, my mother sighs. "Ah! If that taxi driver in Beirut only knew what was happening to you and your children. I don't even know why I'm visiting you. I knew you'd be walking on shifting sands, being buried bit by bit, hardly able to keep your heads above the surface. If only he knew what really goes on in America . . . but he'd never believe it."

The taxi driver had struck his face in a torment of envy when he found that his passenger had a return ticket to the States, and an entry visa.

"Why doesn't your photo with Reagan save us?" we say jokingly to my mother. This is a photo of her with a poster of Reagan behind her, looking so real that some simple people in Beirut believe my mother is friendly with him, and have asked her to use her influence with him to get them a U.S. visa.

We sleep, or rather close our eyes to relax, so that we can make decisions.

My mother and sister take refuge with a friend. Although my nephews assure us that one of their friends will put them up, they are going to sleep on the beach as they have often done before, warmed by the bright stars and wept over by the dew.

My niece will sleep in a friend's car. My mother's heart will be on fire, and icy cold. And I will no longer cling to my memory of an old American woman with earrings like little birds in cages, who gasped in wonder at the Roman ruins in Baalbek, and made me want my grandmother to be able to travel abroad like her. I will forget the feel of the "cowboys," as we used to call jeans, which my father borrowed for me from a friend of his who owned a clothes store. He made me promise only to wear them at the school party. In the end, I never dared wear them at all, but was content to look at them and touch them. When I saw them, I saw a piece of America running ahead of me, disregarding the cries of "Shame!"

Translated from the Arabic by Catherine Cobham

Questions for Discussion and Writing

1. What do you think Hanan al-Shayk expected the United States to be like based on the American influences she had experienced before her visit? How do these impressions change in the course of her trip?
2. The writer left her home country of Lebanon in 1976 because of the civil war there. Find out what the causes of that war were and write a short explanation of the circumstances for a general reader.
3. The writer's mother says that she would rather die than to stay in America. This conflicts with many of the ways we think people from overseas think about the United States. Explore why she might feel this way based on evidence from within the essay.
4. The writer talks about rap music in this piece. Are her comments surprising to you based on the tone of the essay? What points is she making about the role of rap in the lives of her sister's children?
5. This article relies on personal experience to make a point. What are the advantages and disadvantages of using a writer's own story in an article like this one?

Challenging Rest of the World with a New Order

ROGER COHEN, DAVID E. SANGER, AND STEVEN R. WEISMAN

This article appeared in the New York Times *on October 12, 2004, as part of the newspaper's coverage of the 2004 election campaign. Many conservative and right-wing groups have attacked the editorial policy of the* New York Times, *claiming that it is the mouthpiece for liberals and their views. The polarization of ideologues in the country has not helped the discussion, with many previously untouchable media sources under renewed scrutiny for bias. Under intense pressure flagship newspapers like the* New York Times *continue to investigate and challenge issues that many politicians would like to see accepted without critical coverage. The following article examines the changes in the relations between the Bush administration and other nations of the world since 2001 and how the United States has repositioned itself as a member of the global community.*

--------------------   ✦   --------------------

Jorge Castañeda, Mexico's former foreign minister, has two distinct images of George W. Bush: the charmer intent on reinventing Mexican-American ties and the chastiser impatient with Mexico as the promise of a new relationship soured.

The change came with the September 11 attacks. "My sense is that Bush lost and never regained the gift he had shown for making you feel at ease," said Mr. Castañeda, who left office last year. "He became aloof, brusque, and on occasion abrasive."

The brusqueness had a clear message: the United States is at war, it needs everybody's support and that support is not negotiable. Mexico's hesitant stance at the United Nations on the war in Iraq became a source of tension. Yet Mr. Castañeda said, "I was never asked, 'What is it you need in order to be more cooperative with us? What can we do to help?' "

It is a characterization of Mr. Bush's foreign policy style often heard around the world: bullying, unreceptive, brazen. The result, critics of this administration contend, has been a disastrous loss of international support, damage to American credibility, the sullying of America's image and a devastating war that has already taken more than 1,000 American lives. In the first presidential debate, Senator John Kerry argued that only with a change of presidents could the damage be undone.

Mr. Bush had a sharp rebuttal, just as his advisers have long told a different story. In their narrative, Mr. Bush's presidency has been an era of historic change, of new alliances bravely embraced, critical relationships solidified, rapid adaptation to a mortal threat and, above all, a bold undertaking to advance freedom in the Middle East through Iraq.

That was the best way, they argue, to confront the terrorist threat to the United States. Along the way, they say, Mr. Bush has used the North Korea crisis to deepen an American relationship with China, steered Pakistan and India away from the brink of nuclear war, and nurtured a relationship with Vladimir V. Putin, the Russian president, even after scrapping the 1972 Anti-Ballistic Missile Treaty.

"The charge is, 'You guys are unilateralists and it's a strategy of pre-emption,'" Secretary of State Colin L. Powell said in an interview. "I just don't think it's true, but it gets repeated often enough that it starts to take on the aura of truth."

• • •

"Relations between Japan and America have never been better than with Bush," said Hatsuhisa Takashima, the foreign ministry spokesman in Tokyo, where spines have been stiffened by the North Korean threat and Mr. Bush's blunt approach to terrorism. "We have more than 500 troops in Iraq because we believe the American-British action prodded Libya to disarm, sent a strong message to North Korea and showed the price of noncompliance with United Nations resolutions. Failure in Iraq is unthinkable."

But as things stand, failure, with its potentially dire consequences for American world leadership, cannot be ruled out. Mr. Bush has proved to be a gambler in foreign affairs. Revolutions can bring big rewards. They can also deliver disaster.

NEW ATTITUDE, NEW ALLIES

The story of the Bush foreign policy is one of startling change: from the promise of a "humble" approach in 2000 through the "dead or alive" search for the elusive Osama bin Laden to the articulation of a bold, pro-active doctrine summed up last month by Mr. Bush, when he told the United Nations:

"Our security is not merely founded in spheres of influence or some balance of power; the security of our world is found in advancing the rights of mankind."

In other words, less emphasis on containment—the policy of slow-squeeze that defeated communism—and more on the contagion of liberty installed, at least in Iraq, by force of arms. This is stirring stuff that resonates in Eastern Europe, where the wounds of oppression are still felt, as well as with Ayad Allawi, the interim prime minister of Iraq, and many of his compatriots. But it is also the stuff of upheaval, and a policy on which the NATO alliance, long a cornerstone of American security, has been unable to agree.

"We have been worried by the absence of debate, the presentation of faits accomplis," said Javier Solana, a former NATO secretary-general and now the European Union's chief foreign affairs official.

In effect, a new spectrum of relations with Washington has emerged. At one end are estranged allies like France and Germany, angered by the war, convinced it is a losing struggle, alarmed by America's use of overwhelming power.

In the muddy middle are nations like Pakistan, Jordan, Egypt and Saudi Arabia, important allies whose leaders are sometimes supportive, but where many people believe Mr. Bush has ignited a war against Islam. Their reliability is uncertain.

It has not helped that the Mideast peace process has stalled and that Mr. Bush has appeared less engaged in resolving the Israeli-Palestinian dispute than his recent predecessors.

At the other end are nations, including Poland, Italy, Britain and Japan, that have made the choice to fall in line with Mr. Bush after September 11. Others, including Russia, China and Israel, have embraced the war on terror for reasons of their own.

These divisions get little airing when Mr. Bush campaigns for a second term. The rhetoric at his rallies is of an America unbowed and unrestrained. The day after the first presidential debate Mr. Bush said Mr. Kerry would subject decisions on national security to vetoes "by countries like France." The U.N. is often derided at Republican events.

This sort of talk may bring partisan crowds to their feet, but it makes the world uneasy.

"If you want to get a cheap cheer from certain quarters in America, it seems that all you have to do is bash the U.N., or the French or the very idea that allies are entitled to have their own opinions," Chris Patten, the commissioner for external relations for the European Union, said last month. "Multilateralists, we are told, want to outsource American foreign and security policy to a bunch of garlic-chewing, cheese-eating wimps."

• • •

A WORLD ALIENATED

While many nations have criticized Mr. Bush for walking away from certain international institutions and treaties, it is doubtful that any American president would have embraced an International Criminal Court that could put American peacekeepers on trial. Even Mr. Kerry says the Kyoto protocol on global warming that Mr. Bush rejected should be renegotiated. Certainly, any American president would have used force to respond to the attacks on New York and Washington.

But the complaint often heard around the world is that from the outset the Bush administration's dismissive attitude set a pattern of take-it-or-leave-it policies that needlessly alienated friends. The Iraq war accelerated that process. Then, the acknowledgment that there were no stockpiles of weapons of mass destruction and no proven links between Mr. Hussein and Al Qaeda cemented the view in Paris, Berlin and elsewhere that Mr. Bush governed from ideology first, facts second.

"The United States had to react strongly to Sept. 11, a fact often forgotten in Europe," said Alexandre Adler, a French foreign policy expert generally sympathetic to America. "But Bush has given the image of a warmonger without subtleties and the result is no president since Nixon, and perhaps not even then, has been so unpopular here."

• • •

Condoleezza Rice, Mr. Bush's national security adviser, . . . listed several ways she thought the president had improved relations with foreign leaders.

"The best relationship that any administration has had with Russia," she said in an interview. "The best relationship that any administration has had with China. An outstanding relationship with India at the same time that you have a very good relationship with Pakistan. The expansion of NATO into the Baltics without destroying the U.S. relationship with Russia."

China and India, of course, account for more than a third of humanity, a point Ms. Rice underscored as she urged the administration's critics to think hard about who is complaining about alienation and who is not.

But the complaints are often vociferous. "The Bush administration started with a belief that in the past 500 years or more, no greater gap had ever existed between the No. 1 and No. 2 power in the world," said Norman Ornstein, a foreign policy expert at the American Enterprise Institute. "Given this American domination, they believed, especially after 9/11, that it was enough to express the American national interest firmly and everyone would accommodate themselves."

They did not. While there was an outpouring of sympathy for the United States after the September 11 attacks, by the end of 2002 the sympathy had vanished. When Mr. Bush arrived this summer in Ireland, he was spirited off to a castle, miles from anyone. Protests marked Mr. Bush's most recent visit to Britain, home of his most steadfast ally, Prime Minister Tony Blair. Even Mr. Blair had to apologize for the intelligence about unconventional weapons in Iraq, something Mr. Bush has resisted.

Anti-Americanism has become a winning European platform. In the most recent Spanish and German elections, opposing Mr. Bush's policies proved central to both the upset victory of José Luis Rodríguez Zapatero and the re-election of Chancellor Gerhard Schröder, respectively.

• • •

Still, anti-American hostility in the Islamic world is widespread. Last year, Mr. Powell asked Edward P. Djerejian, an experienced diplomat, to travel the world to examine the failures of American public diplomacy in the Arab and Muslim worlds.

Mr. Djerejian returned shocked at the picture of America he saw on Arab television and the absence of any effective American rebuttal. "We did not have anywhere near enough people in place with the right language skills or the right sensitivities to respond," he said.

Mr. Djerejian still believes the outcome in Iraq could be positive, but he added that a chronically unstable Iraq would "set back the key goals we said we were trying to achieve on the Arab-Israeli front, on energy security and certainly on democratizing the region."

His investigation came before the photographs of abuse at Abu Ghraib prison in Iraq emerged. "The photographs shattered our reputation as the world's most admired champion of freedom and justice," said Philip Gordon of the Brookings Institution. "That is grave, because without the world's trust, America cannot flourish."

So three years after September 11, Mr. Bush leads a United States whose image has been tarnished, while Europeans, Asians and Latin Americans still feel far less threatened by terrorism than Americans do.

The president speaks of the threat almost daily, but leaders elsewhere do not. In Europe, terrorism is not new and so seems less menacing; in Asia, the rapid growth of China and India continues to fuel an optimism that dispels, or at least diminishes, the dark clouds from the Middle East; in Latin America, trade and economic issues seem at least as important as Al Qaeda. The shared perception of a common threat that was the cornerstone of America's cold war alliances is gone.

"This America that speaks constantly of war and designates an enemy is not really accepted here," said Nicole Bacharan, a French analyst. "Europeans have a deep desire not to feel threatened. It is sad to observe this divorce in our world views."

IN SPITE OF RIFTS, ADVANCES

Mr. Bush is aware of the divide, and in recent months has tried to bridge it. In Istanbul in June at a NATO summit meeting where Iraq, Afghanistan, Bosnia, and terrorism were on the agenda, he dispensed with his prepared speech in favor of a direct and emotional appeal.

An American diplomat in attendance said that Mr. Bush "spoke strongly, seemed a real leader" and pressed his case that "whatever past differences, we all have a stake in the success of an independent Iraq."

But the next day, President Jacques Chirac of France shot back that NATO would never go into Iraq. "I don't believe it's NATO's job to intervene in Iraq," he said. Mr. Bush was angry, aides say, but pushed on. This summer NATO sent a 40-person team to Baghdad and recently, after long wrangling between the United States and France, agreed to increase the team to about 300 people to train Iraqi officers.

Ms. Rice and Mr. Powell say such missions prove that any tensions with France are overblown. "The relationship's fine," Ms. Rice said, citing the French role in Kosovo and Afghanistan. Relations with France are always "better in practice than they are in theory," she added.

Perhaps, but Mr. Chirac and Mr. Bush are no closer in world views than they ever were. The French president said recently that he sought a multilateral world in which the United Nations set the laws by which all nations abide—code words for limiting American power. Mr. Bush flatly rejects this view.

Ms. Rice insisted that Iraq had not thrust all other issues to the back burner.

"You have the most comprehensive policy toward Africa that any administration has had, including trade rights and AIDS and intervention with American forces to help solve the Liberia situation," she said. "You have China on the front lines against the North Korean nuclear program."

Her voice began to rise. "You want me to keep going?" she asked.

Certainly, Mr. Bush can cite the democratic opening in Afghanistan and Libya's move to abandon its nuclear weapons program as achievements. An Indian-Pakistani dialogue has begun, in part because of Mr. Powell's intervention last year.

At campaign stops, Mr. Bush often mentions the six-party talks with North Korea—involving China, Russia, South Korea and Japan—as an example of his diplomatic style.

"The difference between Iraq and North Korea, for example, is 11 years," Mr. Bush said in his interview. "Diplomacy failed for 11 years in Iraq. And this new diplomatic effort is barely a year old."

But the North Korean talks have also been an example of what happens when international diplomacy gets bogged down between hawks in the Pentagon and the vice president's office, and those in the State Department urging engagement. Not until it was clear that North Korea was probably manufacturing new weapons did Mr. Bush intervene.

"I give credit to Secretary Powell, who has been a lone voice of sanity on this issue, for creating the six-party talks, which now have the possibility of a potential solution," said Gov. Bill Richardson of New Mexico, who was engaged in negotiating efforts as a member of the Clinton administration and is an active supporter of Mr. Kerry. "But we should have engaged bilaterally with North Korea sooner."

Elsewhere, the record seems mixed. In Africa, Mr. Bush followed Mr. Powell's lead to describe events in Sudan as "genocide." The United States is still working with African, Arab and European nations to make Sudan accept a large force of African peacekeeping troops to stabilize the western region of Darfur.

Pakistan's continued help against Al Qaeda appears solid, but Islamabad pardoned Abdul Qadeer Khan, the nuclear scientist who had smuggled nuclear technology to North Korea, Libya and Iran. Mr. Bush uttered not a word of criticism, even after Pakistan refused to allow the United States to interrogate him.

A QUESTION OF CONSULTATION

It often appears to his allies that Mr. Bush offers only a veneer of consultation. To deal with the Israeli-Palestinian conflict, the Bush administration has embraced the "quartet"—the United States, Russia, the European Union and the United Nations—to work on reciprocal steps by Israel and the Palestinians leading to a Palestinian state.

But Europeans, including Prime Minister Blair of Britain, remain frustrated by what they say has been Mr. Bush's failure to become actively engaged in pressing Israel to freeze the growth of settlements and to ease conditions for Palestinians living in the West Bank.

• • •

European states no longer know how to structure their relationship with the United States. They wonder if there is enough stability in "coalitions of the willing"—Mr. Bush's favorite phrase to describe the nations that have joined the United States in Iraq.

Indeed, Iraq, many European officials say, was a costly distraction from fighting terrorism. They argue that the Israeli-Palestinian conflict, whose images feed extremism across the Arab world, has been neglected. Iran, a more real and imminent threat than Iraq, and a source of further European-American division, was ignored for too long.

The resulting splits—those between Europe and America and those between the Arab world and America—are clear. What remains uncertain is whether Mr. Bush's policies will let terrorists exploit those divisions or whether his determination will crush them.

Questions for Discussion and Writing

1. President Bush is quoted in this article as saying: "Our security is not merely founded in spheres of influence or some balance of power; the security of our world is found in advancing the rights of mankind." Using the information in the article, how do you see the writers explaining the effects of this policy in international relations?

2. There are advantages and disadvantages to America dictating policy rather than engaging in consultation. What do you see as being the positive elements and the drawbacks to such a policy move?

3. The final part of this article highlights the Middle East as being the area of the world most in need of positive attention. The writers indicate that much international unrest is generated from this relatively small area of the planet. Investigate the root causes of the Israeli-Palestinian conflict and explain them for a general reader.

4. This article relies heavily on direct interviews with sources. What must a writer be aware of when conducting an interview? How can readers be sure that writers are giving us a fair report of an interview and not slanting it for us? What do we miss as readers that would have been readily apparent to the interviewer and how might that change things?

American Public Diplomacy in the Islamic World

ANDREW KOHUT

Andrew Kohut is Director of the Pew Research Center for The People & The Press (formerly the Times Mirror Center for the People & the Press) in Washington, DC. From 1979 to 1989 he was President of The Gallup Organization, leaving to create Princeton Survey Research Associates, an organization chiefly specializing in media, politics, and public policy studies. Kohut was the founding director of surveys for the Times Mirror Center from 1990 to 1992 and was named its director in 1993. Kohut was President of the American Association of Public Opinion Research (1994–1995), President of the National Council on Public Polls (2000–2001), a member of the Market Research Council, and a member of the Council on Foreign Relations. Andrew Kohut made the following statement to The Senate Foreign Relations Committee Hearing, and the transcript was released on February 27, 2003.

◆

I am delighted to help this committee achieve a better under-standing of how the United States is perceived in the Islamic world. I am not here to make recommendations about how to solve America's image problems, but rather to give you as much as I can on the nature of the problem.

While this committee is primarily interested in the image of United States in the Islamic world, I will put my remarks in context by also discussing attitudes toward the United States around the world more generally. The *Pew Global Attitudes Project* surveyed 38,000 people in 44 countries. We released our results, "What the World Thinks in 2002," in December and you all should have copies of our report.

Despite an initial outpouring of public sympathy for America following the September 11, 2001 terrorist attacks, discontent with the United States has grown around the world over the past two years. Images of the U.S. have been tarnished in all types of nations: among longtime NATO allies, in developing countries, in eastern Europe and, most dramatically, in Muslim societies.

Since 2000, favorability ratings for the U.S. have fallen in 19 of the 27 countries worldwide where trend benchmarks are available. While criticism of America is on the rise, however, a reserve of goodwill toward the United States still remains. The *Pew Global Attitudes* survey finds that the U.S. and its citizens continue to be rated positively by majorities in 35 of the 42 countries in which the question was asked. True dislike, if not hatred, of America is concentrated in the Muslim nations of the Middle East and in Central Asia, today's areas of greatest conflict.

The most serious problem facing the U.S. abroad is its very poor public image in the Muslim world, especially in the Middle East/Conflict Area. Favorable ratings are down sharply in two of America's most important allies in this region, Turkey and Pakistan. The number of people giving the United States a posi- tive rating has dropped by 22 points in Turkey and 13 points in Pakistan in the last three years. And in Egypt, a country for which no comparative data is available, just 6% of the public holds a favorable view of the U.S.

Fully three-quarters of respondents in Jordan, the fourth largest recipient of U.S. assistance, have a poor image of the United States. In Pakistan and Egypt, an even-larger aid recipient, nearly as many (69%) have an unfavorable view and no more than one-in-ten in either country have positive feelings toward the U.S. In Jordan, Pakistan and Egypt, the intensity of this dislike is strong—more than 50% in each country have a very unfavorable view.

Public perceptions of the United States in Turkey have declined sharply in the last few years. In 1999, a slim majority of Turks felt favorably toward the U.S., but now just three-in-ten do. As is the case in Pakistan, Jordan and Egypt, the intensity of negative opinion is strong: 42% of Turks have a very unfavorable view of the U.S. The same pattern is evident in Lebanon, where 59% have a poor opinion of the U.S.

Uzbekistan, a new U.S. ally in the fight against terror, is a notable exception to this negative trend. By nearly eight-to-one (85%−11%) Uzbeks have a positive opinion of the United States and more than a third (35%) hold a very favorable view of the U.S.

Dislike of America undoubtedly reflects dislike of U.S. policies in the Middle East. In a survey of opinion leaders released by the Pew Research Center in December 2001 ("America Admired, Yet Its New Vulnerability Seen as Good Thing, Say Opinion Leaders"), a majority in Islamic countries told us that U.S. support of Israel is the top reason that people in their countries dislike America.

But backlash against the U.S.-led war on terror is also a big part of the problem. Unlike in much of the rest of the world, the war on terrorism is opposed by majorities in 10 of the 11 predominantly Muslim countries surveyed by Pew. This includes countries outside the Middle East/Conflict Area, such as Indonesia and Senegal where majorities still held favorable opinion of the U.S. While they still like us, they don't like our war on terrorism. The principal exception is the overwhelming support for America's anti-terrorist campaign found in Uzbekistan, where the United States currently has troops stationed.

Jordanians, in particular, are overwhelmingly opposed to the war on terror (85%–13%). Majorities in Egypt, Lebanon and Turkey and a plurality in Pakistan, a key U.S. ally in the region, also oppose the U.S.-led war on terror. In Pakistan, Lebanon and Egypt, Muslims are more likely to oppose these efforts to fight terrorism than non-Muslims.

The prevailing opinion among people in this region is that the United States ignores the interests of their countries in deciding its international policies. This view is as dominant in Turkey (74%), a NATO ally, as it is in Lebanon (77%). More specifically, the Pew survey finds a strong sense among most of the countries surveyed that U.S. policies serve to increase the formidable gap between rich and poor countries. Moreover, sizable minorities feel the United States does too little to help solve the world's problems.

The Gallup Poll, which conducted nationwide surveys in nine predominately Muslim countries in January 2002, summed it up well. They concluded that "the perception that Western nations are not fair in their stances toward Palestine fits in with a more generalized view that the West is unfair to the Arab and Islamic worlds . . . it is one of several examples of Western bias that might extend to Afghanistan, Iraq Gulf oil and other situations."

"AMERICANIZATION" REJECTED

But it is all not one way—even in Muslim countries, opinions about the U.S. are complicated and contradictory. As among other people around the world, U.S. global influence is simultaneously embraced and rejected by Muslim publics. America is nearly universally admired for its technological achievements and people in most countries say they enjoy U.S. movies, music and television programs.

Very large majorities of the publics in most of the world admire U.S. technology. This is the case even among people with a low regard for the United States generally. In Jordan, where just a quarter have a favorable opinion of the U.S., 59% say they admire U.S. technological achievements. Even in Pakistan, where one-in-10 have a positive image of the U.S., a 42% plurality says they admire U.S. scientific advances.

Opinion of American popular culture is mixed, but more positive than one might expect. In Lebanon, where most have an unfavorable view of the U.S., 65% say they like American music, movies and television. In African countries with significant Muslim populations such as Senegal and Nigeria, majorities say they like American popular culture. But majorities in Jordan and Cairo dislike U.S. culture, as does a plurality in Turkey. Pakistan stands alone in the extent of its dislike of American popular culture. Eight-in-ten Pakistanis dislike American music, movies and television.

Although people in some Islamic countries like American popular culture while others reject it, there is more of a consensus that people do not like the spread of "Americanism." In general, the spread of U.S. ideas and customs is disliked by majorities in almost every country included in this worldwide survey. In the Middle East/Conflict Area, overwhelming majorities in every country except Uzbekistan have a negative impression of the spread of American ideas and customs. Just 2% of Pakistanis and 6% of Egyptians see this trend as a good thing. Even in generally pro-American Uzbekistan, 56% object to the spread of American ideas and customs.

WAR IN IRAQ

The unpopularity of a potential war with Iraq can only further fuel hostilities—almost no matter how well such a war goes. At the Pew Research Center, we got some sense of this when we conducted another survey in addition to our 44-nation poll. In November, we also surveyed the people of five countries Britain, France, Germany, Turkey and Russia, about their attitudes toward a potential U.S.-led war in Iraq.

Unlike western Europeans and Russians, Turkish respondents were divided on whether the regime in Baghdad is a threat to the stability of the region, and were divided over whether ending Saddam Hussein's rule would be good or bad for Turkey. Further, and of particular interest to this committee, a 53%

majority of Turkish respondents believe the U.S. wants to get rid of Saddam Hussein as part of a war against unfriendly Muslim countries, rather than because the Iraqi leader is a threat to peace.

SUMMARY: OPINION OF U.S. LINKED TO VIEWS OF POLICIES

In summary, antipathy toward the U.S. is shaped by how its international policies are interpreted. Gallup's findings reflected that clearly in showing that large majorities in their nine-nation survey said the West doesn't respect Muslim values, nor show concern for the Islamic and Muslim worlds.

Improving America's image is a tough charge unless we can prove that our critics in the Muslim world are wrong about our intentions and the consequences of our policies. Until that happens, U.S. communication efforts in the region can only be defensive, doing the best possible in a bad situation—correcting misinformation, softening hostility by playing to aspects of America that are still well regarded. But in the end, we will only be affecting opinions on the margins.

However, I think there are some bigger opportunities down the road as I look at the second wave of the *Pew Global Attitudes* polling. We will show a very substantial level of democratic aspirations among Muslim people. People in Muslim countries place a high value on freedom of expression, multi-party systems, equal treatment under the law—in fact, higher than in some nations of eastern Europe. Our upcoming release this spring will detail these aspirations, and show how they exist side-by-side with a desire for a strong role for Islam in governance.

American policies that are seen as encouraging democratization might help establish, or bolster, constituencies for the U.S. in Muslim countries, especially outside of the Middle East—in Africa, particularly, where America's Palestinian policies have not so inflamed opinion. In the Middle East, the establishment of democratic institutions in Iraq after Saddam Hussein could prove to be an important first positive step in that most problematic part of the Muslim world.

Questions for Discussion and Writing

1. What reasons does Kohut give for the problems America has with image since the initial outpouring of support in 2001?
2. In what fields are the United States almost universally admired?

3. How might you explain the apparent contradictions in these surveys—that the cultural influence is generally welcomed while political policy influence is not?
4. Does the focus on the image of America take away from the actual impact of American influence? It is right that the image could project one element of America but the reality might be something wholly different?

Rights to Remember
HAROLD HONGJU KOH

Harold Hongju Koh is a Professor of International Law at Yale Law School and became Dean of the School in 2003. Dr. Koh is a Korean-American who served as Assistant Secretary of State for Democracy, Human Rights and Labor for the Clinton administration under Madeline Albright. He is the author of several books on international relations law and human rights and over 70 articles on international law, constitutional law, and international business transactions. Dr. Koh was educated at Harvard University, Magdalen College, Oxford (UK), and Harvard Law School. The following article appeared in The Economist *on October 30, 2003. In the essay Dr. Koh questions the wisdom and legality of many measures put in place by the U.S. government since September 2001. He also examines how the new American model has led to negative effects on democratic political opposition around the world.*

◆

I would argue that September 11th ended the euphoria brought on by the fall of the Berlin Wall, the belief that American-led global co-operation could solve global problems. The American administration responded to the twin-towers tragedy with a sweeping new global strategy: an emerging "Bush doctrine," if you will.

One element of this doctrine is what I call "Achilles and his heel." September 11th brought upon America, as once upon Achilles, a schizophrenic sense of both exceptional power and exceptional vulnerability. Never has a superpower seemed so powerful and so vulnerable at the same time. The Bush doctrine asked: "How can we use our superpower resources to protect our vulnerability?"

The administration's answer has been "homeland security." To preserve American power and prevent future attack, the government has asserted a novel right under international law to disarm through "pre-emptive self-defence" any country that poses a threat. At home it has instituted sweeping strategies of immigration control, security detention, governmental secrecy and information awareness.

The administration has also radically shifted its emphasis on human rights. In 1941, Franklin Delano Roosevelt called the allies to arms by painting a vision of the world we were trying to make: a post-war world of four fundamental freedoms: freedom of speech, freedom of religion, freedom from want, freedom from fear.

This framework foreshadowed the post-war human-rights construct—embedded in the Universal Declaration of Human Rights and subsequent international covenants—that emphasised comprehensive protection of civil and political rights (freedom of speech and religion), economic, social and cultural rights (freedom from want), and freedom from gross violations and persecution (the Refugee Convention, the Genocide Convention and the Torture Convention). But Bush administration officials have now reprioritised "freedom from fear" as the number-one freedom we need to preserve. Freedom from fear has become the obsessive watchword of America's human-rights policy.

Witness five faces of a human-rights policy fixated on freedom from fear. First, closed government and invasions of privacy. Second, scapegoating immigrants and refugees. Third, creating extra-legal zones, most prominently at the naval base at Guantánamo Bay in Cuba. Fourth, creating extra-legal persons, particularly the detainees of American citizenship labelled "enemy combatants." Fifth, a reduced American human-rights presence through the rest of the globe.

The following vignettes illustrate this transformation of human rights:

- Closed government and invasions of privacy. Two core tenets of a post-Watergate world had been that our government does not spy on its citizens, and that American citizens should see what our government is doing. But since September 11th, classification of government documents has risen to new heights.

  The Patriot Act, passed almost without dissent after September 11th, authorises the Defence Department to develop a project to promote something called "total information awareness." Under this programme, the government may gather huge amounts of information about citizens without proving they have done anything wrong. They can access a citizen's records—whether telephone, financial, rental, internet, medical, educational or library—without showing any involvement with terrorism. Internet service providers may be forced to produce records based solely on FBI declarations that the information is for an anti-terrorism investigation.

Many absurdities follow: the Lawyers Committee for Human Rights, in a study published in September, reports that 20 American peace activists, including nuns and high-school students, were recently flagged as security threats and detained for saying that they were travelling to a rally to protest against military aid to Colombia. The entire high-school wrestling team of Juneau, Alaska, was held up at airports seven times just because one member was the son of a retired Coast Guard officer on the FBI watch-list.

- Scapegoating immigrants. After September 11th, 1,200 immigrants were detained, more than 750 on charges based solely on civil immigration violations. The Justice Department's own inspector-general called the attorney-general's enforcement of immigration laws "indiscriminate and haphazard." The Immigration and Naturalisation Service, which formerly had a mandate for humanitarian relief as well as for border protection, has been converted into an arm of the Department of Homeland Security.

The impact on particular groups has been devastating. The number of refugees resettled in America declined from 90,000 a year before September 11th to less than a third that number, 27,000, this year. The Pakistani population of Atlantic County, New Jersey has fallen by half.

ZONES AND PEOPLE OUTSIDE THE LAW

- The creation of extra-legal zones. Some 660 prisoners from 42 countries are being held in Guantánamo Bay, some for nearly two years. Three children are apparently being detained, including a 13-year-old, several of the detainees are aged over 70, and one claims to be over 100. Courtrooms are being built to try six detainees, including two British subjects who have been declared eligible for trial by military commission. There have been 32 reported suicide attempts. Yet the administration is literally pouring concrete around its detention policy, spending another $25m on buildings in Guantánamo that will increase the detention capacity to 1,100.

- The creation of extra-legal persons. In two cases that are quickly working their way to the Supreme Court, Yasser Hamdi and José Padilla are two American citizens on American soil who have been designated as "enemy combatants," and who have been accorded no legal channels to assert their rights.

   The racial disparities in the use of the "enemy combatant" label are glaring. Contrast, for example, the treatment of Mr Hamdi, from Louisiana but of Saudi Arabian ancestry, with that of John Walker Lindh, the famous "American Taliban," who is a white American from a comfortable family in the San Francisco Bay area. Both are American citizens; both were captured in Afghanistan in late 2001 by the Northern Alliance; both were handed over to American forces, who eventually brought them to the United States. But federal prosecutors brought criminal charges against Mr Lindh, who got an expensive lawyer and eventually plea-bargained to a prison term. Meanwhile, Mr Hamdi has remained in incommunicado detention, without a lawyer, in a South Carolina military brig for the past 16 months.

- The effect on the rest of the world. America's anti-terrorist activities have given cover to many foreign governments who want to use "anti-terrorism" to justify their own crackdowns on human rights. Examples abound. In Indonesia, the army has cited America's use of Guantánamo to propose building an off-shore prison camp on Nasi Island to hold suspected terrorists from Aceh. In Australia, Parliament passed laws mandating the forcible transfer of refugees seeking entry to detention facilities in Nauru, where children as young as three years old are being held, so that Australia does not (in the words of its defence minister) become a "pipeline for terrorists."

   In China, Wang Bingzhang, the founder of the pro-democracy magazine *China Spring*, was recently sentenced to life imprisonment for "organising and leading a terrorist group," the first time, apparently, that the Chinese government has charged a democracy activist with terrorism. In Russia, Vladimir Putin on September 12th 2001 declared that America and Russia "have a common foe" because Osama bin Laden's people are connected to events in Chechnya. Within months the American government had added three Chechen groups to its list of foreign terrorist organisations.

   In Egypt, the government extended for another three years its emergency law, which allows it to detain suspected national-security threats almost indefinitely without charge, to ban public demonstrations, and to try citizens before military tribunals. President Hosni Mubarak announced that America's parallel policies proved that "we were right from the beginning in using all means, including military tribunals, to combat terrorism."

What's wrong with this picture? Each prong of the Bush doctrine places America in the position of promoting double standards, one for itself, and another for the rest of the world. The emerging doctrine has placed startling pressure upon the structure of human-rights and international law that the United States itself designed and supported since 1948. In a remarkably short time, the United States has moved from being the principal supporter of that system to its most visible outlier.

Around the globe, America's human-rights policy has visibly softened, subsumed under the all-encompassing banner of the "war against terrorism." And at home, the Patriot Act, military commissions, Guantánamo and the indefinite detention of American citizens have placed America in the odd position of condoning deep intrusions by law, even while creating zones and persons outside the law.

NOTHING NATURAL ABOUT IT

At this point, you are surely asking: "Why did this happen?" and "What can we do about it?" People living outside America sometimes suggest that the reason is rooted in the American national culture of unilateralism, parochialism and an obsession with power. With respect, let me urge you to see it differently. The Bush doctrine, I believe, is less a broad manifestation of American national character than of short-sighted decisions made by a particularly extreme American administration.

Many, if not most, Americans would have supported dealing with September 11th in a different way. Imagine, for example, the Bush administration dealing with the atrocity through the then prevailing multilateralist strategy of using global co-operation to solve global problems. On the day after the attack, George Bush could have flown to New York to stand in solidarity with the world's ambassadors in front of the United Nations.

He could have supported the International Criminal Court as a way of bringing the Osama bin Ladens and Saddam Husseins of the world to justice. He could have refrained from invading Iraq without a second UN resolution and he could have maintained a host of human-rights treaties to signal the need for even greater global solidarity in a time of terror. I am convinced that the American people would have supported him in all those efforts.

So to those who would blame American culture for America's unilateralism, let me remind you that not every American is equally well-placed to promote American unilateralism. In recent years, such individuals as Mr Bush, Donald Rumsfeld, John Bolton, Jesse Helms and Justice Antonin Scalia have held particularly strategic positions that enabled them to promote this sea-change in human-rights policy.

But if particular politicians and judges are part of the problem, they are also part of the solution. For, in recent months, American human-rights lawyers have launched multiple efforts to counter these trends, particularly through lawsuits seeking to persuade judges to construe American law in light of universal human-rights principles.

What are the signs of this trend? With each passing day, I see growing resistance to these policies among ordinary Americans. Some promising examples:

- Career bureaucrats have started to challenge the administration's policies for undoing years of hard work.
- Military judges and former federal prosecutors have expressed dismay over military commissions.
- A group of former federal judges filed a brief in the Padilla case challenging the president's detention of American citizens without express congressional authorisation.

They were joined in those efforts by two conservative libertarian groups: the Cato Institute and the Rutherford Institute.

- Career diplomats have told me of early retirements by those who refuse to implement what they view as discriminatory visa policies.
- A group of former American diplomats and former American prisoners-of-war have challenged the administration's flouting of the Geneva Conventions before the Supreme Court.
- Librarians and booksellers have joined a bipartisan group of 133 congressional representatives to press for a law, called the Freedom to Read Protection Act, that would shield library and bookstore records from government surveillance.

These grassroots efforts are finally reaching the political actors. The public outcry following the leak of a proposed second Patriot

Act has put that legislation on hold. Resolutions opposing the first Patriot Act have passed in three states and 162 municipalities. The House of Representatives has refused to provide funding for the part of the Patriot Act that allows so-called sneak and peek searches of private property without prompt notice to the resident. A battle is brewing in Congress over whether parts of the current act should be eliminated in 2005.

THE SUPREME COURT TO THE RESCUE?

Most important, the key cases are finally starting to make their way to the United States Supreme Court. Now you may ask: what influence can a combination of international pressure and protest from ordinary Americans have on such a conservative court? But recent cases may give hope. For instance, last June in *Lawrence v Texas*, the Supreme Court finally overruled its 17-year-old decision in *Bowers v Hardwick*, which had permitted states to ban same-sex sodomy among consenting adults. Representing Mary Robinson, the former UN Human Rights High Commissioner, and several other human-rights groups, I had filed an *amicus curiae* brief urging the court to consider two decades of European human-rights precedent rejecting the criminalisation of same-sex sodomy as a violation of the European Convention's right to privacy.

In a six-to-three vote, Justice Anthony Kennedy wrote, citing our brief, that the rationale of Bowers had been rejected by "values we [Americans] share with a wider civilisation."

The court noted that "the right petitioners seek in this case has been accepted as an integral part of human freedom in many other countries" and that "[t]here has been no showing in [the United States] that governmental interest in circumscribing personal choice is somehow more legitimate or urgent."

What this may mean is that when the September 11th cases get to the Supreme Court, American human-rights lawyers can similarly argue that the legality of our policies must be evaluated by "values we [Americans] share with a wider civilisation." Citing *Lawrence*, human-rights advocates can urge the court to decide whether the rights being asserted by detainees like Mr Hamdi, Mr Padilla and those on Guantánamo "have been accepted as an integral part of human freedom in many other countries" and can argue that our government has not demonstrated "that the govern-mental interest in circumscribing [these freedoms] is somehow more legitimate or urgent" in the United States than in other countries that have seen fit to forgo such legal restrictions.

Whether our Supreme Court will accept these arguments remains unclear. But these cases may well determine whether historians will remember these past two years as a fundamental change, or as only a temporary eclipse, in America's human-rights leadership. I, for one, have neither given up hope, nor accepted as inevitable a 21st-century American human-rights policy that is increasingly at odds with core American and universal values.

In our "Declaration of Independence," Thomas Jefferson wrote: "When in the course of human events, it becomes necessary for one people . . . to assume among the Power of the Earth, the separate and equal Station to which the Laws of Nature . . . entitle them, a decent respect to the opinions of mankind requires that they should declare the causes . . . " Most patriotic Americans, I believe, still think that our human-rights policy should pay "decent respect to the opinions of mankind." As a nation conceived in liberty and dedicated to certain inalienable rights, our country has strong primal instincts to address the world not just in the language of power, but through a combination of power and principle.

In 1759, Benjamin Franklin wrote: "They that can give up essential liberty to obtain a little temporary safety deserve neither." In the months ahead, I believe, we can both obtain our security and preserve our essential liberty, but only so long as we have courage from our courts, commitment from our citizens, and pressure from our foreign allies. Even after September 11th, America can still stand for human rights, but we can get there only with a little help from our friends.

Questions for Discussion and Writing

1. What does Dr. Koh see as threats to the inalienable rights of "life, liberty, and the pursuit of happiness" in the current political climate in the United States?
2. How have measures taken in the United States influenced other nation states in the world?
3. What examples does Dr. Koh offer for signs that the American people are resisting inroads made into their liberty and privacy?
4. Argue the advantages and disadvantages of designating some people as "extralegal." Describe what this term means and examine the benefits and detriments to the American legal system of having such a designation.

Symbols of Destruction

ELEMER HANKISS

Elmer Hankiss has been Director of the Hungarian Academy of Sciences Institute of Sociology since 1996. Dr. Hankiss received his bachelor's degree and his PhD from Budapest University. He is also Senior Scientist at The Gallup Organization (Princeton). He has also held the post of Visiting Professor at the European University Institute, Florence, and the Central European University. His research fields include how social values and belief systems interact and construct contemporary Western civilization, contemporary mythologies, and the sociology of the consumer civilization. His recent books include Humans and Antelopes: Conversations About Some Ultimate Concerns *(2001) [in Hungarian] and* Fears and Symbols: An Introduction in the Study of Western Civilization *(2000). In this article he breaks down how the destruction of the World Trade Center in 2001 resonated on a mythical and symbolic level in the United States and around the world.*

◆

THE SHOCK

Since the assassination of President Kennedy nothing has shocked the western world, and not only the USA, more than the terror attack of 11 September.

On the one hand, this is understandable. We are citizens of the same world, heirs of the same civilization, and myriad human relations, institutional contacts, common values and interests, ventures and projects bind us closely and inseparably together. But, on the other hand, the intensity of the shock outside the U.S. is something that is worth a closer scrutiny. Beyond the deep-felt sorrow for those innocent people who lost their lives, and the indignation over the brutality of the attack, people were shaken in their very existence and uncertainty and fear filled their hearts. The question is: Why? There are a few obvious, and some less obvious answers.

CENTRUM MUNDI

In the last few decades America has undoubtedly become the center of the world; both in the literal and the symbolic sense of the word.

Let's take the White House as an example. It has become physically the center of world political power. The most important political decisions are being made inside its walls. But, at the same time, the building itself—with its white walls, serene proportions, classical Greek tympanum and colonnade—has become the symbol of a power that radiates not only strength but also peace, freedom, and harmony. This rich and positive symbolism has been daily reinforced by the media broadcasting throughout the world pictures of this resplendent mansion, the opulent elegance of the Oval Room, the amazing professionalism and impeccable white shirts of the president's men, the beautiful green lawns with a cheerful and self-confident president and his playful dog nimbly stepping out of the helicopter as if he were a Greek God alighting from Olympus.

And the White House has been only one of these real-world plus symbolic centers of the world in America. One might list some of these centers in the following way.

USA
The Center of The World

The World Trade Center	Symbol of globalization, and the glory of the Western World
Wall Street	Real and symbolic center of global financial power
The White House	Global center of political power
The Pentagon	Global center and symbol of military power
Silicon Valley	Center and symbol of digital power and technical development
Harvard, Yale, Stanford	Global centers of knowledge and scientific research
CNN	Global center and source of information. Only those things really happen in the world that are broadcast by CNN
Hollywood	Center of contemporary myths and divinities
San Francisco	Center of "flower power"
California	Center of the new lifestyle and joy of life
U.S. $	The global symbol of wealth and power

September 11 has shattered almost all of these symbols. The World Trade Center physically collapsed and its symbolic message, the triumph of the western world, has been impaired. The Pentagon was seriously hit, and the symbolic invincibility of America's military power has had to be quickly reinforced by a blazing victory in Afghanistan. Wall Street and Silicon Valley trembled. CNN faltered, it lost—even if only for a few days or weeks—its grip on events, and suddenly the pictures of a new television company, al-Jazira, emerging from nowhere, filled the screens around the world. The colors of the "flower power" grew pale. Anxiety crept into the joy of life of California. Hollywood suddenly lost its self-confidence and was not sure if it could go on broadcasting the same illusions, myths, and pictures of virtual terror as before.

America had become a conscious and unconscious, emotional and cognitive reference point for most of the people living in the western world. Beyond being the center of power, wealth, information, it was also the source of a score of fundamental values: freedom, entrepreneurial spirit, the apotheosis of the human personality, new ideas and concepts, new movements, lifestyles, hope. And now, suddenly, this symbolic axis of our world faltered and a fearful vacuum emerged, even if only for some weeks or months, at the center of the world. And our hearts sank. Apparently we need a fixed point in the world to which we may cling. America has been able to function as this Archimedean point in spite of all its inner contradictions and the questions marks around its role in the world. Losing this anchoring point has been a fearful experience for hundreds of millions of people in the western world'.[1]

But in spite of the upsetting impact of this loss, it does not wholly explain the intensity of the shock people suffered on September 11. Further factors, too, must have played a role in it.

DEEP STRUCTURES

This act of terror may have hit some of the deepest chords in our minds and souls. A Freud, a Jung, a Rank, a Roheim, an Eliade, a Campbell would probably argue that the events of September 11 mobilized in our subconscious atavistic fears or archetypal, mythic, symbolic energies and the explosion of these energies may have amplified the shock to terrifying proportions.

Let me refer to some phenomena that may support this sort of interpretation.

The spectacle. The spectacle itself was already horrendous. Who could ever forget the sight of the airplane in the sky of New York, taking an elegant bend and then, suddenly, smashing into the tower and exploding in a fireball. It was stupefying to see this fearful metamorphosis of a beautiful, silver airplane, symbol of peace, freedom, and joy into an awful and destructive weapon. The metamorphosis of a dove of peace into a predator; the transubstantiation of a silvery angel into a fiery demon.

Apocalypse. The destruction was almost apocalyptic. The avenging angel swooping down on our world flashed up pictures of the Revelation of St. John the Divine, or of the Greek goddess, Nemesis.

Apocalypse, Now. In our virtual world created by the media we have already witnessed, many times, the death of hundreds and thousands of people. Think of the newsreels and TV news showing the bombardment of cities, houses ablaze and collapsing, tanks and trucks hit by rockets and their crew stumbling out burning. But there has ever been a time lag. A couple of hours, days, months between the event and the moment we were watching them, often in a bowdlerized version, on the screen. September 11 was perhaps the first time that we faced death "live"; "in real time." We were watching as thousands of women and men fell, helpless, into their death.

The irruption of the irrational. The impossible and unimaginable happened under our very eyes. The irrational broke into our world of Cartesian, Kantian rationality. The impact may prove to be as destructive as was that of the earthquake of Lisbon in 1755, which—according to the testimony of Voltaire—irreparably shook the faith of the Enlightenment in a harmonious and rational universe.

The negative miracle. In the moments of the crash, we were shocked by the sight of a horrendous "negative miracle." Instead of a miraculous act of healing or creation, we witnessed an infernal miracle of destruction. In the mythic world of Hollywood, the American hero was able to victoriously achieve the "Mission

Impossible." It was a shock to see now that it was our adversaries who successfully accomplished the impossible.

The Tower of Babel.   An obvious parallel. The collapse of the two sky-high towers, symbols of the greatness of human achievements, may have invoked in many people's minds the myth of the Tower of Babel, the destruction of which was, according to the Old Testament, God's punishment for humankind's divine ambitions.[2]

Icarus.   Modern American civilization developed an unprecedented cult of the human personality, who—by the help of will power, achievement orientation, self-confidence, positive thinking, a faith in the world and human opportunities, competition, professionalism, courage—is able to overcome all the difficulties, bring peace, freedom, well-being to the peoples of the world. The last few decades were those of the apotheosis of the human personality, soaring into unprecedented heights. And now, on September 11, nothing and nobody could save this victorious Icarus from falling into the depths of destruction.

The Wheel of Fortune.   Another myth, and emblem, of the transience of human wealth, power and glory. The events of September 11 may have invoked this terrifying vision of the fall of human beings from the height of glory and success into the depths of annihilation and non-being. A kindred motif, the **Fall of Princes**, may also have contributed to the shocking effect of the sight of the collapsing towers. It was a stock-in-trade motif in the late Middle Ages, and the Renaissance, but broadsides and highbrow literary works (pulp magazines and Shakespeare's tragedies, for instance) have kept it alive in popular imagination.

Arrows and spears.   The victims of September 11 are mourned as martyrs. Martyrdom may be extended, symbolically to the towers themselves. Several people I have talked to mentioned the martyrdom of St. Sebastian, imprinted on our minds by myriad pictures, icons, frescoes, who, bound to a pole, was pierced by deadly arrows as the towers were run through by the lethal arrows of the airplanes.

Axis mundi.   We know from Mircea Eliade and others that high mountains, trees, towers appear in the mythic imagination of people as axes mundi, i.e. as "axes" that connect the profane world with the realm of the divine, the immanent with the transcendental, humankind with God. The two planes broke this axis, this connection between humankind and the sphere of the divine and self-apotheosis.

The Tablets of Moses.   Would it be too farfetched to say that the two towers, standing and rising upright, as symbols of the triumph and glory of the western world, may have had an at least vague resemblance to the two tablets of Moses, with the fundamental principles of a new civilization carved on them?

Horror vacui.   When the clouds of dust started to settle, it was a painful shock to see the absurd gap, the vacuum, the absence of something that had been there a couple of minutes before, in its full power and reality. We were staring into the invisible depths of non-existence, the existentialists' Néant. With the so-called stop-trick, filmmakers can make objects and persons disappear from a scene in a trice but in reality we have never witnessed this sudden annihilation of life.

Satan.   The minds of contemporary people are far less exempt from mythic elements than we would like to believe in our rational moments. The apparition of Satan, who with his black wings (caftan) spread over the towers, darkened the sky and the universe, seems to have been a rather common experience of those who witnessed the attack. In a picture that got great publicity around the world and showed the infernal flames and smoke of the explosion, lots of people discovered the outlines of Satan's face.

Good and Evil.   The horrendous spectacle may have rekindled in many people's minds the Manichean vision of the battle of Good and Evil, Light and Darkness, the forces of creation and destruction. The Judeo-Christian tradition has ever fought this dualistic vision but it overwhelmed people's and communities' imagination again and again, in times of conflict and crisis. After the end of the Cold War, we hoped that we got rid of this dangerous and destructive dualism forever. But in the aftermath of September 11 it came back with a vengeance.

The sacrilege.   In the Manichean vision people identify themselves with the Good, and their adversaries with Evil. They are likely to believe that their truth is the absolute and only truth in the world, and their adversaries' convictions are dangerous errors and machinations. Una est Veritas. Questioning this Truth, let alone trying to destroy it, is a horrendous sacrilege.

Death, triumphant.   With a certain degree of exaggeration one could say that, together with the towers, the illusion of immortality collapsed as well on September 11. In what sense? We, people living in our contemporary consumer civilization, believe, and want to believe, so strongly in the power of the human being to solve the problems of life that we have almost come to believe that even the ultimate problem of human existence, mortality, can be solved. Or, at least, it can and should be eliminated from human consciousness.

Several scholars have argued that the "denial of death" is one of the main characteristics of citizens of contemporary western civilization, the civilization of consumption.[3] The cult of youth, the joy of life, success, wealth, the exclusion of death from civilized, politically correct conversation, the tactful separation of the elderly from the world of the young, the teeming of angels, spirits, time travelers, those returned from the land of death on the TV screen, the American soldier who must win the war without letting himself get killed: it is beyond doubt that—at least on the surface—our contemporary civilization turns much less about the idea of mortality and death than traditional European civilization (and most other traditional civilizations) have ever done.

And on September 11, we were suddenly and rudely confronted with the fragility of human life. And we could not avert our eyes from the terrible sight. We could not ignore any more the unacceptable fact of death. Even if only temporarily death has moved into our hearts.

All these may have been among the factors that have made September 11 the day of the symbols of destruction.

GLOBAL RESPONSES

It would be important to know whether or not the drama of September 11 was so rich in symbolic and mythic elements also in the Islamic world. What we know is that in the world of Islam visual representation plays a much smaller role than in the Christian tradition. And, as a consequence, the events of September 11 may have triggered off much less visual associations than in the imagination of people in the West. One could also say that in the world of Islam there were relatively less dramatic events and visions; there is no Apocalypse in the Koran; Satan has played a much less picturesque role than in the Judeo-Christian tradition. The Manichean vision of the battle of Good and Evil, which has emerged again and again in Judeo-Christianism, is, if not absent, much less pronounced in the Islam.

It is true, though, that in the twentieth century, and especially since the Algerian, Israeli-Palestinian and other conflicts, anti-western feelings have escalated. But they mostly stayed in the realm of frustrations, anger, and protest against exploitation and injustice. The West has been mythicized into the embodiment of transcendental Evil only within certain extremist groups of funda-mentalists. If, in the mythic imagination of people in the West, bin Laden was quickly and easily identified with a vengeful Satan, the majority of Moslems presumably considered the events of September 11—with much less visual or symbolic drama—simply as the sign of Allah's wrath.

It would be important to know more also about the emotional and symbolic impact of the events of September 11 in the other communities of the world. How did people in India, China, South-America, Africa, Russia respond to it; intellectually and emotionally? Was the impact amplified, or tempered and muffled by the various traditional mythic and symbolic heritages? What was, and what is the balance between various responses to the tragic events in the various communities: Empathy and condo-lence? Aversion, gloating, satisfaction? Anxiety and fear? Or?

If the answers were known, if the various responses could be mapped, this would help a lot people in the west locate themselves in a global public sphere. It would help them better to see their global image(s); to rethink the global role they play; better to develop their norms of global behavior.

Anyway, are we learning a new language, the symbolic language of the civilization of consumption? Or should we rather say that we are already learning the language of a coming "Post-Consumer Civilization"?

Endnotes

1. It would be extremely important to analyze the cognitive, emotional, and symbolic impact of the events of September 11 also on those who are strongly critical of America's role in the globalizing world (accusing America of "imperialism," "neo-colonialism," "wasting of resources," "growing global inequality," "metropolitan ghettos," "crime and drug problems," etc.) but this should be the subject of a series of other studies. Let me only mention here that even those who loathe America have been turning around it, have related themselves to it, have defined themselves in their opposition to it. A third group to be studied would be people in the developing world. The picture must be extremely complex. There certainly are a great many people for whom America seems to be one of the major sources of their misery and suffering (forgetting sometimes that their own feudal and despotic lords may be an even more important source). And there certainly are many people for whom America is, for all its ambiguity, the last glimmer of hope in a hopeless world. A special group would be the Islamic world, with its own deep divisions. I shall come back to it later in this paper.
2. The destruction of the Bastille belongs to a different kind of symbolism.
3. The expression comes from Ernest Becker's *The Denial of Death* (New York: The Free Press, 1973). He applied this concept only to people in America.

Questions for Discussion and Writing

1. Dr. Hankiss focuses on the mythical and symbolic meanings of September 11, 2001. How do you react to that? What are your personal memories, and does this kind of reading impact those memories in any way?
2. In the section on "deep structures" Hankiss mentions that witnessing the attacks may have "mobilized in our subconscious atavistic fears." What is atavism? How does it link to the point that Hankiss is making?
3. Hankiss talks about the attacks undermining the feeling of American invincibility and upsetting a view of the world order. Write about how this looked to an American citizen and how it might have looked to someone in a country such as Somalia, Rwanda, or Chechnya, where civil wars and the struggles against occupation have raged for years.

Responses to 9/11: Individual and Collective Dimensions

RAJEEV BHARGAVA

Rajeev Bhargava is Professor of Political Theory and Indian Political Thought at the University of Delhi, India, and the South Asian editor of Open Democracy. *He was educated at Oxford University in England and has centered his work in the history of political thought and the philosophy of social science. He is the author of* Individualism in Social Science *(1992) and editor of* Secularism and Its Critics *(1998).*

◆

In India, as elsewhere, every person understood that cry for help, the horror and fear writ large on terror stricken faces, the trauma in the choked voices of people who saw it happen, the hopeless struggle to control an imminent breakdown in public, the unspeakable grief. For one moment, the pain and suffering of others became our own. In a flash, everyone recognised what is plain but easily forgotten: that inscribed in our personal selves is not just our separateness from others but also sameness with them, that despite all socially constructed differences of language, culture, religion, nationality, perhaps even race, caste and gender, and over and above every culturally specific collective identity, we share something in common. Amidst terror, acute vulnerability and unbearable sorrow, it was not America alone that rediscovered its lost solidarity but across the globe, almost everyone who heard, saw or read about these cataclysmic events seemed to reclaim a common humanity.

As we empathised with those who escaped or witnessed death and relived the traumatic experience of those who lost their lives, we knew of a grave, irreparable wrong done to individuals, killed, wounded or traumatised by the sudden loss of family and friends. These individuals were not just subjected to physical hurt or mental trauma, they were recipients and carriers of a message embodied in that heinous act: from now on they must live with a dreadful sense of their own vulnerability. This message was transmitted first to other individuals in New York and Washington, then quickly to citizens through out the democratic world. The catastrophe on the U.S. east coast has deepened the sense of insecurity of every individual on this planet.

However, this was not the entire text of messages sent by the perpetrators. The rest is revealed when we focus on our collective identities or rather on the collective dimensions of the tragedy that unfolded on that terrible, terrible Tuesday. Unlike the first, which allows a plain and simple good to be distinguished from unambiguous evil, these messages were disturbingly ambivalent, morally fuzzy and less likely to sift good from evil, more likely to divide rather than unite people across the world. One such message which the poor, the powerless and the culturally marginalised would always like to have communicated to the rich, powerful and the culturally dominant, although not in this beastly manner, is this: we have grasped that any injustice done to us is erased before it is seen or spoken about, that in the current international social order, we count for very little; our ways of life are hopelessly marginalised, our lives utterly valueless. Even middle class Indians with cosmopolitan aspirations became painfully aware of this when a country-wise list of missing or dead persons was flashed on an international news channel: hundreds of Britons, scores of Japanese, some Germans, three Australians, two Italians, one Swede. A few buttons away, a South Asian channel listed names of several hundred missing or dead Indians, while another flashed the names of thousands with messages of their safety to relatives back home.

Hard as it was to acknowledge in the immediate aftermath of September 11, it must be admitted that the attacks on New York and Washington were also meant to lower the collective self-esteem of Americans, to rupture their pride. Not all intentional wrongdoing is physically injurious to the victim but every intentionally generated physical suffering is invariably accompanied by intangible wounds. The attack on September 11 did not merely demolish concrete buildings and individual people. It tried to destroy the American measure of its own self-worth, to diminish the self-esteem of Americans. Quite separate from the immorality of physical suffering caused, isn't this attempt itself morally condemnable? Yes, if the act further lowered the self-worth of a people already devoid of it. But this is hardly relevant in the case of America, where sections of the ruling elite ensure that its collective self-worth borders on supreme arrogance, always over the top. Does not the Pentagon symbolise this false collective pride? Amidst this carnage, then, is the sobering thought that occurs more naturally to poor people of powerless countries that occasionally even the mighty can be humbled. In such societies, the genuine anguish of people at disasters faced by the rich is mixed up with an unspeakable emotion which, on such apocalyptic occasions, people experience only in private or talk about only in whispers.

The whispering did not continue for long. Soon, left-oriented intellectuals the world over appealed vociferously to the Americans to explore the deeper reasons that underlie terrorism, pointing towards America's dubious foreign policy that has caused millions to suffer in Vietnam, Chile, Palestine, Iraq and Sudan, to name just a few countries. Madeline Albright's infamous remark that justified the suffering and death of Iraqi children ricocheted from newspaper reports to television channels. Americans were coaxed to re-examine what their leaders do in their name. American ignorance and innocence were ridiculed: if only ordinary Americans cared to look at what was really going on alongside the American way of life and the rhetoric of freedom, they would begin to understand what happened on September 11 and why many ordinary people in the non-western world were overcome with the feeling that it was more or less what America deserved.

Naturally, American intellectuals reacted with horror and disdain toward such "ideological excuses for terrorism." They asked if a grave wrong committed today can be justified by a wrong committed in the past, in a different context and time? Could America never do anything right and Americans never allowed to be victims? Surely, there has to be a deep rooted anti-American prejudice in most such intellectual responses from the non-western world. They could respectfully listen to reasoned political opposition to American foreign policy but not accept the pathetic ideological reflex that was characteristic of these anti-American responses.

It is hard to deny the presence of prejudice, rhetoric and the sledgehammer of ideology in current critiques of America. And, even harder to accept the view of the skeptic that denies the very distinction between rhetoric and argument, between ideology and reasoned political theory. It is true of course that both reasoned political argument and ideology seek to win over others, but they do so in dramatically opposite ways. One, steadfastly committed to transparency, provides every conceivable reason for its principles and value-based conclusions, the other short-circuits moral values, reduces principles to formulae, almost always privileges the use of rhetoric over reason and permits half-truths, even lies.

Yet, for all the validity and usefulness of the distinction between reasoned political argument and ideology, we must try not to seal them off altogether or wholly overlook what they have in common. For a start, the world of the political theorist is not entirely devoid of rhetoric and emotion, nor is the universe of the ideologist completely lacking in reflexiveness, internal coherence or rational thought. Likewise, no matter how well justified, a rationally defended belief system still contains an element of extra-rational preference and some prejudice. For all the justified complaints against ideology, in the end, we must also acknowledge the grain of truth it might contain about us and our world. No matter how exasperating its form and how crude its technique, we must attend to its content. At any rate, ideologies are shaped by their practical function, by the inherent logic of what they are meant to deliver, i.e., a broad conceptual map of the social and political world without which a political agent can not think, decide or act. Ideologies are necessarily gestural, uncertain steps in the dark that may lead to invaluable and indispensable insights about the social and political world. Surely, it must be admitted that reasoned political argument is not always necessary for this purpose and never sufficient. Reason may fine tune some ideologies or help defeat others but it cannot replace them. Alas, even those of us who loath the form of ideology must closely attend to its content. The ideology of anti-Americanism must not be dismissed as prejudice standing against enlightened reason.

However, what appears to have invaded the public sphere well before and certainly after the air strikes is galaxies away from not only the careful, issue-based reasoned opposition to U.S. foreign policy but also from the ideology of anti-Americanism. Way beneath the anti-Americanism of the ideologue lies a magma of impression, emotion and confused thought of ordinary people that just a while ago was self-directed and is now suddenly targeted at the other. It is this chaotic, sweltering, cesspool that non-western intellectuals are trying to hold in their hands and then carry into the international public domain. It is quite wrong to call this ideology. Such mixtures of impressions and feelings, having settled slowly over the years, independent of our will, suddenly and unexpectedly reveal themselves under the impact of cataclysmic events. They are not content-less, however. Often, they are beliefs masquerading as feelings, the common man's interpretation of larger social and political situations based on directly felt experience and the itsy-bitsy information filtering through to him, the ordinary person's very own causal account of her suffering, produced in her view by a chain of oppression that resides in her home but originates and begins its devious journey from somewhere in America. The cognitive content of these feelings is this: the world is governed by two sets of international laws, one exclusive to American and its allies, and the other for the rest of the non-western world. A single American life is worth more than a thousand others. Is it such a remarkable fact that struggling, harried people, breathing a trifle freely for the first time, sometimes in an incipient egalitarian society, wish not to take any personal responsibility for their own enduring woes? [T]hat they overreact with anger, blame and schadenfreude? Not any more than to discover that people with excessive wealth and power are generally insensitive to those without it, that they do not even notice their existence.

Non-western intellectuals are trying to open a chink for people in America and give them a glimpse of these convoluted feelings. This is frequently done not in the language of reasoned political theory but in a somewhat defective, coarse, shockingly brazen or insensitive form that, alas, is yet another import from the west. The irony is that many of these non-western intellectuals are personally committed to the best ethical ideals developed in the west and are close cultural cousins of a typical western intellectual. In all probability, they are not even liked by the people whose message they so earnestly carry. Culturally estranged, they appear shallow and hypocritical to them. In aligning themselves with the oppressed, and in trying to communicate their feelings, these intellectuals sow in themselves the seeds of a permanent schizophrenia.

I have pleaded with American intellectuals that they should pay attention to the content of feelings, not obsessively demand that they be expressed in their preferred form. However, I have a few sobering thoughts to share with my own non-American intellectual brethren. Insensitivity and ignorance is not a unique American fault. Much of the Indian elite is shockingly insensitive to the appalling conditions under which their fellow citizens live and alarmingly ignorant of the horrors in large parts of Africa. How can we then expect the even more wealthy, powerful and privileged to be any different? Humans everywhere in the world tend to build a wall around themselves and the more comfortable they are within these walls the less likely they are to notice those outside such walls. Perhaps this is a time for all of us to look within and catch this ugly, decidedly uncomfortable truth about ourselves.

I had also spoken above of two dimensions to the message hidden in the mangled remains of the destruction of September 11. The moral horror of the individual dimension of the carnage was unambiguous and overwhelming. But as we examined its collective dimension, a less clear, more confusing moral picture emerged. How, on balance, after putting together these two dimensions, were we to evaluate this complicated moral terrain? The answer had to be swift and unwavering. The focus then had to remain on the individual and the humanitarian. To have shifted our ethical compass in the direction of the collective would have weakened the moral claims of the suffering and the dead. And this was plainly wrong. Nor was it enough to have merely made a passing reference to the tragedy of individuals, a grudging concession before considering the weightier political crimes of a neo-imperial state. Then, as always in such situations, the moral claims of individuals are supreme. To have aggressively emphasised the collective dimension of the tragedy at an inopportune time was horribly indecent. But equally, to have screened off the collective dimension, to have ignored what ordinary people in the non-western world feel, would have obstructed our understanding of how tragedies of individuals can be prevented in future; surely, this would only perpetuate another already existing moral wrong.

Questions for Discussion and Writing

1. Dr. Bharagava writes that "Humans everywhere in the world tend to build a wall around themselves and the more comfortable they are within these walls the less likely they are to notice those outside such walls." Do you agree with him that this has been the case with the United States?
2. The writer points out how Indians were excluded from mentions of the lost and missing in the 2001 attacks. Were you aware of this exclusion? Is it consistent with his claim that often one U.S. life is seen as worth more than a thousand others? Examine, for example, the U.S. media response to the losses of 2001 with the coverage of the Madrid train attacks or the massacre at Beslan, Russia.
3. Dr. Bharagava suggests that the 2001 attacks were as much about puncturing American pride as anything else. Explain how this was intended to work and what the American response has been in the years since.
4. Does the upsurge in patriotism since the attacks of 2001 address the underlying problems that are discussed in this article or might they make them worse? How would you explain to Dr. Bharagava the changes that you have seen in your own community, for example?

What We Think of America (2)

RAJA SHEHADEH

Raja Shehadeh is an attorney who lives and works in Ramallah, Palestine, where he was born in 1951. He is a founder of the human rights organization al-Haq. He has written several books on international law, human rights, and the Middle East. His family was forcibly moved from Jaffa by Israelis in 1948, and Shehadeh sees that event as a key to his identity, remembering that as a child his parents would point out the lights of Jaffa on the horizon as his true home. His memoir, Strangers in the House: Coming of Age in Occupied Palestine, *was published in the United States in 2002. In this article Raja Shehadeh reflects on American influence on his community, family, and landscape in Ramallah—both directly, and through support given to Israel.*

✦

Ever since I was a child I have been losing friends and relatives to America. I remember one summer afternoon sitting on a green wicker chair, which had first to be cleared of dry pine needles, in the garden of the Ramallah Grand Hotel. Trees rustled in the breeze. I was just ten years old. My friend, Issa Mitri and I had been allowed to join a group of older guys who were saying farewell to Issa's brother. He was leaving the next day for the U.S., the first member of his family to emigrate.

I had not heard that word before. Did it mean he would never come back? Issa solemnly confirmed that this was so. He was more proud than sad. I looked at his brother Elias, a tall, slightly stooped young man with a shy face. He didn't look particularly happy. I could not understand why. Travelling to America was to me then like going to heaven. I could not understand why he was not utterly blissful.

A few years later Issa left Ramallah to finish high school in America. This was soon after the 1967 war and Israel's occupation of the West Bank, and the Mitri family had decided he would be safer there. His mother went with him to keep house. His father, who reported for *Newsweek*, remained alone for a few months and then decided to pack his bags. I remember seeing him before he left and asking him if he was happy to be leaving. There was rancour in his voice as he told me: "I have long been dreaming of the time when I would no longer have to follow your father around to get his comments on the situation." My father was a political maverick. A few days after the war he had called for a peaceful resolution of the conflict based on the partition of the land into two states, Israel and Palestine, the Palestinian state to be created in the areas occupied by Israel in 1967. That was then a novel proposal, and it earned him few friends among Palestinians or Israelis.

There are tens of thousands of Ramallah people, like the Mitris, who have settled permanently in America. The few who come back for brief summer visits parade up and down Main Street in their Bermudas and baseball hats, stopping at the ice cream parlour to reminisce with its proprietor in an old accent that you hardly ever hear in Ramallah today. The migration has been going on since the end of the nineteenth century; today there are more Ramallah people in the U.S. than in Ramallah. Before 1967 that was how most Palestinians related to America—via the good things about the country that they heard from their migrant friends and relations. After 1967, America entered our life in a different way.

After Israel occupied the Palestinian territories, it began almost immediately to claim large areas of land surrounding our towns and villages for the building of Jewish settlements. This was an expensive enterprise. Without American largesse, both official and private, this massive assault on our countryside would not have been possible. When the British ruled Palestine during the Mandate period, they didn't expropriate Arab land to build Jewish settlements. They fulfilled the terms of the mandate that called for the creation of a national home for the Jews in Palestine in other less provocative and costly ways. The roads they built were cheap. They followed the contours of the hills. And they were still used well after the Mandate ended in May 1948. In the early Eighties, when I accompanied my father, whose driving was as perilous as his politics, to the court in Nablus I would hear him curse the British as he took the turns so abruptly that my stomach jumped. "Instead of cutting through in a straight line they had to go around every damn hill," he would complain. He had just returned from his first trip to the U.S. and was captivated by the American spirit. He believed the Middle East should follow the American example and open up its borders for immigration. The influx of new blood would rid us of our interminable squabbles. How he proposed to convince Israel to abandon its dream of Jewish purity I never knew. In any case, I had no time to ask; it was only a passing fancy.

My father began his legal practice in Jaffa in 1935 when Palestine was still undivided. By the time I began to practise law, the West Bank was under Israeli occupation. On my way to courts in different parts of the country, I could see heavy Israeli machinery flattening the tops of hills. Many of the settlers were enthusiastic American Jews who dreamed of being pioneers. They used the tactics of colonizers everywhere: surveying, mapping, developing spurious legal arguments to justify their plunder, and terrorizing local Palestinians who stood in their way. "Transfer" was the euphemism used by the Israeli parties which advocated ethnic cleansing. To many Palestinians it appeared that American money funded this settlement project just as America's pioneering history vindicated it.

Within a few years Israeli settlements came to dominate the Palestinian landscape. Next came the need for new roads to connect them to Israel; not the old British-style meandering roads but American-style straight four-lane highways that cut through the hills that stood in the way. Palestine is tiny and its countryside precious, yet by 1984 Israeli planners had developed a fully fledged road plan which superimposed on the old north–south road grid a scheme of east–west highways that would cut in half the commuting time between the West Bank's new dormitory settlements and the centre of Israel. The plan needed billions of America dollars to implement. Funding was again no problem.

In the context of the Middle East conflict, roads may seem a small thing, but they have done a kind of spiritual damage. Gone is that attractive stretch of serpentine road that meandered downhill into the lower wadi that led into Nablus, an ancient city cupped between the mountains of Ebal and Gerizim. Gone are the gorgeous, dramatic views. Now the expensive new highway cuts through the hill and all you can see as you drive is a cutting.

But American assistance did not stop at the funding of ideologically motivated programmes. Last July my cousin was at a wedding reception in a hotel on the southern outskirts of Ramallah when an F16 fighter jet dropped a hundred-pound bomb on a nearby building. Everything had been quiet. There had not been any warning of an imminent air attack. The young couple were exchanging rings. The wedding cake was about to be served. When the missile zoomed over the hotel, the aluminium frames of the large French windows were torn asunder, all the glass shattered, the powerful security doors burst out of their frames. The wedding cake became encrusted with glass and the guests along with the waiters all hit the floor. The target, an old house next to the hotel where the reception was being held, was obliterated. You could not tell that a house had ever stood on that land. Something happened to my cousin that evening. He felt he had been through the worst. He felt he had died and was surprised afterwards to find he was still alive. He was also emboldened. Fear had been wrested out of him. He did not hate America. He studied there. On his last trip to New York he had visited the Twin Towers in New York. He fully appreciated the immensity of the tragedy. When the bombing took place he was worried about his brother who often takes the Boston–Los Angeles flight in the course of his work. Yet when I asked him what he thought of the country he indicated that he dismissed it as a lackey of Israel, giving it unlimited military assistance and never censoring its use of U.S. weaponry against innocent civilians.

Most Americans may never know why my cousin turned his back on their country. But in America the parts are larger than the whole. It is still possible that the optimism, energy and opposition of Americans in their diversity may yet turn the tide and make America listen.

Questions for Discussion and Writing

1. Raja Shehadeh makes a distinction between the occupation of the British and the imperialism of the Americans. What kinds of examples are used and how does the influence on Palestine differ?
2. This article indicates a complex interaction between admiration of the United States and anger at its tactics in the Middle East. Look at both sides of this discussion and examine the issue from each point of view.
3. What do the actions of the ex-Ramallahans returning to visit from their new homes in the United States indicate? How do you think that those who still live in Ramallah would have reacted to them?
4. The author makes a link between the colonization of the American west and the way that American Jews move into the hills of Palestine. In both cases the indigenous peoples were moved to make way for new settlers. How do you react to this? Is this consistent with American values?
5. Raja Shehadeh makes the point that new American-style roads changed the landscape of Palestine and inflicted great damage on the state's natural beauty and heritage. Others might argue that they merely increased the ease and efficiency of transportation. Examine both sides of the argument and make a case for one side or the other.

It's Time We All Signed Up for the Rest of the World Team

MATTHEW PARRIS

Matthew Parris was born in Johannesburg, South Africa, in 1949 and was educated in Africa, at Clare College, Cambridge in England, and Yale University in the United States. His political career saw him working for the Thatcher government in the United Kingdom as a member of the Foreign Office staff in the 1970s, before he became a journalist, commentator, and television analyst in the mid-1980s. He has worked as Parliamentary Sketchwriter for The Times *of London and for the* Investor's Chronicle. *He has won numerous awards for reporting and commentary writing. An active traveler and sportsman, Parris has led expeditions to Mount Kilimanjaro, Zaire, the Sahara, Bolivia, and Peru. This article appeared in* The Times *(UK) newspaper on April 12, 2003.*

---- ✦ ----

Once upon a time, when East was East and West was West and two great hegemons snorted at each other over a high ideological fence, there browsed in the international jungle a herd which called itself the Nonaligned Bloc. To join the nonaligned did not signal hostility to the great powers so much as collective determination not to be eaten by a hegemon. But hegemony collapsed, and for some time now there has been no nation in the jungle so fearsome as to scare the rest into a defensive grouping. The nonaligned broke up. The bloc was forgotten.

It is time to reinvent it. Hegemony was not dead, but sleeping. Today there is only one hegemon, the United States of America; but there is no less a need than existed during the Cold War for a wary defensiveness towards the appetite, the pretensions and the dreams of a great and unchallenged power. If the U.S. eagle is to be contained, collective action is needed by the smaller mammals.

Not all will sign up: some will throw in their lot with the great power and hope for protection and, whenever the eagle dines, for scraps from the feast. But those who choose to stay outside the American cage will need to unite, however loosely, for their own protection. They will have to keep their wits about them.

Yesterday the leaders of Russia, Germany and France met in St Petersburg to talk about the future. They carried with them worries about America shared by many other nations, large and small: Canada, China, New Zealand, Sweden, India, South Africa . . . I could make a list that included most of the rest of the world. That meeting, and others to come, could mark the beginnings of some sense of commonality between those civilised nations that have not chosen to fly with the great eagle, and some sense of the need for collective action in clipping its wings. To call this "The U.S. versus the Rest of the World" oversimplifies, but conveys the spirit. To put it more modestly, those nations that do not choose to take Washington's whip are going to need to coordinate their positions and keep in touch. The balance of power needs rebalancing. For want of a better term, I shall call the grouping of which Russia, Germany and France now form a putative core, the Rest of the World.

For Iraq may not be the last American adventure. Certainly it was not intended to be by those in Washington who were the authors of this invasion: they see it as a bridgehead, the beginning of a new and swelling American assertiveness worldwide. Their argument has been clear: that, however dubious or partial the logic of attacking Iraq today may have seemed, there is a deeper logic—a tomorrow—to the strategy, a taking command with such decisiveness that forces of disorder and un-Americanism in the world will bow, one by one, to Washington's will.

Unless America now takes that command we will have to assume that Washington has thought better of the strategy. To argue (as Tony Blair tries to) that Iraq was some kind of a one-off is to mistake (or cloak) America's purpose. While Damascus arms Hezbollah murderers, for the United States to stop at Baghdad would be a sign of failure.

It is, however, just possible that failure will be faced. The peace in Iraq may prove dirtier than the war, and the American people (as distinguished from their Defence Secretary) are ambivalent about empire and squeamish about becoming other nations' policemen . . .

However grisly and sad, horrors in Iraq now could head U.S. foreign policy off a course which within a decade will lead to grislier entanglements at greater costs. For empires are seldom lucky enough to have their pretensions dashed early by a single, defining, defeat. More often they are drawn in deeper by a series of small apparent successes. Finally they thrash around, unloved, over-extended and harried on all sides. If only the way into this ambush had been blocked earlier.

Success [in Iraq] is, on balance, the likelihood; and a more frightening prospect than failure. As America grows more confident of its muscle and command, it will be clashing again and again, not just with old enemies but with former friends—over trade, the environment, "pre-emptive" defence, regime change, international law, extradition . . . the list is speculative, but let us speculate.

Take trade. The free-trading instincts of the United States are not robust—no stronger than the "old" Europe's. Especially during a recession, protectionist voices will be loud in America. And there will be calls for sanctions against those who disappoint it politically. What will Britain do if the U.S. Congress tries to discriminate against French and German business, offering the United Kingdom favoured status, formal or informal? This will look like British treachery to the European Union. If America gets serious about protectionism, the Rest of the World will have to get serious about threatening a response.

Or take the environment. Less and less does Washington feel the need to pay even lip-service to international processes such as Kyoto. The Rest of the World may conclude it is better to abandon the attempt to keep America on board, rather than continually diluting and postponing action. The same may be true of the International Criminal Court from which it has already excluded itself: countries such as Britain try to see this as mere delay; but it might be better for those nations that wish to submit themselves properly to supranational rules of law to decide to go full steam ahead without America.

I am not suggesting the Rest of the World bring down a new Iron Curtain between a troublesome giant and an informal gang of wary smaller powers. But it is time to throw off habits of thought that are stuck in a past where "the international community," "the West" or "the civilised world" had become sloppy, lazy expressions for a big stockade in which the good guys all resided, America foremost among equals. We must learn to envisage a world where we are not in the American stockade and do not need to be because there is no huge enemy we share with it. We should consider the means and institutions through which we can protect our own collective interests against a great power with interests of its own to pursue. We need to clip the eagle's wings, and we shall not do so singly.

I say "we." But to the regret of some of us in Britain, our own country has passed up the chance to join the Rest of the World. Finding himself halfway across a swaying transatlantic bridge, our Prime Minister scuttled in panic to the American side—an act which we are now being urged to see as brave. But it happened more through miscalculation than valour. Tony Blair thought the bridge could be repaired and that he might be the bridgemaker. Now he is marooned on the other side and will have to take his chances there. Fellow Conservatives who, super-sensitive to the most trivial European encroachment on British sovereignty, used to bawl themselves hoarse in defence of the fat content of the British sausage, have over the past month witnessed the most spectacular ceding of our independence in foreign and military policy since Suez—and all without a peep. Secretly they smile. Blair's European affair is over.

The "new" Europe that he has boasted about assembling will scatter. Italy has already gone quiet, and in Spain Mr Blair's friend, José María Aznar, looks in danger of being ejected by the electorate. Other members of the group will scamper back into the Franco-German fold. Getting your friends to sign a joint letter to a world newspaper—this newspaper—is a great achievement but it does not amount to creating a permanent force in European politics, and signatories to that letter must wonder whether choosing Mr Blair as their pied piper was wise. Britain is on the margins of European politics now. And what of the United Nations? It is the organisation's good luck that America no longer cares to invite its complicity, even to mop up. Tony Blair's observations on the legality of this adventure have been so bizarre that it is futile to try constructing from them any kind of theoretical basis, but as I understand it he and the Attorney-General think the U.S.-UK coalition has occupied Iraq as an agent of the UN. Luckily, his senior coalition partners take a scornful view of the idea. I hope Washington maintains this attitude, for the day is coming when the UN must ask whether it is appropriate for its headquarters to remain in New York, whether it is appropriate to act as stretcher-bearers for U.S. imperialism—or whether it might be better to rejoin the Rest of the World. The sooner that day comes, the better.

Questions for Discussion and Writing

1. Parris suggests that the United States needs reigning in by the rest of the world forming an adequate resistance to its hegemonic power. How do you react to this? What might be the benefits and drawbacks of such resistance?
2. In the article Parris talks about the dangers of forming an empire. What elements constitute an empire? Is it fair to say that the United States is now in the realm of empire building?

General Questions for Chapter Two

1. There are many international voices represented in this chapter. Collate a representative view of the United States based on these articles and write a piece that accurately presents the positive and negative aspects of the United States as seen by those overseas.

2. Is the core of international perception about the United States generated from within other nations or imposed by the power and influence of the United States itself? Use examples from the essays in this chapter to explain your point of view. Also, to demonstrate that you can appreciate the other side of the discussion, acknowledge it and refute it in your writing. The use of valid examples is crucial to this exercise. Use the essays here and incorporate your own research.

3. Write definitions of the following terms and concepts, being sure to illustrate them with examples from the essays in this chapter: ideology; fundamentalist; multilateralist.

4. Analyze the various types of audiences addressed by the articles in this section. For each article estimate who you think it was written for and then see what it is about the style of the article, the language, and the approach that gives you this information.

CHAPTER 3

A New World Order

In the final article of the last chapter Matthew Parris indicated that many nations around the world now see the United States as forming, and expanding, an empire. Throughout history the most powerful nations have looked to expand their security, ideological influence, resources, and military reach through the construction of empire. In most cases the downfall of such empires has been messy, painful, and costly. Those who are claimed as the subjects of empire actively resist imperialism, and when resistance to the power of an empire reaches critical mass, it usually causes the empire to fall apart. However noble the ideologies behind a burgeoning empire, the larger it gets, the more likely it is to alienate, oppress, and antagonize. Currently the United States, seen by many as the empire builder of the new century, claims its mission as spreading peace and democracy around the world. Lofty and worthy as these ideals are, we cannot expect all of the world's citizens to see these standards as appealing or suitable to their own cultures and systems. Criticism, often valid, is leveled at the United States on the grounds that it sees itself as the world, rather than as being part of it.

However uncomfortable for us to acknowledge it, there have been historical occasions when systems other than democracy have preserved a balance and a peace that would be otherwise difficult or impossible to achieve. For example, under President Tito, who acted as a military dictator, Yugoslavia managed to resist the ethnic tensions that had been torturing the Balkans for centuries. Following Tito's death and the compartmentalizing of the Yugoslavia, ethic tensions rose again, leading to the atrocities that characterized the last part of the twentieth century in Bosnia and Serbia. World history now records the names of Slobodan Milosevic and Srebrenica as synonymous with torture and massacre, documents the siege of Sarajevo, and made us sadly familiar with the term "ethnic cleansing." In Iraq, currently the major theater of war for the United States, the barbaric rule of Saddam Hussein prevented civil war between the Sunni and Shiite factions and stifled the Kurdish quest for autonomy in the north of the country. The United States has removed Hussein from power and introduced a democratic system of polls and government, but the cost to the country has been (by some estimates) over 100,000 civilian deaths, and the number of American military casualties is (at the time of writing) 2375 with over 17,000 wounded.

It is hard for many of us to imagine a situation where our country would be controlled by an outside force, but for millions around the world this is the case, and for many the controlling influence is the United States. The assumption that U.S. culture is the best and that as a nation the United States knows better than others how to run a country is sure to alienate many. Nuclear arms negotiations are often conducted under the implicit understanding that the United States can be trusted with weapons of mass destruction but other nations cannot.

The twentieth century was known as the American century, as the United States extended its power and influence around the globe, using the military, technology, and its hold and influence over resources as a lever. However, there were already signs that such influence and control were built on shaky foundations. For example, the crisis in the early 1970s, an oil embargo by Arab nations against the supporters of Israel in the Yom Kippur War, threatened the U.S. economy and led to gasoline rationing and the fall in the value of the dollar. When a huge nation like the United States is reliant on natural resources from other nations to feed it and keep it functioning, there are always opportunities for it to be held hostage to its own appetite. During the Gulf War of 1991 the charge was made that the war was less about restoring sovereignty to Kuwait than about securing oil fields vital to the U.S. economy. This charge gained credence with the U.S. reluctance to enter genocidal conflicts in the Balkans and Rwanda, where, despite massive loss of life, there were no vital energy resources at stake.

Following the terrorist attacks of 2001 and to the present day, the Bush administration has been clear about security priorities and how they should be achieved. Many of the actions taken since 2001 are in line with a policy advocated by a group called the Project for the New American Century (PNAC). In this chapter we will look at President Bush's policy statement and sample the writing of Gary Schmitt, one of the architects of the PNAC. In response, we will see the reflections of other writers on the international stage who are concerned about a new policy of American imperialism and who are calling for resistance and a change in the path of U.S. policy. At this point it is unclear whether the twenty-first century will be the New American Century or whether the American "empire" will undergo an adjustment under a new world order.

The National Security Strategy of the United States
GEORGE W. BUSH

George W. Bush is the forty-third President of the United States. Mr. Bush was born in 1946 and is the son of George H. W. Bush, the forty-first president of the United States. Bush was elected to a second term in office in 2004. Prior to being elected President, he was Governor of Texas for six years. The National Security Strategy document is released periodically by the administration of the President, and is prepared by the executive branch of the government. Until recent times this document was classified, being seen publicly only after declassification years later. In 1950 the document NSC-68 emphasized the importance of halting the spread of Soviet Communism and set the strategy for the Cold War period. This version of the document was published on September 17, 2002. It includes the Hertz doctrine of military preeminence and makes clear that the United States will make preemptive strikes if it feels threatened. The sections included here emphasize the way the administration sees its relationship to other countries of the world. There are also controversial passages in the document, including the assertion that the International Criminal Court has no jurisdiction over U.S. citizens who may be accused of war crimes. Although written in the early years of the twenty-first century, it is clear that the implementation of these policies will impact the United States and the rest of the world for most of the one hundred years that follow.

◆

The great struggles of the twentieth century between liberty and totalitarianism ended with a decisive victory for the forces of freedom—and a single sustainable model for national success: freedom, democracy, and free enterprise. In the twenty-first century, only nations that share a commitment to protecting basic human rights and guaranteeing political and economic freedom will be able to unleash the potential of their people and assure their future prosperity.

People everywhere want to be able to speak freely; choose who will govern them; worship as they please; educate their children—male and female; own property; and enjoy the benefits of their labor. These values of freedom are right and true for every person, in every society—and the duty of protecting these values against their enemies is the common calling of freedom-loving people across the globe and across the ages.

Today, the United States enjoys a position of unparalleled military strength and great economic and political influence. In keeping with our heritage and principles, we do not use our strength to press for unilateral advantage. We seek instead to create a balance of power that favors human freedom: conditions in which all nations and all societies can choose for themselves the rewards and challenges of political and economic liberty. In a world that is safe, people will be able to make their own lives better. We will defend the peace by fighting terrorists and tyrants. We will preserve the peace by building good relations among the great powers. We will extend the peace by encouraging free and open societies on every continent.

Defending our Nation against its enemies is the first and fundamental commitment of the Federal Government. Today, that task has changed dramatically. Enemies in the past needed great armies and great industrial capabilities to endanger America. Now, shadowy networks of individuals can bring great chaos and suffering to our shores for less than it costs to purchase a single tank. Terrorists are organized to penetrate open societies and to turn the power of modern technologies against us.

To defeat this threat we must make use of every tool in our arsenal—military power, better homeland defenses, law enforcement, intelligence, and vigorous efforts to cut off terrorist financing. The war against terrorists of global reach is a global enterprise of uncertain duration.

America will help nations that need our assistance in combating terror. And America will hold to account nations that are compromised by terror, including those who harbor terrorists—because the allies of terror are the enemies of civilization. The United States and countries cooperating with us must not allow the terrorists to develop new home bases. Together, we will seek to deny them sanctuary at every turn.

The gravest danger our Nation faces lies at the crossroads of radicalism and technology. Our enemies have openly declared that they are seeking weapons of mass destruction, and evidence indicates that they are doing so with determination. The United States will not allow these efforts to succeed. We will build defenses against ballistic missiles and other means of delivery.

We will cooperate with other nations to deny, contain, and curtail our enemies' efforts to acquire dangerous technologies. And, as a matter of common sense and self-defense, America will act against such emerging threats before they are fully formed. We cannot defend America and our friends by hoping for the best. So we must be prepared to defeat our enemies' plans, using the best intelligence and proceeding with deliberation. History will judge harshly those who saw this coming danger but failed to act. In the new world we have entered, the only path to peace and security is the path of action.

As we defend the peace, we will also take advantage of an historic opportunity to preserve the peace. Today, the international community has the best chance since the rise of the nation-state in the seventeenth century to build a world where great powers compete in peace instead of continually prepare for war. Today, the world's great powers find ourselves on the same side—united by common dangers of terrorist violence and chaos. The United States will build on these common interests to promote global security. We are also increasingly united by common values. Russia is in the midst of a hopeful transition, reaching for its democratic future and a partner in the war on terror. Chinese leaders are discovering that economic freedom is the only source of national wealth. In time, they will find that social and political freedom is the only source of national greatness. America will encourage the advancement of democracy and economic openness in both nations, because these are the best foundations for domestic stability and international order. We will strongly resist aggression from other great powers—even as we welcome their peaceful pursuit of prosperity, trade, and cultural advancement. Finally, the United States will use this moment of opportunity to extend the benefits of freedom across the globe. We will actively work to bring the hope of democracy, development, free markets, and free trade to every corner of the world. The events of September 11, 2001, taught us that weak states, like Afghanistan, can pose as great a danger to our national interests as strong states. Poverty does not make poor people into terrorists and murderers. Yet poverty, weak institutions, and corruption can make weak states vulnerable to terrorist networks and drug cartels within their borders.

The United States will stand beside any nation determined to build a better future by seeking the rewards of liberty for its people. Free trade and free markets have proven their ability to lift whole societies out of poverty—so the United States will work with individual nations, entire regions, and the entire global trading community to build a world that trades in freedom and therefore grows in prosperity. The United States will deliver greater development assistance through the New Millennium Challenge Account to nations that govern justly, invest in their people, and encourage economic freedom. We will also continue to lead the world in efforts to reduce the terrible toll of HIV/AIDS and other infectious diseases.

In building a balance of power that favors freedom, the United States is guided by the conviction that all nations have important responsibilities. Nations that enjoy freedom must actively fight terror. Nations that depend on international stability must help prevent the spread of weapons of mass destruction. Nations that seek international aid must govern themselves wisely, so that aid is well spent. For freedom to thrive, accountability must be expected and required.

We are also guided by the conviction that no nation can build a safer, better world alone. Alliances and multilateral institutions can multiply the strength of freedom-loving nations.

The United States is committed to lasting institutions like the United Nations, the World Trade Organization, the Organization of American States, and NATO as well as other long-standing alliances. Coalitions of the willing can augment these permanent institutions. In all cases, international obligations are to be taken seriously. They are not to be undertaken symbolically to rally support for an ideal without furthering its attainment.

Freedom is the non-negotiable demand of human dignity; the birthright of every person—in every civilization. Throughout history, freedom has been threatened by war and terror; it has been challenged by the clashing wills of powerful states and the evil designs of tyrants; and it has been tested by widespread poverty and disease. Today, humanity holds in its hands the opportunity to further freedom's triumph over all these foes. The United States welcomes our responsibility to lead in this great mission.

● ● ●

Extracts from the full document follow.

● ● ●

IV. Work with Others to Defuse Regional Conflicts

"We build a world of justice, or we will live in a world of coercion. The magnitude of our shared responsibilities makes our disagreements look so small."

> President Bush
> Berlin, Germany
> May 23, 2002

Concerned nations must remain actively engaged in critical regional disputes to avoid explosive escalation and minimize human suffering. In an increasingly interconnected world, regional crisis can strain our alliances, rekindle rivalries among the major powers, and create horrifying affronts to human dignity. When violence erupts and states falter, the United States will work with friends and partners to alleviate suffering and restore stability.

No doctrine can anticipate every circumstance in which U.S. action—direct or indirect—is warranted. We have finite political, economic, and military resources to meet our global priorities. The United States will approach each case with these strategic principles in mind:

The United States should invest time and resources into building international relationships and institutions that can help manage local crises when they emerge.

The United States should be realistic about its ability to help those who are unwilling or unready to help themselves. Where and when people are ready to do their part, we will be willing to move decisively.

The Israeli-Palestinian conflict is critical because of the toll of human suffering, because of America's close relationship with the state of Israel and key Arab states, and because of that region's importance to other global priorities of the United States. There can be no peace for either side without freedom for both sides. America stands committed to an independent and democratic Palestine, living beside Israel in peace and security. Like all other people, Palestinians deserve a government that serves their interests and listens to their voices. The United States will continue to encourage all parties to step up to their responsibilities as we seek a just and comprehensive settlement to the conflict.

• • •

In South Asia, the United States has also emphasized the need for India and Pakistan to resolve their disputes. This Administration invested time and resources building strong bilateral relations with India and Pakistan. These strong relations then gave us leverage to play a constructive role when tensions in the region became acute. With Pakistan, our bilateral relations have been bolstered by Pakistan's choice to join the war against terror and move toward building a more open and tolerant society. The Administration sees India's potential to become one of the great democratic powers of the twenty-first century and has worked hard to transform our relationship accordingly. Our involvement in this regional dispute, building on earlier investments in bilateral relations, looks first to concrete steps by India and Pakistan that can help defuse military confrontation. Indonesia took courageous steps to create a working democracy and respect for the rule of law. By tolerating ethnic minorities, respecting the rule of law, and accepting open markets, Indonesia may be able to employ the engine of opportunity that has helped lift some of its neighbors out of poverty and desperation. It is the initiative by Indonesia that allows U.S. assistance to make a difference.

In the Western Hemisphere we have formed flexible coalitions with countries that share our priorities, particularly Mexico, Brazil, Canada, Chile, and Colombia. Together we will promote a truly democratic hemisphere where our integration advances security, prosperity, opportunity, and hope. We will work with regional institutions, such as the Summit of the Americas process, the Organization of American States (OAS), and the Defense Ministerial of the Americas for the benefit of the entire hemisphere.

Parts of Latin America confront regional conflict, especially arising from the violence of drug cartels and their accomplices. This conflict and unrestrained narcotics trafficking could imperil the health and security of the United States. Therefore we have developed an active strategy to help the Andean nations adjust their economies, enforce their laws, defeat terrorist organizations, and cut off the supply of drugs, while—as important—we work to reduce the demand for drugs in our own country.

In Colombia, we recognize the link between terrorist and extremist groups that challenge the security of the state and drug trafficking activities that help finance the operations of such groups. We are working to help Colombia defend its democratic institutions and defeat illegal armed groups of both the left and right by extending effective sovereignty over the entire national territory and provide basic security to the Colombian people.

In Africa, promise and opportunity sit side by side with disease, war, and desperate poverty. This threatens both a core value of the United States—preserving human dignity—and our strategic priority—combating global terror. American interests and American principles, therefore, lead in the same direction: we will work with others for an African continent that lives in liberty, peace, and growing prosperity. Together with our European allies, we must help strengthen Africa's fragile states, help build indigenous capability to secure porous borders, and help build up the law enforcement and intelligence infrastructure to deny havens for terrorists.

An ever more lethal environment exists in Africa as local civil wars spread beyond borders to create regional war zones. Forming coalitions of the willing and cooperative security arrangements are key to confronting these emerging transnational threats.

Africa's great size and diversity requires a security strategy that focuses on bilateral engagement and builds coalitions of the willing. This Administration will focus on three interlocking strategies for the region: countries with major impact on their neighborhood such as South Africa, Nigeria, Kenya, and Ethiopia are anchors for regional engagement and require focused attention; coordination with European allies and international institutions is essential for constructive conflict mediation and successful peace operations; and Africa's capable reforming states and sub-regional organizations must be strengthened as the primary means to address transnational threats on a sustained basis.

Ultimately the path of political and economic freedom presents the surest route to progress in sub-Saharan Africa, where most wars are conflicts over material resources and political access often tragically waged on the basis of ethnic and religious difference. The transition to the African Union with its stated commitment to good governance and a common responsibility for democratic political systems offers opportunities to strengthen democracy on the continent.

• • •

VII. Expand the Circle of Development by Opening Societies and Building the Infrastructure of Democracy

"In World War II we fought to make the world safer, then worked to rebuild it. As we wage war today to keep the world safe from terror, we must also work to make the world a better place for all its citizens."

> President Bush
> Washington, D.C. (Inter-American Development Bank)
> March 14, 2002

A world where some live in comfort and plenty, while half of the human race lives on less than $2 a day, is neither just nor stable. Including all of the world's poor in an expanding circle of development—and opportunity—is a moral imperative and one of the top priorities of U.S. international policy.

Decades of massive development assistance have failed to spur economic growth in the poorest countries. Worse, development aid has often served to prop up failed policies, relieving the pressure for reform and perpetuating misery. Results of aid are typically measured in dollars spent by donors, not in the rates of growth and poverty reduction achieved by recipients. These are the indicators of a failed strategy.

Working with other nations, the United States is confronting this failure. We forged a new consensus at the U.N. Conference on Financing for Development in Monterrey that the objectives of assistance—and the strategies to achieve those objectives—must change.

This Administration's goal is to help unleash the productive potential of individuals in all nations. Sustained growth and poverty reduction is impossible without the right national policies. Where governments have implemented real policy changes, we will provide significant new levels of assistance. The United States and other developed countries should set an ambitious and specific target: to double the size of the world's poorest economies within a decade.

• • •

IX. Transform America's National Security Institutions to Meet the Challenges and Opportunities of the Twenty-First Century

"Terrorists attacked a symbol of American prosperity. They did not touch its source. America is successful because of the hard work, creativity, and enterprise of our people."

President Bush
Washington, D.C. (Joint Session of Congress)
September 20, 2001

The major institutions of American national security were designed in a different era to meet different requirements. All of them must be transformed.

It is time to reaffirm the essential role of American military strength. We must build and maintain our defenses beyond challenge. Our military's highest priority is to defend the United States. To do so effectively, our military must:

- assure our allies and friends;
- dissuade future military competition;
- deter threats against U.S. interests, allies, and friends; and
- decisively defeat any adversary if deterrence fails.

• • •

The presence of American forces overseas is one of the most profound symbols of the U.S. commitments to allies and friends. Through our willingness to use force in our own defense and in defense of others, the United States demonstrates its resolve to maintain a balance of power that favors freedom. To contend with uncertainty and to meet the many security challenges we face, the United States will require bases and stations within and beyond Western Europe and Northeast Asia, as well as temporary access arrangements for the long-distance deployment of U.S. forces. . . .

As the United States Government relies on the armed forces to defend America's interests, it must rely on diplomacy to interact with other nations. We will ensure that the Department of State receives funding sufficient to ensure the success of American diplomacy. The State Department takes the lead in managing our bilateral relationships with other governments. And in this new era, its people and institutions must be able to interact equally adroitly with non-governmental organizations and international institutions. Officials trained mainly in international politics must also extend their reach to understand complex issues of domestic governance around the world, including public health, education, law enforcement, the judiciary, and public diplomacy.

Our diplomats serve at the front line of complex negotiations, civil wars, and other humanitarian catastrophes. As humanitarian relief requirements are better understood, we must also be able to help build police forces, court systems, and legal codes, local and provincial government institutions, and electoral systems. Effective international cooperation is needed to accomplish these goals, backed by American readiness to play our part.

Just as our diplomatic institutions must adapt so that we can reach out to others, we also need a different and more comprehensive approach to public information efforts that can help people around the world learn about and understand America. The war on terrorism is not a clash of civilizations. It does, however, reveal the clash inside a civilization, a battle for the future of the Muslim world. This is a struggle of ideas and this is an area where America must excel.

We will take the actions necessary to ensure that our efforts to meet our global security commitments and protect Americans are not impaired by the potential for investigations, inquiry, or prosecution by the International Criminal Court (ICC), whose jurisdiction does not extend to Americans and which we do not accept. We will work together with other nations to avoid complications in our military operations and cooperation, through such mechanisms as multilateral and bilateral agreements that will protect U.S. nationals from the ICC. We will implement fully the American Service members Protection Act, whose provisions are intended to ensure and enhance the protection of U.S. personnel and officials.

We will make hard choices in the coming year and beyond to ensure the right level and allocation of government spending on national security. The United States Government must strengthen its defenses to win this war. At home, our most important priority is to protect the homeland for the American people.

Today, the distinction between domestic and foreign affairs is diminishing. In a globalized world, events beyond America's borders have a greater impact inside them. Our society must be open to people, ideas, and goods from across the globe. The characteristics we most cherish—our freedom, our cities, our systems of movement, and modern life—are vulnerable to terrorism. This vulnerability will persist long after we bring to justice those responsible for the September 11 attacks. As time passes, individuals may gain access to means of destruction that until now could be wielded only by armies, fleets, and squadrons. This is a new condition of life. We will adjust to it and thrive—in spite of it.

In exercising our leadership, we will respect the values, judgment, and interests of our friends and partners. Still, we will be prepared to act apart when our interests and unique responsibilities require. When we disagree on particulars, we will explain forthrightly the grounds for our concerns and strive to forge viable alternatives. We will not allow such disagreements to obscure our determination to secure together, with our allies and our friends, our shared fundamental interests and values.

Ultimately, the foundation of American strength is at home. It is in the skills of our people, the dynamism of our economy, and the resilience of our institutions. A diverse, modern society has inherent, ambitious, entrepreneurial energy. Our strength comes from what we do with that energy. That is where our national security begins.

Questions for Discussion and Writing

1. This policy was written and published in 2002. Much has changed since then, notably the war in Iraq, which has been a polarizing event around the world and within the United States itself. Evaluate areas of this policy that have been followed through and successfully implemented.

2. Are there areas of the policy that seem to need change given the way the world has changed since September 2002?

3. Are there areas of this policy document that surprise you? Why? What do you make of the sections that deal with economic aid rather than directly with security? What is the strategy here?

4. Imagine you are a citizen of Afghanistan, Iraq, India, China, or North Korea and you were to read this document. How might you feel? How do you think your reactions might differ from those of a U.S. citizen?

5. As pointed out in the introduction, this kind of security strategy document used to be kept secret. What are the advantages and disadvantages of making it public? Write an argument that supports classification or publication.

The New American Century
ARUNDHATI ROY

Arundhati Roy is the prize-winning novelist of The God of Small Things *(1997). When she won the Booker Prize for her novel, she was the first non-expatriate and the first Indian woman to do so. She was born in Bengal, India, in 1961, and was raised in Kerala. She has a degree in architecture but gravitated towards writing screenplays for television and film. She lives in New Delhi with her husband, the film-maker Pradeep Kishen. Despite the fact that her novel appeared to great acclaim, Roy has declared it unlikely that she will write another. Instead, she has become a political activist, speaking around the world on the dangers of imperialism and actively protesting military action by the United States and its allies. When asked by Michael Sontheimer why she might not write fiction again, Roy responded: "Because I have the strong feeling that we are living in a time in which writers have to take a position. I feel under a tremendous amount of pressure just now to respond to things." This article is taken from the February 9, 2004, issue of* The Nation.

———————— ✦ ————————

In January 2003 thousands of us from across the world gathered in Porto Alegre in Brazil and declared—reiterated—that "Another World Is Possible." A few thousand miles north, in Washington, George W. Bush and his aides were thinking the same thing. Our project was the World Social Forum. Theirs—to further what many call the Project for the New American Century.

In the great cities of Europe and America, where a few years ago these things would only have been whispered, now people are openly talking about the good side of imperialism and the need for a strong empire to police an unruly world. The new missionaries want order at the cost of justice. Discipline at the cost of dignity. And ascendancy at any price. Occasionally some of us are invited to "debate" the issue on "neutral" platforms provided by the corporate media. Debating imperialism is a bit like debating the pros and cons of rape. What can we say? That we really miss it?

In any case, New Imperialism is already upon us. It's a remodeled, streamlined version of what we once knew. For the first time in history, a single empire with an arsenal of weapons that could obliterate the world in an afternoon has complete, unipolar, economic and military hegemony. It uses different weapons to break open different markets. There isn't a country on God's earth that is not caught in the cross-hairs of the American cruise missile and the IMF checkbook. Argentina's the model if you want to be the poster boy of neoliberal capitalism, Iraq if you're the black sheep. Poor countries that are geopolitically of strategic value to Empire, or have a "market" of any size, or infrastructure that can be privatized, or, God forbid, natural resources of value—oil, gold, diamonds, cobalt, coal—must do as they're told or become military targets. Those with the greatest reserves of natural wealth are most at risk. Unless they surrender their resources willingly to the corporate machine, civil unrest will be fomented or war will be waged.

In this new age of empire, when nothing is as it appears to be, executives of concerned companies are allowed to influence foreign policy decisions. The Center for Public Integrity in Washington found that at least nine out of the thirty members of the Bush Administration's Defense Policy Board were connected to companies that were awarded military contracts for $76 billion between 2001 and 2002. George Shultz, former Secretary of State, was chairman of the Committee for the Liberation of Iraq. He is also on the board of directors of the Bechtel Group. When asked about a conflict of interest in the case of war in Iraq he said, "I don't know that Bechtel would particularly benefit from it. But if there's work to be done, Bechtel is the type of company that could do it. But nobody looks at it as something you benefit from." In April 2003, Bechtel signed a $680 million contract for reconstruction.

This brutal blueprint has been used over and over again across Latin America, in Africa and in Central and Southeast Asia. It has cost millions of lives. It goes without saying that every war Empire wages becomes a Just War. This, in large part, is due to the role of the corporate media. It's important to understand that the corporate media don't just support the neoliberal project. They *are* the neoliberal project. This is not a moral position they have chosen to take; it's structural. It's intrinsic to the economics of how the mass media work.

Most nations have adequately hideous family secrets. So it isn't often necessary for the media to lie. It's all in the editing—what's emphasized and what's ignored. Say, for example, India was chosen as the target for a righteous war. The fact that about 80,000 people have been killed in Kashmir since 1989, most of them Muslim, most of them by Indian security forces (making the average death toll about 6,000 a year); the fact that in February and March of 2002 more than 2,000 Muslims were murdered on the streets of Gujarat, that women were gang-raped and children were burned alive and 150,000 driven from their homes while the police and administration watched and sometimes actively participated; the fact that no one has been punished for these crimes and the government that oversaw them was re-elected . . . all of this would make perfect headlines in international newspapers in the run-up to war.

Next thing we know, our cities will be leveled by cruise missiles, our villages fenced in with razor wire, U.S. soldiers will patrol our streets, and Narendra Modi, Pravin Togadia or any of our popular bigots will, like Saddam Hussein, be in U.S. custody having their hair checked for lice and the fillings in their teeth examined on prime-time TV.

But as long as our "markets" are open, as long as corporations like Enron, Bechtel, Halliburton and Arthur Andersen are given a free hand to take over our infrastructure and take away our jobs, our "democratically elected" leaders can fearlessly blur the lines between democracy, majoritarianism and fascism.

Our government's craven willingness to abandon India's proud tradition of being non-aligned, its rush to fight its way to the head of the queue of the Completely Aligned (the fashionable phrase is "natural ally"—India, Israel and the United States are "natural allies"), has given it the leg room to turn into a repressive regime without compromising its legitimacy.

A government's victims are not only those it kills and imprisons. Those who are displaced and dispossessed and sentenced to a lifetime of starvation and deprivation must count among them too. Millions of people have been dispossessed by "development" projects. In the past fifty-five years, big dams alone have displaced between 33 million and 55 million in India. They have no recourse to justice. In the past two years there have been a series of incidents in which police have opened fire on peaceful protesters, most of them Adivasi and Dalit. When it comes to the poor, and in particular Dalit and Adivasi communities, they get killed for encroaching on forest land, and killed when they're trying to protect forest land from encroachments—by dams, mines, steel plants and other "development" projects. In almost every instance in which the police opened fire, the government's strategy has been to say the firing was provoked by an act of violence. Those who have been fired upon are immediately called militants.

Across the country, thousands of innocent people, including minors, have been arrested under the Prevention of Terrorism Act and are being held in jail indefinitely and without trial. In the era of the War against Terror, poverty is being slyly conflated with terrorism. In the era of corporate globalization, poverty is a crime. Protesting against further impoverishment is terrorism. And now our Supreme Court says that going on strike is a crime. Criticizing the court is a crime too, of course. They're sealing the exits.

Like Old Imperialism, New Imperialism relies for its success on a network of agents—corrupt local elites who service Empire. We all know the sordid story of Enron in India. The then-Maharashtra government signed a power purchase agreement that gave Enron profits that amounted to 60 percent of India's entire rural development budget. A single American company was guaranteed a profit equivalent to funds for infrastructural development for about 500 million people!

Unlike in the old days, the New Imperialist doesn't need to trudge around the tropics risking malaria or diarrhea or early death. New Imperialism can be conducted on e-mail. The vulgar, hands-on racism of Old Imperialism is outdated. The cornerstone of New Imperialism is New Racism.

The best allegory for New Racism is the tradition of "turkey pardoning" in the United States. Every year since 1947, the National Turkey Federation has presented the U.S. President with a turkey for Thanksgiving. Every year, in a show of ceremonial magnanimity, the President spares that particular bird (and eats another one). After receiving the presidential pardon, the Chosen One is sent to Frying Pan Park in Virginia to live out its natural life. The rest of the 50 million turkeys raised for Thanksgiving are slaughtered and eaten on Thanksgiving Day. ConAgra Foods, the company that has won the Presidential Turkey contract, says it trains the lucky birds to be sociable, to interact with dignitaries, school children and the press. (Soon they'll even speak English!)

That's how New Racism in the corporate era works. A few carefully bred turkeys—the local elites of various countries, a community of wealthy immigrants, investment bankers, the occasional Colin Powell or Condoleezza Rice, some singers, some writers (like myself)—are given absolution and a pass to Frying Pan Park. The remaining millions lose their jobs, are evicted from their homes, have their water and electricity connections cut, and die of AIDS. Basically they're for the pot. But the Fortunate Fowls in Frying Pan Park are doing fine. Some of them even work for the IMF and the WTO—so who can accuse those organizations of being antiturkey? Some serve as board members on the Turkey Choosing Committee—so who can say that turkeys are against Thanksgiving? They participate in it! Who can say the poor are anti-corporate globalization? There's a stampede to get into Frying Pan Park. So what if most perish on the way?

As part of the project of New Racism we also have New Genocide. New Genocide in this new era of economic interdependence can be facilitated by economic sanctions. New Genocide means creating conditions that lead to mass death without actually going out and killing people. Denis Halliday, who was the UN humanitarian coordinator in Iraq between 1997 and 1998 (after which he resigned in disgust), used the term genocide to describe the sanctions in Iraq. In Iraq the sanctions outdid Saddam Hussein's best efforts by claiming more than half a million children's lives.

In the new era, apartheid as formal policy is antiquated and unnecessary. International instruments of trade and finance oversee a complex system of multilateral trade laws and financial agreements that keep the poor in their bantustans anyway. Its whole purpose is to institutionalize inequity. Why else would it be that the U.S. taxes a garment made by a Bangladeshi manufacturer twenty times more than a garment made in Britain? Why else would it be that countries that grow cocoa beans, like the Ivory Coast and Ghana, are taxed out of the market if they try to turn it into chocolate? Why else would it be that countries that grow 90 percent of the world's cocoa beans produce only 5 percent of the world's chocolate? Why else would it be that rich countries that spend over a billion dollars a day on subsidies to farmers demand that poor countries like India withdraw all agricultural subsidies, including subsidized electricity? Why else would it be that after having been plundered by colonizing regimes for more than half a century, former colonies are steeped in debt to those same regimes and repay them some $382 *billion* a year?

For all these reasons, the derailing of trade agreements at Cancún was crucial for us. Though our governments try to take the credit, we know that it was the result of years of struggle by many millions of people in many, many countries. What Cancún taught us is that in order to inflict real damage and force radical change, it is vital for local resistance movements to make international alliances. From Cancún we learned the importance of globalizing resistance.

No individual nation can stand up to the project of corporate globalization on its own. Time and again we have seen that when it comes to the neoliberal project, the heroes of our times are suddenly diminished. Extraordinary, charismatic men, giants in the opposition, when they seize power and become heads of state, are rendered powerless on the global stage. I'm thinking here of President Lula of Brazil. Lula was the hero of the World Social Forum last year. This year he's busy implementing IMF guidelines, reducing pension benefits and purging radicals from the Workers' Party. I'm thinking also of the former president of South Africa, Nelson Mandela. Within two years of taking office in 1994, his government genuflected with hardly a caveat to the Market God. It instituted a massive program of privatization and structural adjustment that has left millions of people homeless, jobless and without water and electricity.

Why does this happen? There's little point in beating our breasts and feeling betrayed. Lula and Mandela are, by any reckoning, magnificent men. But the moment they cross the floor from the opposition into government they become hostage to a spectrum of threats—most malevolent among them the threat of capital flight, which can destroy any government overnight. To imagine that a leader's personal charisma and a c.v. of struggle will dent the corporate cartel is to have no understanding of how capitalism works or, for that matter, how power works. Radical change cannot be negotiated by governments; it can only be enforced by people.

At the World Social Forum some of the best minds in the world come together to exchange ideas about what is happening around us. These conversations refine our vision of the kind of world we're fighting for. It is a vital process that must not be undermined. However, if all our energies are diverted into this process at the cost of real political action, then the WSF, which has played such a crucial role in the movement for global justice, runs the risk of becoming an asset to our enemies. What we need to discuss urgently is strategies of resistance. We need to aim at real targets, wage real battles and inflict real damage. Gandhi's salt march was not just political theater. When, in a simple act of defiance, thousands of Indians marched to the sea and made their own salt, they broke the salt tax laws. It was a direct strike at the economic underpinning of the British Empire. It was real. While our movement has won some important victories, we must not allow nonviolent resistance to atrophy into ineffectual, feel-good, political theater. It is a very precious weapon that must be constantly honed and reimagined. It cannot be allowed to become a mere spectacle, a photo opportunity for the media.

It was wonderful that on February 15 last year, in a spectacular display of public morality, 10 million people on five continents marched against the war on Iraq. It was wonderful, but it was not enough. February 15 was a weekend. Nobody had to so much as miss a day of work. Holiday protests don't stop wars. George Bush knows that. The confidence with which he disregarded overwhelming public opinion should be a lesson to us all. Bush believes that Iraq can be occupied and colonized as Afghanistan has been, as Tibet has been, as Chechnya is being, as East Timor once was and Palestine still is. He thinks that all he has to do is hunker down and wait until a crisis-driven media, having picked this crisis to the bone, drops it and moves on. Soon the carcass will slip off the bestseller charts, and all of us outraged folks will lose interest. Or so he hopes.

This movement of ours needs a major, global victory. It's not good enough to be right. Sometimes, if only in order to test our resolve, it's important to win something. In order to win something, we need to agree on something. That something does not need to be an overarching preordained ideology into which we force-fit our delightfully factious, argumentative selves. It does not need to be an unquestioning allegiance to one or another form of resistance to the exclusion of everything else. It could be a minimum agenda.

If all of us are indeed against imperialism and against the project of neoliberalism, then let's turn our gaze on Iraq. Iraq is the inevitable culmination of both. Plenty of antiwar activists have retreated in confusion since the capture of Saddam Hussein. Isn't the world better off without Saddam Hussein? they ask timidly.

Let's look this thing in the eye once and for all. To applaud the U.S. Army's capture of Saddam Hussein, and therefore in retrospect justify its invasion and occupation of Iraq, is like deifying Jack the Ripper for disemboweling the Boston Strangler. And that after a quarter-century partnership in which the Ripping and Strangling was a joint enterprise. It's an in-house quarrel.

They're business partners who fell out over a dirty deal. Jack's the CEO.

So if we are against imperialism, shall we agree that we are against the U.S. occupation and that we believe the United States must withdraw from Iraq and pay reparations to the Iraqi people for the damage that the war has inflicted?

How do we begin to mount our resistance? Let's start with something really small. The issue is not about *supporting* the resistance in Iraq against the occupation or discussing who exactly constitutes the resistance. (Are they old killer Baathists, are they Islamic fundamentalists?)

We have to *become* the global resistance to the occupation.

Our resistance has to begin with a refusal to accept the legitimacy of the U.S. occupation of Iraq. It means acting to make it materially impossible for Empire to achieve its aims. It means soldiers should refuse to fight, reservists should refuse to serve, workers should refuse to load ships and aircraft with weapons. It certainly means that in countries like India and Pakistan we must block the U.S. government's plans to have Indian and Pakistani soldiers sent to Iraq to clean up after them.

I suggest we choose by some means two of the major corporations that are profiting from the destruction of Iraq. We could then list every project they are involved in. We could locate their offices in every city and every country across the world. We could go after them. We could shut them down. It's a question of bringing our collective wisdom and experience of past struggles to bear on a single target. It's a question of the desire to win.

The Project for the New American Century seeks to perpetuate inequity and establish American hegemony at any price, even if it's apocalyptic. The World Social Forum demands justice and survival.

For these reasons, we must consider ourselves at war.

Questions for Discussion and Writing

1. Roy labels a lot of things as "new" in her article—new imperialism and new racism, for example. How does she justify labeling these elements as new phenomena?

2. Summarize Roy's position on free trade and respond to it. Do you support it based on your own knowledge and reading or do you oppose it? Why?

3. Examine Roy's claims about the link between capitalism and military action. What examples can you think of where this seems to have been the case? Can you argue for the use of military power to protect the use of natural resources? Can you argue effectively against it?

4. List some of Roy's examples of American influence being detrimental to the people of other countries. Have you heard of any of these instances before? How might the coverage of the media affect what we know of U.S. actions around the world? For research, look at the Union Carbide factory disaster in Bhopal, India. Did you know about this? How might Roy explain the lack of media coverage in the United States?

America and World Power
IMMANUEL WALLERSTEIN

Dr. Wallerstein was born in 1930 in New York, and was educated at Columbia University. He taught at McGill University, the State University of New York at Binghampton until his retirement in 1999. He has acted as a visiting professor at universities around the world and headed the Fernand Braudel Center for the Study of Economics, Historical Systems and Civilization. Dr. Wallerstein was President of the International Sociological Association from 1994 to 1998, and currently holds the post of Senior Research Scholar at Yale University. He is the author of many books, some of the more recent being Utopistics: Or, Historical Choices of the Twenty-first Century *(1998),* The End of the World As We Know It: Social Science for the Twenty-first Century *(1999), and* Decline of American Power: The U.S. in a Chaotic World *(2003). Consistent with his concerns about the role of the United States in this new century, his article on America and world power addresses many of his concerns, particularly the unilateral nature of America's approach to the rest of the world. The article has been edited for length.*

———————— ✦ ————————

I t is a rare president of the United States, in the twentieth century at least, who has not at some point made the statement that the United States is the greatest country in the world. I'm not sure our omnipresent public opinion polling agencies have ever put the question directly to the American public, but I suspect that the percentage of the U.S. population that would agree with such a statement is very large indeed. I ask you to reflect on how such a statement sounds, not merely to persons from poor countries with cultures that are very different from ours but to our close friends and allies—to Canadians, to the English, and of course to the French. Does Tony Blair think the United States is the greatest country in the world, greater than Great Britain? Would he dare think that? Does Pope John Paul II think it? Who, besides Americans and those who wish to migrate to the United States, believe this?

Nationalism is of course not a phenomenon limited to people in the United States. The citizens of almost every country are patriotic and often chauvinistic. Americans are aware of that, no doubt. But they nonetheless tend to note the fact that many people across the world wish to emigrate to the United States, and that no other locus of immigration seems to be quite as popular, and they take this as confirmation of their belief in American superior virtue as a nation.

• • •

There is nothing so blinding as success. And the United States has had its fair share of success in the past 200 years. Success has the vicious consequence that it seems to breed almost inevitably the conviction that it will necessarily continue. Success is a poor guide to wise policy. Failure at least often leads to reflection; success seldom does.

Fifty years ago, U.S. hegemony in the world-system was based on a combination of productive efficiency (outstripping by far any rivals), a world political agenda that was warmly endorsed by its allies in Europe and Asia, and military superiority. Today, the productive efficiency of U.S. enterprises faces very extensive competition, competition first of all coming from the enterprises of its closest allies. As a result, the world political agenda of the United States is no longer so warmly endorsed and is often clearly contested even by its allies, especially given the disappearance of the Soviet Union. What remains for the moment is military superiority.

It is worth thinking about the objectives of U.S. foreign policy, as pursued for the last 50 years by successive U.S. governments. Obviously, the U.S. has been concerned with threats posed by governments it considered hostile or at least inimical to U.S. interests. There is nothing wrong or exceptional about this. This is true of the foreign policy of any state in the modern world-system, especially any powerful state. The question is how the U.S. thought it could deal with such threats.

In the 1950s and 1960s, the U.S. seemed to be so strong that it could arrange, without too much difficulty and with a minimal use of force, that governments it did not like either could be neutralized (we called that containment) or, in the case of weaker governments, could be overthrown by internal forces supported covertly by the U.S. government, assisted occasionally by a little old-fashioned gunship diplomacy.

Neutralization was the tactic employed vis-a-vis the Communist world. The U.S. did not seek to overthrow the Soviet Union or any of its satellite regimes in east and central Europe. Basically, it did not seek this because it was not in a military position to carry this out against the expected resistance by the government of the U.S.S.R. Instead, the U.S. government entered into a tacit accord with the U.S.S.R. that it would not even try to do this, in return for a pledge by the Soviet Union that it would not try to expand its zone. We refer to this in code as the Yalta agreement. If one doubts the reality of this agreement, just review U.S. foreign policy vis-a-vis the German Democratic Republic in 1953, Hungary in 1956, Czechoslovakia in 1968, and Poland in 1981.

The accord was not however intended to apply to East Asia, where Soviet troops were absent, thanks primarily to the insistence of the Communist regimes in China and North Korea. So the U.S.

did in fact try to overthrow these regimes as well as that in Vietnam. It did not however succeed. And these failed attempts left a serious scar on American public opinion.

The United States, however, was able to enforce its will in the rest of the world, and did so without compunction. Think of Iran in 1953, Guatemala in 1954, Lebanon in 1956, the Dominican Republic in 1965, and Chile in 1973. The coup in Chile by Gen. Pinochet against the freely-elected government of Salvador Allende, with the active support of the U.S. government, occurred on September 11. I do not know whether or not Osama bin Laden or his followers were aware of this coincidence of dates, but it is nonetheless a symbolic coincidence that many, especially in Latin America, will notice. It also points to a further metaphor of the Twin Towers. The Twin Towers were a marvelous technological achievement. But technological achievements can and will be copied. The Malaysians have already copied the Twin Towers architecturally, and a bigger skyscraper is being built right now in Shanghai. Symbols too can be copied. Now we have two September 11 anniversaries, on which victims mourn.

In the 1970s, U.S. foreign policy methods changed, had to change. Chile was the last major instance in which the U.S. was able so cavalierly to arrange other governments to its preferences. (I do not count the cases of either Grenada or Panama, which were very small countries with no serious mode of military defense.) What had caused this change was the end of U.S. economic dominance of the world-economy, combined with the military defeat of the United States in Vietnam. Geopolitical reality had changed. The U.S. government could no longer concentrate on maintaining, even less on expanding, its power; instead its prime goal became preventing a too rapid erosion of its power—both in the world-economy and in the military arena.

In the world-economy, the U.S. faced not only the hot breath of its competitors in western Europe and Japan but the seeming success of "developmentalist" policies in large parts of the rest of the world, policies that had been designed expressly to constrain the ability of countries in the core zone to accumulate capital at what was seen to be the expense of countries in the periphery. We should remember that the 1970s was declared by the United Nations the "decade of development." In the 1970s, there was much talk of creating a "new international economic order," and in UNESCO of creating a "new international information order." The 1970s was the time of the two famous OPEC oil price rises, which sent waves of panic into the American public.

The U.S. position on all these thrusts was either ambiguous discomfort or outright opposition. Globally, a counterthrust was launched. It involved the aggressive assertion of neoliberalism and the so-called Washington Consensus, the transformation of GATT into the World Trade Organization, the Davos meetings, and the spreading of the concept of globalization with its corollary, TINA (there is no alternative). Essentially, all these efforts combined amounted to a dismantlement of the "developmentalist" policies throughout the world, and of course particularly in the peripheral zones of the world-economy. In the short run, that is in the 1980s and 1990s, this counteroffensive led by the U.S. government seemed to succeed.

These policies on the front of the world-economy were matched by a persistent world military policy which might be summarized as the "anti-proliferation" policy. When the United States successfully made the first atomic bombs in 1945, it was determined to maintain a monopoly on such very powerful weapons. It was willing to share this monopoly with its faithful junior partner, Great Britain, but that was it. Of course, as we know, the other "great powers" simply ignored this claim. First the Soviet Union, then France, then China achieved nuclear capacity. So then did India and later Pakistan. So did South Africa, whose apartheid government however admitted this only as it was leaving power and was careful to dismantle this capacity before it turned over power to the successor, more democratic, government of the Black African majority. And so did Israel, although it has always denied this publicly.

Then there are the almost nuclear powers, if indeed they are still in the almost category—North Korea, Iran, Iraq (whose facilities Israel bombed in the 1980s in order to keep it in the "almost" category), Libya, and maybe Argentina. And there are in addition the former Soviet countries which inherited this capacity—Ukraine, Belorussia, and Kazakhstan. To this must be added the other lethal technologies—biological and chemical warfare. These are so much easier to create, store, and employ, that we are not sure how many countries have some capacity, even a considerable capacity in these fields.

The United States has had a simple straightforward policy. By hook or by crook, by force or by bribery, it wishes to deny everybody access to these weapons. It has obviously not been successful, but its efforts over the past years have at least slowed down the process of proliferation. There is a further catch in U.S. policy. Insofar as it tries to employ international agreements to limit proliferation, it simultaneously tries not itself to be bound by such constraints, or to be minimally bound.

The U.S. government has made it clear that it will renounce any such restraints whenever it deems it necessary to do so, while loudly condemning any other government that seeks to do the same.

As a policy, non-proliferation seems doomed to failure, not only in the long run but even in the middle run. The best that the U.S. will be able to do in the next 25 years is to slow the process down somewhat. But there is also a moral/political question here. The United States trusts itself, but trusts no one else. The U.S. government wishes to inspect North Korean locations to see if it is violating these norms. It has not offered the U.N. or anyone else the right to inspect U.S. locations. The U.S. trusts itself to use such weapons wisely, and in the defense of liberty (a concept seemingly identical with U.S. national interests). It assumes that anyone else might intend to use such weapons against liberty (a concept seemingly identical here too with U.S. national interests). Personally, I do not trust any government to use such weapons wisely. I would be happy to see them all banned, but do not believe this is truly enforceable in the contemporary interstate system. So personally I abstain from moralizing on this issue. Moralizing opens one to the charge of hypocrisy. And while a cynical neorealist (a category that probably includes me) would say that all governments are hypocritical, moralizing jars badly if one wishes to attract support in other countries on the basis of one's comparative virtue.

• • •

Americans, especially American politicians and publicists, like to speak about our ideals. An advertisement for the "bestselling" book of Chris Matthews, *Now, Let Me Tell You What I Really Think*, offers this excerpt: "When you think about it, we Americans are different. That word 'freedom' isn't just in our documents; it's in our cowboy souls." "Cowboy souls"—I could not have said it better. Our ideals are perhaps special. But the same people who remind us of that do not like to talk about our privileges, which are also perhaps special. Indeed, they denounce those who do talk of them. But the ideals and the privileges go together. They may seem to be in conflict, but they presuppose each other.

I am not someone who denigrates American ideals. I find them quite wonderful, even refreshing. I cherish them, I invoke them, I further them. Take for example the First Amendment to the U.S. Constitution—something correctly remembered at all the appropriate ceremonies as incarnating American ideals. Let us, however, recall two things about the First Amendment. It wasn't in the original Constitution, which means it wasn't considered a founding principle. And public opinion polls have often shown that a majority of the American public would change, diminish, or even eliminate these guarantees, in whole or in part, even in so-called ordinary times. When we are in a "war" such as the "war on terrorism," then neither the U.S. government nor the U.S. public can be counted on to defend these ideals, and not even the Supreme Court can be relied upon to hold fast to them in an "emergency." Such defense is left largely to an often timid organization with at best minority support in public opinion, the American Civil Liberties Union, membership in which is often cited as a reason not to vote for someone in a general election. So, I am in favor of freedom of speech and freedom of religion and all the other freedoms, but sometimes I must wonder if America is.

• • •

The question before Americans is really the following. If American hegemony is in slow decline, and I believe it unquestionably is, will we lose the ideals because we will have less power to override them? Will our cowboy souls erect barbed wire around our national ranch in order to guard our privileges in danger of decline, as though they could not escape through the barbed wire? Let me suggest here another metaphor that comes from the Twin Towers. Towers that are destroyed can be rebuilt. But will we rebuild them in the same way—with the same assurance that we are reaching for the stars and doing it right, with the same certainty that they will be seen as a beacon to the world? Or will we rebuild in other ways, after careful reflection about what we really need and what is really possible for us, and really desirable for us?

• • •

The future of the United States, the future of the world, in the short run, but even more in the medium run, is absolutely uncertain. Certainty may seem desirable if one reflects on one's privileges. It seems less desirable if one thinks that the privileges are doomed to decline, even disappear. And if it were certain that the Osama bin Ladens of this world, in all camps, were to prevail, who would cherish that certainty?

After the Civil War, the United States spent some 80 years pursuing its manifest destiny. It was not sure, all that time, whether it wished to be an isolationist or an imperial power. And when, in 1945, it had finally achieved hegemony in the world-system, when it had (in Shakespeare's choice) not only achieved greatness but had greatness thrust upon it, the American people were not fully prepared for the role they now had to play. We spent thirty years learning how to "assume our responsibilities" in the world. And just when we had learned this reasonably well, our hegemony passed its peak.

We have spent the last thirty years insisting very loudly that we are still hegemonic and that everyone needs to continue to acknowledge it. If one is truly hegemonic, one does not need to make such a request. We have wasted the past thirty years. What the United States needs now to do is to learn how to live with the new reality— that it no longer has the power to decide unilaterally what is good for everyone. It may not even be in a position to decide unilaterally what is good for itself. It has to come to terms with the world. It is not Osama bin Laden with whom we must conduct a dialogue. We must start with our near friends and allies—with Canada and Mexico, with Europe, with Japan. And once we have trained ourselves to hear them and to believe that they too have ideals and interests, that they too have ideas and hopes and aspirations, then and only then perhaps shall we be ready to dialogue with the rest of the world, that is, with the majority of the world.

This dialogue, once we begin to enter into it, will not be easy, and may not even be pleasant. For they shall ask us to renounce some privileges. They will ask us to fulfill our ideals. They will ask us to learn. Fifty years ago, the great African poet/politician, Léopold-Sédar Senghor, called on the world to come to the "rendez-vous du donner et du recevoir." Americans know what they have to give in such a rendez-vous. But are they aware of something they wish to receive?

We are being called upon these days to return to spiritual values, as though we had ever observed these values. But what are these values? Let me remind you. In the Christian tradition (Matthew 19:24), it is said: "It is easier for a camel to pass through the eye of a needle than for a rich man to enter the kingdom of God." And in the Jewish tradition, Hillel tells us: "Do unto others as you would have them do unto you." And in the Muslim tradition, the Koran (52.36) tells us: "Or did they create the heavens and the earth? Nay! They have no certainty." Are these our values?

• • •

Osama bin Laden will soon be forgotten, but the kind of political violence we call terrorism will remain very much with us in the

30–50 years to come. Terrorism is to be sure a very ineffective way to change the world. It is counterproductive and leads to counterforce, which can often wipe out the immediate set of actors. But it will nonetheless continue to occur. An America that continues to relate to the world by a unilateral assertion that it represents civilization, whether it does so in the form of isolationist withdrawal or in that of active interventionism, cannot live in peace with the world, and therefore will not live in peace with itself. What we do to the world, we do to ourselves. Can the land of liberty and privilege, even amidst its decline, learn to be a land that treats everyone everywhere as equals? And can we deal as equal to equal in the world-system if we do not deal as equal to equal within our own frontiers?

Questions for Discussion and Writing

1. Dr. Wallerstein points out that the United States has often supported governments that were not democratically elected. How does this influence the current mission statement of the United States and the way that other countries might react to it?

2. The independence of the United States itself was achieved by the actions of a citizenry against a controlling power that often included guerilla warfare tactics. What kind of argument might be formed by citizens of a nation rebelling against U.S. influence or control based on this historical fact.

3. The writer argues that the hegemony of the United States has passed its peak. What characterized the hegemony and what moves does Wallerstein advocate for moving forward into the new century?

Power & Duty: U.S. Action Is Crucial to Maintaining World Order

Gary Schmitt

Dr. Gary Schmitt was educated at the University of Dallas and the University of Chicago. He has served as a member of the professional staff of the Senate Select Committee on intelligence, and under President Reagan he was executive director of the President's Foreign Intelligence Advisory Board, the White House. Since he left that position in 1988, Dr. Schmitt has held various visiting fellowships at the Brookings Institution and the National Interest and has acted as a consultant to the Department of Defense. He is the coauthor of The Future of U.S. Intelligence *(1996) and* Silent Warfare: Understanding the World of Intelligence *(2002) with Abram N. Shulsky. Dr. Schmitt is executive director of the Project for the New American Century (PNAC), described on its website as "a non-profit educational organization dedicated to a few fundamental propositions: that American leadership is good both for America and for the world; and that such leadership requires military strength, diplomatic energy and commitment to moral principle." The goal of the PNAC is to use military power and preemptive-strike capabilities to promote "a foreign policy that boldly and purposefully promotes American principles abroad; and national leadership that accepts the United States' global responsibilities." This article appeared in the* Los Angeles Times *on March 23, 2003.*

---◆---

As the war in Iraq unfolds, the awesome military power of the United States is on exhibit for the whole world to see. Despite the real but mostly tacit support of friends and allies around the world, America is exercising its power in the face of world opinion decidedly opposed to the war. In some respects, the very fact that the United States can do so is even more confirmation to its critics around the world that American power seemingly unhinged from all restraints—be it the United Nations or world opinion—is as much a danger to world order as perhaps Saddam Hussein himself.

Critics of America's preeminent role in the world, like France's president, are quick to see the supposed problems related to a unipolar world. What they are far slower to offer is a realistic alternative. For example, for all the huffing and puffing about the need to have this war sanctioned by the United Nations, it goes without saying that neither Paris nor Beijing is especially eager to constrain its national security decisions because of U.N. mandates. Indeed, in the continuing case of North Korea's violation of the Nuclear Nonproliferation Treaty, France and China have actively sought to push the matter away from U.N. consideration.

The fact is, the U.N. can only operate by majority consensus, and this means that its decisions will be governed by the particular interests of the individual member states of the Security Council—not some disembodied, benign voice of the "international community." As the failure to back up its own resolutions on Iraq and to act decisively in the cases of Rwanda and Kosovo in the 1990s shows, the U.N. cannot be trusted to be the sole arbiter of these matters.

No. The unavoidable reality is that the exercise of American power is key to maintaining what peace and order there is in the world today. Imagine a world in which the U.S. didn't exercise this power. Who would handle a nuclear-armed North Korea? Who would prevent the one-party state of China from acting on its pledge to gather democratic Taiwan into its fold? Who would be left to hunt down Islamic terrorists increasingly interested in getting their hands on weapons of mass destruction? Who could have contained, let alone defeated, a tyrant like Hussein, preventing him from becoming the dominant power in the Middle East? Who can prevent the Balkans from slipping back into chaos? Who is going to confront regimes like those of Iran, Syria and Libya as they rush to get their own weapons of mass destruction? Given how little most of our allies and critics spend on defense, certainly not them.

As Robert Kagan notes in "Of Paradise and Power," his seminal examination of the growing distance between the strategic perspectives of America and Europe, the United States today is in much the same position as Marshal Will Kane, played by Gary Cooper in the movie "High Noon." The townspeople are more than happy to live in the peace brought by his law enforcement but are nervous and resentful when the bad guys come back to town looking for him, to enact their revenge. The residents shortsightedly believe that if the marshal would just leave town, there would be no trouble. Of course, the reverse is true. Without Kane to protect them, the town would quickly fall into an anarchic state, paralyzed by ruthless gunslingers.

The simple but fundamental point is that it matters more what purposes our power serves than that we have power. President Bush made it clear in his address to the nation last week that removing Hussein was necessary not only because of the threat he poses but also because it could begin a process of reform in a region long in need of it. Cutting the nexus between weapons of mass destruction and terrorists requires transforming regimes that possess these weapons and cooperate with or spawn terrorists.

Like the townsfolk in "High Noon," this naturally makes many in the world anxious. Change always brings risk and instability. But the danger in doing nothing—of pretending that the volatile Middle East mix of failing regimes, rogue states, weapons of mass destruction and terrorism can be contained safely if we only let it alone—is far greater. As British Prime Minister Tony Blair said on the floor of Parliament during a debate over Iraq last week, "What was shocking about 11 September was not just the slaughter of the innocent, but the knowledge that had the terrorists been able to, there would have been not 3,000 innocent dead, but 30,000 or 300,000, and the more the suffering, the greater the terrorists' rejoicing."

But change also brings opportunity. The president's decision to remove Hussein from power and his work to create a viable, democratic Iraq has already led to a number of positive steps in the region. In Iran, moderates, emboldened by the possibility of a democratic Iraq, are again pushing to reform that cleric-dominated state. In Saudi Arabia, the homeland of 15 of the 19 terrorists who carried out the attacks on the United States, the royal family has for the first time begun serious deliberations with reformers on how to transform and democratize the country. In the Palestinian territories, Yasser Arafat reluctantly agreed to give up much of his day-to-day control over the Palestinian Authority to a new prime minister. And in Egypt, the government has just released its most vocal human-rights advocate.

None of these steps amounts to a revolution in the region. Nor do they mean that positive political transformation throughout the Islamic world will happen easily or without fits, starts and dead ends. However, the early signs suggest that the president is right to believe that the instinct for liberty is not missing from Middle East genes.

Finally, and lest we forget, America is employing its power in this war to free a people who have suffered under one of history's most terrible tyrants. As *New York Times* correspondent John Burns reported from Baghdad on the eve of the start of the war, "Iraqis have suffered beyond, I think, the common understanding of the United States from the repression of the past 30 years here. And many, many Iraqis are telling us now, not always in the whispers we have heard in the past but now in quite candid conversations, that they are waiting for America to come and bring them liberty." And, he said on PBS, "while they are very, very fearful of course of the bombing, of damage to Iraq's infrastructure . . . there is also no doubt—no doubt—that there are many, many Iraqis who see what is about to happen here as the moment of liberation."

That's a dream only American power can inspire.

Questions for Discussion and Writing

1. When Dr. Schmitt uses the reference to *High Noon* in his article what point is he trying to make and why do you think he chooses this image to advance it?
2. According to the writer, what are the advantages and disadvantages of the United States deciding security issues unilaterally?
3. Examine and comment on the use of the following words in this article: revolution; power; reform; liberty.

Over There

ERIC SCHLOSSER

Eric Schlosser was born in 1959 in New York City. Schlosser is a regular writer for the Atlantic Monthly *and is regularly interviewed for opinion on CNN, Fox News, and CBS Evening News. His first book,* Fast Food Nation *(2001), became a huge success in hardback and paperback, spending over two years on the* New York Times *bestseller list. His latest book,* Reefer Madness: Sex, Drugs and Cheap Labor in the American Black Market, *was published in 2003. Schlosser's next book will be about the American prison system. In this article Schlosser looks back to the problems caused by American imperialism at the beginning of the twentieth century and asks if the nation is falling into the same trap as we enter the twenty-first.*

◆

When Ronald Reagan was President, I spent a few years studying British imperial history, trying to comprehend why empires rise and fall. I was particularly interested in the period between 1898 and 1902, when the British Empire began to stumble, America's empire was born, and a "special relationship" between the two nations was secretly formed amid colonial wars in South Africa and the Philippines. The end of the century marked a historic turning point, a convergence of imperial paths that soon transformed the world. Long-standing attitudes changed, and traditional roles were reversed. At the beginning of the 1890s, Americans still embraced a revolutionary foreign policy: friendship with all nations, entangling alliances with none.

The United States was the world's leading industrial power, but did not possess a single battleship and had only 25,000 men in its army. Great Britain was the world's dominant financial and military power. Its banks supplied capital to Wall Street, and its navy maintained eleven bases and thirty-three coaling stations in the seas around the United States, ensuring those loans would be repaid. Although wealthy members of the East Coast establishment admired the British Empire and sought entry to its upper class, most Americans despised both.

In 1898 the Spanish–American War provided the United States with an opportunity to emulate British imperial policies. The war was initially justified, however, as an anti-imperial crusade to liberate the Cuban people from tyrannical Spanish rule. American newspapers, especially those owned by William Randolph Hearst, stressed the necessity of extending American freedom and democracy overseas. Doing nothing might lead to disaster. "Within a few days," one New York paper warned, "Spain will have it within her power to lay waste and ravage this city as the volcano of Vesuvius ravaged Herculaneum." The sinking of an American battleship, the USS *Maine*, supplied the requisite casus belli. The U.S. Navy claimed that the ship had been sunk by a mine in Havana harbour, an outrageous act of terrorism; historians later concluded that this was misinformation. The powerful explosion aboard the *Maine* was most likely the result of an accident. Just five days after being declared, the noble war to liberate Cuba was somehow transmuted into a campaign to secure coaling stations and port facilities in the Far East. The United States soon annexed Hawaii, Guam, Wake Island and the Philippines.

Many Filipinos were unhappy to find themselves being traded from one imperial power to another. The American occupation sparked guerrilla warfare and a popular uprising that lasted for years. The conquest of the Philippines provoked an angry debate in the United States about imperialism. William Jennings Bryan, the Democratic candidate for President in 1900, argued that the most important question of the campaign was: "Republic or Empire?" Bryan was soundly defeated by Wall Street's candidate, William McKinley, but popular distrust of militarism and imperialism endured in the United States for another fifty years.

In retrospect, the same fundamental issue was at stake during the presidential elections of 1900 and of 2000: republic or empire? Imperial power has once again become fashionable. In London and Washington DC, you hear suggestions that perhaps the British Empire wasn't such a bad idea after all—and that an

American empire, properly administered, might do a lot of good. Such arguments have been well received in today's political climate. For some reason, celebrations of the British Empire are not welcomed the same way in India, Pakistan, Kenya or South Africa. The whole notion of selfless conquest, of a "White Man's Burden," was always a lie. Outside of Rudyard Kipling's poem (written in 1899 to persuade Americans to keep the Philippines), the real burden was borne by the colonized, not the colonizer. Although British rule may have conferred some lasting benefits, altruism was hardly the guiding force of that empire—or of any other. "Destiny" can also be ruled out as a plausible explanation, despite the many attempts throughout history to claim it as one. President McKinley described America's acquisition of the Philippines as "a gift from the gods," failing to mention that the undersecretary of the navy, Theodore Roosevelt (a great man, yes, but not divine), had secretly ordered the American fleet to Manila. As the historian A. K. Weinberg once observed, "destiny" tends to be invoked in the very circumstances which, upon further analysis, seem to give it least justification.

In November 2000, only months before becoming the director of policy planning at the State Department, Richard N. Haas gave a speech entitled "Imperial America." Haas argued that the United States should assume a world role similar to that of Great Britain in the nineteenth century, exerting control through both informal and formal means. "America's destiny is to police the world," says another prominent supporter of President George W. Bush's foreign policy. Although members of the Bush administration have strongly denied that they are seeking to create a new American empire, their current plans for administering Iraq seem vaguely familiar. "We come, not as invaders or conquerors," President McKinley told the Filipino people, "but as friends, to protect the natives in their homes, in their employments, and in their personal and religious rights." McKinley called his policy "benevolent assimilation." An estimated 200,000 civilians died between 1899 and 1902, as the United States benevolently assimilated the Philippines.

A century ago those who questioned America's god-given right to rule the world were often accused of treason, an accusation frequently made today. Mark Twain is now considered the quintessential American novelist, yet he too was called a traitor for opposing the annexation of the Philippines. Twain was thought un-American. *"Shall we?"* he asked, attacking McKinley's foreign policy. "Shall we go on conferring our Civilization upon the peoples that sit in darkness, or shall we give those poor things a rest? Shall we bang right ahead in our old-time, loud, pious way, and commit the new century to the game; or shall we sober up and sit down and think it over first?" Twain suggested a new flag for America's imperial conquest: the American flag, with the white stripes painted black, and the stars replaced by a skull and crossbones.

Questions for Discussion and Writing

1. Discuss the similarities and differences between the international "missions" of the United States in the early 1900s and the early 2000s.
2. The writer Mark Twain opposed America's imperialist policy in the Philippines. In our own time many writers and entertainment figures also air their political views freely. Write an essay that discusses the positive and negative elements of such political involvement by nonelected figures.

America the Ignorant
LAURA MILLER

This article appeared in the online magazine Salon.com *on September 27, 2001. Coming two weeks after the terrorist attacks on the World Trade Center in New York, Miller's article was part of the new evaluation of the American role in the world. Her voice joined others that discussed whether American ignorance of other nations could have been a trigger for the hostility that had led to the appalling events of September 11. Laura Miller is a senior editor at* Salon. *Miller has also written for newspapers and magazines, such as the* New York Times, *the* San Francisco Examiner, *and* Wired, *covering movies, books, theater, digital culture, and social issues.*

--------- ◆ ---------

Almost as soon as rescue workers began sifting through the rubble at the sites of the September 11 terrorist attacks on the World Trade Center and the Pentagon, many Americans launched another search—not quite as desperate, perhaps, but crucial nonetheless. Citizens scrambled for information about the places the killers came from and the ideas and beliefs that could drive men to lay down their lives for the chance to massacre ordinary American office workers. Foreign correspondents with expertise in the Middle East say their phones have been ringing off the hook, and virtually every newspaper in every town across the nation has run a variation on two basic stories: "What is Islam?" and "Why Do They Hate Us?" Adding to the shock of thousands of violent deaths was the bewildering information that the people who so passionately want us dead belong to nations and groups that many Americans had never even heard of.

Why are Americans so ignorant of what's going on in the world outside our borders, even when our own government is playing a key role in those events? That's a question that dogged Anne Kelleher, a professor of political science at Pacific Lutheran University in Washington state, while she was lecturing in Ankara, Turkey, last year on a Fulbright scholarship. "I tried to explain to the teachers and students there why, during the U.S. presidential election, foreign policy wasn't front and center. For them, it's unfathomable that the most militarily powerful, the most politically influential country, with the most impact on the global economy, plus a culture that's transformed the world via its media—how a country with that kind of far-flung influence can choose its leader with no attention to the issues that it faces worldwide." Kelleher cited a January 2000 Gallup poll in which Americans asked to rank the importance of issues in the presidential campaign relegated the U.S. role in world affairs to 20th place.

Ignorance of history, as well as of current events, can have dire consequences. President George W. Bush's use of the word "crusade" in describing his planned war on terrorism was a stunning misstep at a time when the U.S. badly needs to reassure the Muslim world that we aren't on the verge of a new holy war. If that's not disturbing enough, only a year ago the president's national security advisor, Condoleezza Rice, was talking nonsense to the New York Times and USA Today about Iran trying to spread Islamic fundamentalism to the Taliban and "doing all kinds of things with Pakistan"; Iran, a Shiite Muslim nation, is a foe of the Sunni Muslim governments of both Afghanistan and Pakistan. On Sunday, the Times reported that the "outline" of the U.S.'s war plan "often emerges from the private conversations" between Bush and Rice.

Eric Ransdell, a foreign correspondent for nine years in Africa and Asia and currently a documentary filmmaker living in Shanghai, China, blames the American education system for producing know-nothing citizens, people who in turn are unlikely to protest the decline in news coverage of foreign affairs. Recent surveys by such institutions as Harvard and the University of Maryland show that reporting on world events has dramatically shrunk in both the print and broadcast news media.

"For decades we've been reading about how American school-children can't find Mexico or Canada on a map, and yet nothing seems to change," says Ransdell. "These people who don't know the difference between Switzerland and Swaziland then become the main consumers of news. And in poll after poll they tell us that they want less foreign news and more of what I call 'selfish journalism'—which stocks to buy, sex and beauty tips, 10 steps to a healthier colon and so on. It becomes this horrible feedback loop where people are sent out of our schools in a state of complete ignorance of the rest of the world and then, maybe because they're embarrassed, clamor for even less information on something they know almost nothing about."

Orville Schell, dean of the journalism school at the University of California at Berkeley, says that while "Americans are ever more involved in the world and ever less knowledgeable about it," it's the bosses at U.S. media companies who deserve the blame. "The broadcast media has decided to cut back on foreign news coverage in its infinitely craven efforts to pander to the largest and the lowest common denominator. This last week we've seen what the broadcast media is capable of when they're let out of the constraints of ratings and the bottom line mentality. I'm hearing journalists saying 'Wow, this past two weeks we felt dignified again. We're able to do what we want to do and know how to do. We had the time and the resources and the suits were off our backs.'"

But even Schell can't claim that any more than an "elite" of American news consumers craves reporting on world events. "Other people would prefer just to read the ball scores," he concedes. Ransdell recalls, "When I was at U.S. News & World Report I heard about these focus groups we did with our readers where almost every time foreign news came in dead last in terms of what our audience wanted us to deliver. Mike Ruby and the other editors I was working for at the time all wanted more foreign coverage, more overseas bureaus and a bigger foreign news hole, but what could they do? The fact that as much foreign news finds its way into print and onto television as it does today is, frankly, a miracle given the yodeling ignorance of the American public."

Editors of Web sites, who can track the actual number of readers who click on each story, confirm that foreign stories simply don't draw readers. "Until the current crisis, our foreign news stories have generally attracted disappointing numbers of readers," says Salon executive editor Gary Kamiya.

This national indifference has its foundation in a lack of the most elementary facts. When Osama bin Laden emerged as the prime suspect behind the attacks, demand for maps of Afghanistan and Central Asia reportedly skyrocketed. Kenneth Davis, a writer who has found a niche for himself by filling in the gaps in readers' knowledge with his "Don't Know Much About . . ." book series (including "Don't Know Much About Geography"), says such rushes are nothing new. "We don't usually know where these places are when the troops hit the beaches. It was no different in 1945, when people were scrambling to learn about Normandy."

The roots of Americans' global cluelessness are tangled. Davis traces a recent worsening of the problem "over the last 30 or 40 years" back to our educational system. "Geography is no longer taught in a lot of schools. It got morphed into something called 'social studies,' along with history and political science. As less actual geography was taught, we then had a lot of teachers who don't know geography." Although Davis feels geography is currently enjoying a revival at the elementary school level, most adult Americans were educated during the decline. "A vast number of Americans are utterly lost when it comes to knowing where we are in the world," he explains.

Davis also blames the traditional "dry, boring" method of teaching geography—the old "principal products of Peru" approach—for the disinterest many people feel in the topic. Combining geography with history and other subjects into a dumbed-down category called "social studies" may have been a well-meaning attempt to make it more interesting, but the truth is that many Americans are also sorely lacking in rudimentary historical literacy. Kelleher, who at her "midsize, midlevel, comprehensive university" sees a great many average American college freshmen, says, "You find that a large cross section of students, even when you mention major events of world history—and I'm just talking about European history, things like the Renaissance—will give you blank stares."

Some outsiders see American's lack of interest in world affairs as springing from our national character as well as our educational shortcomings. Jonathan Clarke, a former British diplomat who is a foreign affairs scholar at the Cato Institute and writes a syndicated column about foreign policy for the *Los Angeles Times*, observes that some of this disregard results from the country's "geographical isolation between the two oceans and with friendly neighbors. In Britain, you're up against foreign affairs all the time. In America, you can go about your business without relating to the rest of the world, at least on the level of detail. You have to have some reason to know about foreign affairs and most Americans don't need to." Not, at least, until September 11, when a nightmare version of "foreign affairs" showed up at America's doorstep.

It's also true, says Davis, that a certain isolationist tendency "goes back to the beginning of American political history. Washington and Jefferson talked about the dangers of foreign entanglements." Clarke sees that vein of thought as a key part of America's identity: "The first waves of people coming to the U.S. and many of the subsequent ones were people fleeing conflicts. And so when they came to the U.S., they said, 'We don't want to hear about that stuff anymore. We don't want to be involved with choosing between, for example, Catholic and Protestant. We left that behind.' People don't want to carry with them the woes of Cambodia or wherever. The U.S. is an oasis, a cultural escape from quarrels that, when you get to the U.S., seem a bit petty. When the former Yugoslavia broke up, we said to them 'Come on, grow up. Your differences are not that significant.' Americans think they are beyond that sort of thing."

But not, as we have bitterly learned, beyond the reach of those conflicts. In fact, the U.S. has long been deeply involved in the political affairs of the regions that the September 11 hijackers hail from. Past U.S. actions have contributed to conditions that have allowed terrorism to flourish. In Afghanistan, for example, the U.S. withdrew from the region entirely once Soviet troops left in 1989, ignoring pleas from Afghans for help in getting their war-devastated country back on its feet. In the resulting anarchy, the Taliban took over, and Afghans continue to resent the U.S. for letting them bear the brunt of Western efforts to contain communism.

"I remember when that happened," says Clarke. "We had people in the British diplomatic corps going to the Americans every day saying you can't just walk away. They got absolutely no response."

One of the ugly ironies of Osama bin Laden's declared war on American citizens is that he is, in a way, calling us on one of our points of pride. Although many Americans aren't fully aware of their nation's policies, and the impact of those policies in the Middle East and Asia, if ours truly is a government "of the people, by the people and for the people," then aren't we responsible for its actions?

If more Americans do decide, in the aftermath of the September 11 attacks, to get up to speed on geopolitics, they're in for a rude awakening. Vivienne Walt, a South Africa-born U.S. citizen currently living in Paris and covering international news for a variety of American newspapers, sees Americans' understanding of their role in world affairs as hobbled by political naiveté. "Americans have an extremely positive view of their country and political system," she observes. Unfortunately, though, most Americans aren't paying close enough attention to object when U.S. policy goes against that view. There's a big gap between what many starry-eyed Americans perceive to be their nation's noble role in world affairs and the routine self-interest that guides most governments' foreign policy— including our own.

"One of the great grievances about America is that they're supporting the Saudi [regime]," says Walt. "The Saudis themselves feel that America is supposed to stand for democracy, yet here they are propping up the totally repressive government they live under as long as it supports their economic interests. Here's this huge power built on notions of freedom and democracy, yet they are living in an awful country with a terrible government and there's no American support for change there." (Most of the hijackers involved in the September 11 attacks appear to have been Saudis.)

Walt thinks Americans get a bad rap for having the kind of provincial outlook common in other Western nations ("if you go to some little town in Burgundy or in the heartland of France or the middle of England, people are exceptionally parochial"), but she nevertheless feels that "America sets itself up for its own fall. It proclaims freedom and democracy as central to what it stands for, so when they're propping up someone horrible it's very glaring. The French support the worst people in the world, but no one makes a fuss about it."

Most observers agree that once the American public can be convinced to pay attention to problems in other countries, their concern is genuine. "When they do get exposed to the issues," says Walt, "Americans seem to care very much. They get intrigued and want to help. In France, people are so blasé and cynical." But even that practical impulse has its drawbacks. "Americans like straight answers to problems," says Kelleher. "They're the activist problem-solvers of the world. If there's a problem out there, Americans think it should be fixed. And Americans like a situation that can be fixed in the foreseeable future. Look at terrorism: Does it lend itself to that kind of fix? No." The complicated, delicate, sometimes centuries-old political conflicts of the Middle East seem custom-designed to exasperate an impatient people with little interest in the past.

In the past, the American public's response to the madden-
ing complexities of geopolitics has been to turn away, leaving the
nation's diplomatic elites to craft and execute U.S. foreign policy
in a nearly scrutiny-free zone. That attitude now seems woefully
outdated. With their own safety on the line, will American citizens finally give geopolitics the attention it deserves? Clarke
hopes so. "If you look back to the most ill-informed action in
U.S. foreign policy over the past 50 years," he says, "I'd have to
say it was the [Gulf of] Tonkin Resolution, and it was the elite
who did that. All the guys you thought would take a more
measured approach didn't. So you can't lay all the blame on
ignorant Joe Six Pack."

Kelleher sees the response to the current crisis as "going in
two different directions. Some moderate, well-meaning people
want to get their minds around the issues in the region. The
second reaction will be a strong 'Let's bomb the Middle East.
This is Christian vs. Muslim. Why bother to understand the people and why bother working with all the nations in the region to
build a political position and strategize with them?'" She calls
this second reaction "almost a glory in ignorance. It's a pride in
not understanding complexity in political issues," arising in
part from a long-standing anti-intellectual strain in American
society.

Now, with the 21st century off to a shaky start, that prejudice
may be one more dangerous luxury we can no longer afford.
"When you start asking questions," says Kelleher, "like Who are
we going to bomb? Are we going to land ground troops? What
are the ramifications of these actions? Who do we alienate? And
the answer is the very people we need in order to effect an anti-
terrorist policy: Arabs—to have to think through that is irritating
because you need to know something, and people do not like to be
confronted with their own ignorance."

Questions for Discussion and Writing

1. How would you characterize the tone of this article? How would you
   respond to this tone if you were asked to write a response to Miller?
2. Miller refers to the "cluelessness" of many Americans to matters outside
   their own borders. Do you consider this a fair assessment? What evidence
   could you offer to confirm or refute this assertion?
3. Do some research about the policy of isolationism that the United States
   has practiced from time to time in the past. Why did it change? Was there
   resistance to changes in U.S. foreign policy regarding, for example, the situation in the Philippines at the start of the twentieth century?

The Globalization of Politics: American Foreign Policy for a New Century

JAMES M. LINDSAY AND IVO H. DAALDER

Ivo H. Daalder is a senior fellow in the Brookings Foreign Policy Studies program at The Brookings Institution. Daalder was born in the Netherlands and is a specialist in European and national security matters. He served as a member of President Clinton's National Security Council staff from 1995 to 1996. He is the author of ten books, including America Unbound: The Bush Revolution in Foreign Policy *(with James Lindsay). James M. Lindsay is currently the vice president and Maurice R. Greenberg chair at the Council on Foreign Relations based in New York. Lindsay was a senior fellow at The Brookings Institution from 1999 to 2003. He is an expert on domestic influences on American foreign policy, globalization, and immigration. He was educated at the University of Michigan and at Yale University. The opening of the article, published under the auspices of the Brookings Institution, lays out the purpose for the essay: to explore how the United States can use its power to shape a global system that works to its advantage. The Brookings Institution came into being in 1927 when the Robert Brookings Graduate School, the Institute of Economics, and the Institute of Government Research merged, bringing together the ideals of independent research into matters of importance with regard to economics and the problems of government. The Institution took as its model the Institute of Government Research, which had been in existence since 1916; the key was to have a privately funded and independent research agenda that would monitor public policy on a national (and later an international) scale. It is based in Washington, D.C. This article appeared in the* Brookings Review *in the winter of 2003.*

---◆---

September 11 signaled the end of the age of geopolitics and the advent of a new age—the era of global politics. The challenge U.S. policymakers face today is to recognize that fundamental change in world politics and to use America's unrivaled military, economic, and political power to fashion an international environment conducive to its interests and values.

For much of the 20th century, geopolitics drove American foreign policy. Successive presidents sought to prevent any single country from dominating the centers of strategic power in Europe and Asia. To that end the United States fought two world wars and carried on its four-decade-long Cold War with the Soviet Union. The collapse of the Soviet empire ended the last serious challenge for territorial dominion over Eurasia. The primary goal of American foreign policy was achieved.

During the 1990s, American foreign policy focused on consolidating its success. Together with its European allies, the United States set out to create, for the first time in history, a peaceful, undivided, and democratic Europe. That effort is now all but complete. The European Union—which will encompass most of Europe with the expected accession of 10 new members in 2004—has become the focal point for European policy on a wide range of issues. The North Atlantic Treaty Organization has evolved from a collective defense alliance into Europe's main security institution. A new relationship with Russia is being forged.

Progress has been slower, though still significant, in Asia. U.S. relations with its two key regional partners, Japan and South Korea, remain the foundation of regional stability. Democracy is taking root in South Korea, the Philippines, Indonesia, and Taiwan. U.S. engagement with China is slowly tying an economically surging Beijing into the global economy.

The success of American policy over the past decade means that no power—not Russia, not Germany, not a united Europe, and not China or Japan—today poses a hegemonic threat to Eurasia. In this new era, American foreign policy will no longer pivot on geography. Instead, it will be defined by the combination of America's unrivaled power in world affairs and the extensive and growing globalization of world politics.

THE SOLE GLOBAL POWER

The United States is today the only truly global power. Its military reach—whether on land, at sea, or in the air—extends to every point on the globe. Its economic prowess fuels world trade and industry. Its political and cultural appeal—what Joseph Nye has called soft power—is so extensive that most international institutions reflect American interests. America's position in the world is unique—no other country in history has ever come close.

But is America's exalted position sustainable? Militarily, the vast gap between the United States and everyone else is growing. Whereas defense spending in most other countries is falling, U.S. defense spending is rising rapidly. This year's requested increase in defense spending is greater than the entire Chinese defense budget. Most remarkably, America can afford to spend more. Defense spending takes a smaller share of the U.S. gross domestic product than it did a decade ago—and even the Bush administration's projected increases will produce an overall budget equal to only about 3.5 percent of GDP, about half of Cold War highs. There is little prospect of any country or group of countries devoting the resources necessary to begin competing with the United States militarily, let alone surpassing it.

Economically, the United States may not widen its edge over its competitors, but neither is it likely to fall behind. The U.S. economy has proven itself at least as adept as its major competitors in realizing the productivity gains made possible by information technology. Europe and Japan face severe demographic challenges as their populations rapidly age, creating likely labor shortages and severe budgetary pressures. China is modernizing rapidly, and Russia may have turned the corner, but their economies today are comparable in output to those of Italy and Belgium—and they have yet to develop a political infrastructure that can support sustained economic growth.

Which brings us to the issue of how to transform this unquestioned power into influence. Unless employed deftly, America's military and economic superiority can breed resentment, even among its friends. A growing perception that Washington cares only about its own interests and is willing to use its muscle to get its way has fueled a worrisome gap between U.S. and European attitudes. European elites increasingly criticize the United States as being morally, socially, and culturally retrograde—especially in its perceived embrace of the death penalty, predatory capitalism, and fast food and mass entertainment. Europe has also begun to exercise diplomatic muscle in international institutions and other arenas, seeking to create new international regimes designed to limit America's recourse to its hard power.

The sustainability of American power ultimately depends on the extent to which others believe it is employed not just in U.S. interests but in their interests as well. Following its victory in World War II, the United States led the effort to create not only new security institutions, such as the United Nations and NATO, but also new regimes to promote economic recovery, development, and prosperity, such as the Marshall Plan, the Bretton Woods monetary system, and the

General Agreement on Trade and Tariffs to promote free trade. These institutions and agreements preserved and extended American power—but in a way that benefited all who participated. The challenge for the United States is to do the same today.

GLOBALIZATION

Globalization is not just an economic phenomenon, but a political, cultural, military, and environmental one as well. Nor is globalization new; networks of interdependence spanning continents were increasing rapidly in the decades before the First World War as the steam engine and the telegraph reduced the cost of transportation and information. What distinguishes globalization today is the speed and volume of cross-border contacts. The prophets of globalization have trumpeted its benefits, particularly how the increased flow of goods, services, and capital across borders can boost economic activity and enhance prosperity. During the 1990s the more globalized economies grew an average of 5 percent a year, while the less globalized economies contracted by an average of 1 percent a year. The spread of ideas and information across the Internet and other global media has broadened cultural horizons and empowered people around the world to challenge autocratic rulers and advance the cause of human rights and democracy. Globalization can even lessen the chance of war. Fearing that war with Pakistan would disrupt their ties to U.S.-based multinationals, India's powerful electronic sector successfully pressed New Delhi in mid-2002 to deescalate its conflict with Pakistan. But globalization also brings terrible new perils. A handful of men from halfway across the globe can hijack four commercial airliners and slam them into key symbols of American power, killing thousands. A computer hacker in the Philippines can shut down the Internet and disrupt e-commerce thousands of miles away. Speculators can produce a run on the Thai currency, plunging Russia and Brazil into recession, robbing American exporters of markets, and costing American jobs. Greenhouse gases accumulating in the atmosphere in newly booming economies can raise global temperatures, possibly flooding coastal plains and turning mountain meadows into deserts.

Worse, for the United States, is that its power makes it a magnet for terrorism. As Richard Betts has argued, America's power "animates both the terrorists' purposes and their choice of tactics. . . . Political and cultural power makes the United States a target for those who blame it for their problems. At the same time, American economic and military power prevents them from resisting or retaliating against the United States on its own terms. To smite the only superpower requires unconventional modes of force and tactics [which] offer hope to the weak that they can work their will despite their overall deficit in power." Worse still, other weak countries might decide to buy their security by turning a blind eye to terrorist activities on their soil, thereby increasing the risk to the United States.

AMERICANISTS VS. GLOBALISTS: THE UTILITY OF POWER

Much of the foreign policy debate in the United States today revolves around assessments of the fundamental importance of American primacy and globalization. Americanists, so-called because they emphasize American primacy, see a world in which the United States can use its predominant power to get its way, regardless of what others want. They believe the United States must summon the will to go it alone if necessary. Globalists emphasize globalization. They see a world that defies unilateral U.S. solutions and instead requires international cooperation. They warn against thinking that America can go it alone.

Americanists see two great virtues in America's primacy. First, it enables the United States to set its own foreign policy objectives and to achieve them without relying on others. The result is a preference for unilateral action, unbound by international agreements or institutions that would otherwise constrain America's ability to act. As Charles Krauthammer puts it, "An unprecedentedly dominant United States . . . is in the unique position of being able to fashion its own foreign policy. After a decade of Prometheus playing pygmy, the first task of the new [Bush] administration is precisely to reassert American freedom of action." The views, preferences, and interests of allies, friends, or anyone else should therefore have no influence on American action.

Second, because American power enables the United States to pursue its interests as it pleases, American foreign policy should seek to maintain, extend, and strengthen that relative position of power. As President Bush told graduating West Point cadets last June, "America has, and intends to keep, military strength beyond challenge, thereby making the destabilizing arms races of other eras pointless, and limiting rivalries to trade and other pursuits of peace." In other words, the United States can achieve its policy objectives best if it can prevent others from acquiring the power necessary to oppose it effectively when interests clash. It is as good a definition of what would constitute an American empire as one can get.

In contrast, Globalists stress how globalization both limits and transforms America's capacity to use its power to influence events overseas. At bottom, the challenges and opportunities created by the forces of globalization are not susceptible to America acting on its own. Combating the spread of infectious diseases, preventing the spread of weapons of mass destruction, defeating terrorism, securing access to open markets, protecting human rights, promoting democracy, and preserving the environment all require the cooperation of other countries. As British Prime Minister Tony Blair put it succinctly following the September 11 attacks, "we are all internationalists now."

But, Globalists argue, it is not simply that the nature of the issues arising from globalization limits the reach of American power and compels international cooperation. Globalization transforms the nature of power itself. No one has grappled with this problem more thoughtfully than Joseph Nye in his latest book, *The Paradox of American Power.* As Nye explains, "power today is distributed among countries in a pattern that resembles a complex three-dimensional chess game." One dimension is military power, where the United States enjoys an unrivaled advantage, and the power distribution is therefore unipolar. The second dimension is economic, where power among the United States, Europe, and Japan is distributed more equally. The third dimension is transnational relations, where power is widely dispersed and essentially beyond government control. This is the realm of nonstate actors—from multinational companies and money managers to terrorist organizations and crime syndicates to nongovernmental organizations and the international media. "Those who recommend a hegemonic [or power-based] American foreign policy," Nye concludes, "are relying on woefully inadequate analysis. When you are in a three-dimensional game, you will lose if you focus on the interstate military board and fail to notice the other boards and the vertical connections among them."

WHO IS RIGHT?

Both Americanists and Globalists are right in important ways. Take the Americanists first. Despite globalization, power remains the coin of the realm in international politics. Five decades of concerted U.S. and allied efforts may have transformed Europe into a Kantian zone of perpetual peace where the rule of law has triumphed, but in much of the rest of the world military might continues to hold sway. True, no country, not even China, poses the geostrategic threat to the United States that first Germany and then the Soviet Union did in the previous century. Still, lesser-order threats abound, from Pyongyang to Teheran to Baghdad, and U.S. military and economic power will be needed to contain, if not extinguish, them. More broadly, the rule of law demands more than simply codifying rules of behavior. It also requires the willingness and ability to enforce them. But that requirement, as Mancur Olson demonstrated years ago, runs into a fundamental collective-action problem—if the potential costs of action are great and the benefits widely shared, few will be willing to incur the costs. That is where overwhelming power, and the concomitant willingness and ability to provide for global public goods, makes a crucial difference. So, without American primacy—or something like it—it is doubtful that the rule of law can be sustained.

The wise application of American primacy can further U.S. values and interests. The use (or threat) of American military might have evicted Iraqi troops from Kuwait, convinced Haiti's military junta to relinquish power, ended Serbian atrocities in Kosovo, and broke al-Qaida's hold over Afghanistan. Nor does American primacy advance only U.S. interests and values. As the one country willing and able to break deadlocks and stalemates preventing progress on issues from promoting peace in the Balkans, Northern Ireland, and the Middle East to preserving financial stability around the world, the United States frequently advances the interests of most other democratic states as well. Often, the United States is exactly what Madeleine Albright said it was—the indispensable nation that makes it possible to mobilize the world into effective action.

And the United States does differ from other countries. Unique among past hegemons in not seeking to expand its power through territorial gains, it is also unique among its contemporaries. Its primacy and global interests prompt others both to seek its assistance in addressing their problems and to resent it for meddling in their affairs. The ambivalence the world feels about American engagement—as well as the unique nature of that engagement—makes it imperative that the United States not mistake the conduct of foreign policy for a popularity contest. Doing the right thing may not always be popular—but it is vitally important nevertheless.

But Globalists are right that while America is powerful, it is not omnipotent. Far more able than most countries to protect itself against the pernicious consequences of globalization, it is by no means invulnerable. Some crucial problems do defy unilateral solutions. Global warming is perhaps the most obvious case, but others include stopping the spread of weapons of mass destruction and fighting global terrorism. In other cases, such as protecting the American homeland from terrorist attack, unilateral action can reduce but not eliminate risks.

Similarly, unilateral American power may not be enough to sustain the benefits of globalization. Globalization is not irreversible. World War I, the Russian Revolution, and the Great Depression combined to strangle the economic and social interactions that emerged early in the 20th century. Economic globalization today rests on an intricate web of international trade and financial institutions. Extending, developing, and improving these institutions requires the cooperation of others. Without it, the benefits of globalization, which help to underwrite American power, could erode.

Globalization has greatly broadened America's foreign policy agenda. Infectious diseases, poverty, and poor governance not only offend our moral sensibilities but also represent potential new security threats. Failed and failing states endanger not just their own citizens but Americans as well. If the United States cannot find ways to encourage prosperity and good governance, it runs the risk of seeing threats to its security multiply. It could eventually find itself harmed not by bears in the woods but by swarms of tiny pests.

Finally, cooperation can extend the life of American primacy. Working with others can spread the costs of action over a wider array of actors, enabling the United States to do more with less. By creating international regimes and organizations Washington can imbed its interests and values in institutions that will shape and constrain countries for decades, regardless of the vicissitudes of American power. And cooperation can build bonds with other countries, lessening the chances of cultural and political tactics that can over the years sap U.S. power.

IMPLICATIONS FOR AMERICAN FOREIGN POLICY

Both Americanists and Globalists understand essential truths about the world today. Power continues to matter, but power alone will often not be enough to achieve our goals. A pragmatic

American internationalism would recognize that we do not need to pick between these two truths. Both should guide American foreign policy. But what should America seek to accomplish abroad? The indisputable first objective must be to safeguard and enhance our liberty, security, and prosperity. The question is how. In the new age of global politics, the best way to accomplish these goals is to promote an international order based on democracy, human rights, and free enterprise—to extend the zone of peace and prosperity that the United States helped establish in Europe to every other region of the world. Put differently, the United States needs to integrate the world's have-nots into the globalized West. Pursuing that goal is not charity. Creating an international order in which more people are free and prosperous is profoundly in America's self-interest. In a world of market democracies, America and Americans are likely to be both more prosperous and more secure. In such a world we are most likely to realize the promise of globalization while minimizing its dangers.

Ensuring that a commitment to democracy and open markets triumphs on a global scale entails four broad strategies. First, it is necessary to sustain and strengthen the bases of American power. This, most of all, requires ensuring that the fundamentals of the nation's economy remain sound. It is important not to spend today what the country may need tomorrow. It also requires maintaining America's military edge, both technologically and in terms of the overall capacity to bring force to bear at a time and place of America's own choosing. And it requires persistent diplomatic engagement on Washington's part to demonstrate awareness that what happens abroad and matters to others can also have a profound impact on security and prosperity at home.

Second, U.S. policy should seek to extend and adapt proven international institutions and arrangements. NATO's recent transformation is a prime example. During the 1990s, the collective defense organization that had safeguarded the territorial integrity of its members against the Soviet Union for four decades gradually took on a new role: providing security for every state and its citizens in an ever enlarging north Atlantic area. By taking the lead in stabilizing conflict-ridden regions like the Balkans, as well as by opening its doors to new members, NATO began to do for Europe's east what it had done for Europe's west. The world trading system is also ripe for change. Barriers to the free flow of goods, capital, and services have steadily fallen over the years, and more and more countries have joined the free trading regime.

Now it is time to lower the most pernicious barriers, especially those for agricultural goods, and bring poor countries into the global economic system.

Third, U.S. policy should enforce compliance with existing international agreements and strengthen the ability of institutions to monitor and compel compliance. Too many favor the negotiation of new sets of rules or new institutions for their own sake, and too few pay attention to making sure new rules are upheld and new institutions function effectively.

• • •

Finally, U.S. policy must take the lead in creating effective international institutions and arrangements to handle new challenges, especially those arising from the downside of globalization. The United States must lead not only because it alone can help the international community overcome its collective-action problems, but because it is most likely to be hurt by inaction. Just as one example, an international system for reporting and monitoring research in dangerous pathogens could provide early warning if biotechnologists create such pathogens either deliberately or inadvertently.

As these strategies make clear, promoting an international order based on market democracies will require the United States to lead as well as listen, to give as well as take. Arguing that American foreign policy should be either unilateral or multilateral is to posit a false choice as well as to confuse means with ends. Unilateralism can be put to good or bad uses. The flaw in the Bush administration's decision to withdraw the United States from the Kyoto Treaty was not so much that Washington went its own way—though the peremptory manner of the withdrawal maximized bad feelings—but that it has failed to propose a better strategy for dealing with a rise in global temperatures that its own EPA scientists acknowledge. In this case, what is needed is not more multilateralism, but more unilateral action on the part of the United States to curtail its greenhouse gas emissions. Likewise, multilateralism can produce a modern day Kellogg-Briand Treaty just as easily as it produces a Gulf War coalition or a World Trade Organization.

Can U.S. foreign policy promote a liberal world order in the new age of global politics? In many ways it has no other choice. The pernicious effects of globalization, which empower tiny groups of people to inflict grievous harm, make it essential to create a world community that shares American values. But there is also good reason to believe that the United States can succeed in integrating the rest of the world into the western world order. Immediately after World War II, the United States forged a series of bold political, economic, and military arrangements that made allies of former enemies and set the stage for victory in the age of geopolitics. U.S. policymakers at the time took a broad view of American interests and understood that their efforts would be for naught if America's partners did not see them as being in the interest of all. U.S. policymakers in the age of global politics must do likewise.

Questions for Discussion and Writing

1. The authors make it clear that the best path for globalization is to operate on an American model and an American-set agenda. How do you feel about this? What might be the shortcomings and problems associated with this point of view?

2. There is a possibility that smaller nations could group together to offset American power and influence. There are also small and independent groups of techno-terrorists, or those who resort to real violence to show disagreement with American policy. How might Lindsay and Daalder answer such fears? Do you have your own solutions?

3. Do you think it is a safer and more secure world with the United States as the sole superpower? Argue for and against the benefits of one superpower over a balance of power between multiple nations.

4. The article refers to the Marshall Plan, the Bretton Woods monetary system, and the General Agreement on Trade and Tariffs. Research what these are and how they influence the United States and other nations and write a brief description of each.

5. Write a brief paper that explains the relationship between the United States and the North Atlantic Treaty Organization (NATO). How has it changed over the years since NATO was formed?

The American Military Empire
JOHN M. SWOMLEY, JR.

Dr. Swomley is Professor Emeritus of Christian Social Ethics at St. Paul School of Theology in Kansas City, Missouri. He is a frequent contributor to Christian Ethics Today—*from where this article was taken—and the author of many books on the subject of ethics, religion, and politics, including* The Politics of Liberation *(1984),* Confronting Systems of Violence—Memoirs of a Peace Activist *(1998), and* Religious Liberty and the Secular State: The Constitutional Context *(1987). Dr. Swomley visited North Korea in 1994 and 1995 and started the American Committee on Korea to examine American policy in the region, which he sees as military and political brinkmanship. He is a United Methodist minister and served as President of Americans for Religious Freedom.*

———————— ✦ ————————

America's role as the world's only "superpower" is obvious, and many Americans take pride in that role. Few, however, are aware that America's armed forces have built a worldwide empire that has led millions of people to fear and even hate the presence of uniformed American personnel. American journalists and the media do not describe life in the satellites, colonies, and bases that are a part of the imperial complex, or report the disregard of human rights, environmental damage, land seizures and other abuses that characterize the American presence.

The Pentagon maintains some 800 stations and air bases around the world. Some entire countries are virtual colonies. In South Korea, for example, the U.S. Army has 37,000 combat troops at 96 bases occupying 65,500 acres of that country's land. It has for many years controlled a South Korean armed force of 670,000: 460 combat aircraft, 44 destroyers and frigates, as well as four attack submarines, all under a command structure led by U.S. military personnel. All of this happened when there was no Russian or Chinese occupation of North Korea to threaten control of South Korea. Even the less well-armed North Koreans never threatened the South when the U.S. commander and South Koreans withdrew a South Korean border division to deal with riots in South Korea. The North Koreans, although not a threat, were always used by the Pentagon as a rationale for the military occupation of South Korea and for periodic aerial and naval war games against the North.

The U.S. Central Intelligence Agency, which has long been active in South Korea, helped create the Korean Central Intelligence Agency (KCIA), as a secret police organized to prevent dissent, including student protests and labor unrest, and in the process maintain censorship of the press. After its early organization it grew to about 350,000 agents within a country of only thirty million.

General Park Chung-hee was the President and virtual dictator of South Korea from 1961 to 1979, accepted by the U.S. Army and theoretically in charge of the KCIA. However, in October 1979 the KCIA commander shot the President's bodyguard and then the President. No motive surfaced, but many in South Korea assumed that the U.S. had given the order to kill him because he was a nationalist, pursuing policies opposed by the U.S. such as a program to develop nuclear weapons.

A new President, Choi, and a new commanding general, Chun who was also acting director of the KCIA, took power in 1980. This led to widespread student protests and then to martial law, the closing of the universities, and the banning of political activities. There was a general assumption that all of this repression had taken place with at least the tacit consent of the United States. One reaction was the rebellion of whole populations in some areas, including an appeal to the U.S. embassy to intervene, but the U.S. commander had already given permission to Korean forces to act independently. In the city of Kwangju about 150,000 civilians seized weapons and ammunition from arsenals as well as armored personnel carriers, trucks and buses.

As a result of a decision in Washington, U.S. General John Wickham withdrew the Korean Division on the border of North Korea and turned it and other South Korean forces loose to engage in what later was called the Kwangju Massacre. South Koreans knew that the United States was involved in the killing of thousands of South Koreans, but the American people remained ignorant of the deaths and repression.

Under the leadership of Kim Dae-jung, the current democratically elected President of South Korea, some conditions have improved, such as relations with North Korea. The U.S. Army, however, continues its widespread control at many points and the Korean economy is still heavily influenced by the United States.

Another more tightly controlled U.S. military colony is Okinawa. Although there are eight major bases in Japan itself, there are forty-seven bases in Okinawa which nominally belongs to Japan but since the end of World War II has been largely controlled by U.S. armed forces. Neither the Okinawan nor Japanese police or courts have any control of the land, sea and air spaces occupied and used by the United States. The U.S. bases occupy 20% of Okinawa's land, including the most fertile farm areas of a mountainous island.

During the 1950s, the U.S. took the land by armed force, burned and bulldozed houses and land without compensating the owners, and used the CIA to fund and encourage political control friendly to U.S. occupation. Okinawans are left with little arable land and most food is imported. Of all Japanese prefectures, Okinawa has the highest unemployment rate, highest prices and lowest wages.

The U.S. bases at best provide only about 5 percent of the gross domestic product of Okinawa, while tourism has become the main source of income.

U.S. damage to the environment is extensive. Fifty-five years of live shelling in U.S. artillery practice has resulted in severe erosion of mountains and fields, the destruction of coral reefs and oceans, the loss of livelihood of fishermen and the endangerment of rare species of birds and animals. Over 1,500 depleted uranium shells were fired into an offshore island.

Since 1972, 5,000 crimes (including rapes, murders, robberies and burglaries) have been committed by U.S. military personnel against Okinawans. The rape of an Okinawan schoolgirl by three American marines in 1999 resulted in a people's rally of 815,000 Okinawans, parents, teachers, students, labor unions, women's groups, civic organizations and people from all political parties. U.S. Admiral Richard Macke, commander of all U.S. forces in the Pacific, was quoted in the press as calling the rape "absolutely stupid. For the price they paid to rent the car (used to kidnap the child) they could have had a girl." No U.S. official review or inquiry was conducted.

In addition to the bases just described, there is Kadina Airbase, the largest in the Far East, and Futenma Marine Air Station, which covers a huge area in the center of Ginowan, second-largest city in Okinawa.

Within the United States there is the Commonwealth of Puerto Rico, which is often treated as part of the colonial empire. The small island of Vieques off the coast of Puerto Rico's main island has approximately 9,300 residents. In the 1940s the U.S. Navy took three-fourths of its land for military use and relocated its residents to a tiny area between a live firing range and a munitions storage area. The Navy uses the island for bombing practice and amphibious landings. The lives of residents have been threatened, as has the environment. There is 50% unemployment and cancer rates are much higher than in the rest of Puerto Rico.

In July 1999, Puerto Ricans marched to the naval base to demand that the Navy leave Vieques. The residents want the island demilitarized and the contamination cleaned up. Other civil disobedience has continued, with demands for community economic development. The Navy has responded by promising a vote in November 2001, and if voters want to expel the Navy they agree to leave by May 2003.

Congress could have removed the Navy long ago if it were not for the power of the military industrial complex and its devotion to superpower status.

When referring to U.S. bases, we speak not only of huge military facilities, but also of soldiers and their dependents, housing complexes, swimming pools, golf courses, post exchanges, and nearby bars, brothels, and STD disease clinics. When I taught in the Philippines in 1973, the U.S. naval base at Subic Bay was near the town of Olongapo, whose only industry was entertainment houses which included almost 55,000 prostitutes, along with various other places offering rest and recreation to U.S. naval and military personnel.

In Australia, according to an Australian Encyclopedia, the U.S. maintains more than two dozen installations concerned with military matters. However, there are many more joint facilities manned by Australians and Americans, but funded by and for the U.S., such as a Joint Defense Space Research Facility. In addition there are U.S. Air Force land and sea surveillance flights that operate over the Indian Ocean, and a transit point for aircraft carriers, nuclear-powered attack submarines, missile cruisers and destroyers. One facility for communicating with U.S. submarines is the largest and most powerful of all the stations in America's worldwide submarine communications system. It covers U.S. military operations in the Indian and western Pacific Oceans. In fact, Australia is integrated into the American military system via a thorough military alliance. It is host to more U.S. operations than any other country except for the United Kingdom, Canada and Germany.

The American military empire includes storage facilities for nuclear weapons. The November-December 1999 issue of the Bulletin of the Atomic Scientists lists the following total nuclear deployments in places in the Pacific of 1700 weapons in Okinawa, Guam, Taiwan and the Philippines. Almost 800 were at Kadena Airbase in Okinawa. Presumably they have been withdrawn, but B-61 bombers are listed as still remaining at ten airbases in seven European countries.

The military empire also includes a program called Joint Combined Exchange Training (JCET) whereby the Pentagon sends specially-trained U.S. forces for training missions in 110 countries to establish close relations with their officers for possible future operations and for training them in espionage and other skills. The U.S. officers also get invaluable information about those countries and their terrain while preparing the country's officers for internal defense against rebel groups in their own countries. Indonesia was a prime example of this during the Suharto regime, where U.S. trained officers opposed the independence of East Timor.

These are illustrations, by no means complete, of the American Military Empire. They can be considered positive and useful only if one approves of imperialism. Certainly its victims do not approve of it, and there have been numerous demonstrations against the bases in Korea and Okinawa, almost all of them nonviolent.

The most recent example of U.S. imperialist sabotage of international law and order is our opposition to a treaty to establish an international criminal court to hold accountable soldiers and political leaders charged with war crimes and crimes against humanity. The world's leading democracies support such a treaty but the U.S., China, Israel, Libya and Yemen voted against it in the United Nations. The U.S. wants to keep its soldiers, CIA officers, and other operatives who are part of the 200,000 imperial agents deployed in at least 40 countries from being tried for rape, murder, torture, and other crimes or infractions of human rights.

The cost of U.S. imperialism, with all its liabilities in terms of financial outlay, hatred engendered against Americans abroad, terrorist activities, and the bad reputation that comes from CIA "secret" operations, is too high a price to pay. Its ultimate cost is, in fact, nearly irreparable damage to future world order.

Questions for Discussion and Writing

1. Dr. Swomley's views seem in direct opposition to the idea that the United States is always a force for good. Examine the evidence he offers here and discuss whether he is making strong or weak points and explain why.
2. The situation of Vieques has been controversial for a while. Research the use of Vieques and the kinds of protests that have been held to change U.S. policy. Explain the history of this conflict for a general reader, being sure to present the opinions of both sides involved.
3. Swomley refers to "American imperialism" and the "American military empire." Examine this use of language—what do those terms mean? Are they accurate in this case? How does he justify the use of these labels?
4. One of the writer's chief complaints seems to be a lack of ethical action and accountability on the part of the U.S. military. List some of the examples he

gives and discuss whether the U.S. military should be held responsible for them or what circumstances would free it from liability.

General Questions for Chapter Three

1. Define the following terms using examples from the essays in this chapter: imperialism; geostrategic; unilateralism.
2. Many of the writers in this chapter seem to think that the there is great difficulty in balancing the needs of national security with a favorable image around the globe. Using examples drawn from this chapter explain some of the strategic moves that are, and could be, made to ease this conundrum.
3. Discuss the benefits and problems of an imperialist policy, being sure to analyze the possible impact on the country building an empire and the countries being brought under that country's umbrella of influence.

CHAPTER 4

The International
Influence of American
Culture

In this chapter we will be reading articles that address the reach and impact of American culture around the world. There are many books on this subject that go into great depth about how and why this influence is so great. I have pulled together essays that are reflective of many areas of influence—the purpose being to provide a grounding in some of the main issues and to encourage readers and writers to pursue the subject beyond the scope of this reader. So, for example, our writers here discuss areas such as television, sport, commercial products as symbols of the culture, and the impact of an American icon like Walt Disney.

The export of cultural influence is an interesting phenomenon; for it to work effectively there has to be a supply from the providing country and a desire to receive it from other countries. The other key element, of course, is that the cultural elements admired or abhorred by other cultures come to be a representation of the country itself. For countries with a strict code regarding the viewing of the human body, for example, soap operas and singers like Britney Spears and Christina Aguilera come to represent American decadence and low moral values, even if many millions of people in the United States are equally opposed to such corporeal display. One element becomes representative of the whole, even if that representation is false. In the same way, American products come to represent the nation. Jeans are synonymous with America. McDonald's is a piece of America in whatever country a franchise appears. Some years ago I was in Rome, Italy, enjoying the beauty and vibrancy of the area around the Spanish Steps. Many Roman teenagers were returning from a day at the beach, glowing from the sun, and heading to the McDonald's adjacent to the house where the poet John Keats died. It seemed incongruous to me then that Italians with a great sense of taste and style, in the center of all of that wonderful Italian cuisine, would be heading to a fast-food restaurant. After talking to some of them I realized that it wasn't the food they came for, it was the idea. America, they explained to me, was cool, and McDonald's represented America to them.

This, of course, was before 2001 and before the war in Iraq. In his essay in this chapter, Dan Roberts talks about how the changing image of America around the world is likely to change that "cool" image and lead to a distancing of American products that "mean" America to people around the world.

This said, however, the influence of American music, television, and cinema is undeniable. Not only does the United States have great financial and technological resources to produce block-busters like the *Star Wars* series and *Titanic* and television series that are syndicated around the world (programs produced in massive profusion compared to those in other countries), but also the business structure surrounding entertainment ensures that global distribution is successful and pervasive. It is from American movies and television shows that millions of people around the world learn what America is "like." It is through seeing performers from the United States that young people learn what they should be wearing or how they should be adorning their bodies. It is through lyrics and the scripts of American shows that language is changed. Think about the influence of a film like *Clueless*, for example, and the way that the term "Whatever!" has become a cover-all sentiment. A show like *Buffy the Vampire Slayer* has generated its own "Buffyspeak" with books of slayer slang and a whole lexicon published internationally. In Japan, groups of teenagers gather in Harajuku (a district of Tokyo) to compare their versions of American style. In Japan, also, the culture of hip-hop and rap has been adopted—appealing in its antithesis of Japanese culture. In Tokyo alone over 300 stores specialize in hip-hop clothing styles and accessories. At the same time, we have started to see a return of the influence—see, for example, how Gwen Stefani has used her four Japanese "Harajuku Girls" as part of her new image and stage act (and we will get to that in Chapter Five).

This chapter, therefore, will offer some ideas and impressions of American cultural influence around the world. Some writers see the U.S. effect in commercial terms; others in terms of "cultural imperialism." One of the central issues to remember at all times is that the impression that American culture gives around the world becomes how other nations get to know the United States. Think about the popular culture that you are familiar with, and it becomes easier to understand why the international image of America is of a country where everyone is rich, has a gun, wears little clothing, eats pizza and McDonald's, drinks Budweiser and Rolling Rock, and drives a SUV. We also need to understand why there is also a growing resistance in some areas of the world to exactly what U.S. culture represents and fears that national identity will be lost in the flood of American media and product.

Bored with USA?
BRENDON O'CONNOR

Dr. Brendon O'Connor is a senior lecturer at the School of Politics and Public Policy—Griffith University in Brisbane, Australia. He was educated at Monash University and LaTrobe University, and in 2000 he was invited to Harvard University as Visiting Scholar From 1998 to 1999 he worked as Social Research Officer for the national Development Research Institutes in New York City. Dr. O'Connor has extensive publications and conference experience, and his research interests focus on American politics, cultural influence, and welfare reform. In 2003 the Fulbright Commission funded a symposium organized by Dr. O'Connor that discussed Americanization and anti-Americanism. This article, which appeared in the The Courier Mail *in Brisbane on June 21, 2003, was published to coincide with that event.*

———————— ✦ ————————

American culture is part of Australian mass consumer culture, like it or not, dude! It dominates our television, radio stations, movie theatres, fashion and our imagination. We are effectively governed from Washington DC with our cultural menu set by producers in Los Angeles and designers in New York. Resistance is futile and likely to mean you are totally uncool. In short, we are all Americans now. This summary of affairs is, of course, an exaggerated view of reality, although plenty of Australians probably watch American sitcoms, own American CDs and DVDs, and dress in American fashion labels right down to their Calvin Klein underwear.

Those who reject claims of American cultural imperialism in Australia might respond: Isn't talk of American songs or underwear an overly nationalistic outlook? Isn't a lot of American culture just part of mass consumer culture, as the U.S. has the biggest studios, media empires, fashion companies, and marketing machines? And don't American talent houses draw on the best ideas and individuals from around the globe?

However, such responses present only part of the story.

Global and Australian culture clearly has been Americanized, particularly since World War II. Although put-downs of American culture often run roughshod over the sheer diversity of American cultural output, it is entirely understandable that people worry about local business and art being overrun by American cultural icons such as McDonald's, Coca-Cola, Time AOL and so on.

Others worry about our obsession with middle class American life via the tube. The world of TV viewers often knows far more about American high schools and colleges, American court rooms and police precincts, and American hospitals and office life than they know about their own society.

I worry that Australians are familiar with *Frasier*'s Seattle and *Ally McBeal*'s Chicago but have no popular equivalents set in Darwin, let alone Jakarta. Familiarity may breed contempt (recent outpourings of anti-Americanism are a case in point), but familiarity can also lead to greater awareness, comfort with difference and a sense of who we are.

My fellow university colleagues sometimes remark that the basic knowledge students have of how the American legal and political system works is often drawn from *Law and Order* or *West Wing* rather than from their own high school education. It certainly is hard to compete with American TV. One of my students recently commented that lecturers in my department needed to be more like American professors. I told them that with make-up on and viewed on TV, I sound a lot more impressive. I am not sure they were convinced; maybe I need to work on my New England accent.

The relative size of the American cultural industry makes it an increasing part of Australian language and the way we describe ourselves—for instance, an Australian is just as likely as an American to say: "Lleyton Hewitt is like such a *Rocky* wannabe."

Faced with this situation, is resisting American cultural colonization futile—the cultural equivalent of being a Luddite? I favor a dialogue between cultures, recognizing that our culture is fluid and open to outside influences. But dialogue is difficult when you're the smaller and poorer cousin. Because of our size we have to keep asserting our differences and supporting local talent, ideas and products. To have a vibrant Australian culture, particularly in the entertainment and arts industries, we also need to subsidize local performances and artists, and maintain Australian content regulations. The lure of freer trade with the U.S. is certainly no reason to back down on these cultural values.

I worry about the conformity and blandness that comes with much American popular culture. I would add to this concern an unease with the power of American advertising and marketing. Because of this, parents feel pressured into buying their children expensive label clothes, teenage girls starve themselves to look like Video Hits dancers, and every second individual seems to think that "Whatever!" is a witty way of telling someone you don't want to listen to their point of view. These superficialities aren't solely the fault of American culture but it does deserve a fair amount of the blame. For me they reflect a worrying conformity in our culture.

My gripes aren't meant to imply a total rejection of American popular culture or a retreat to some mythical Aussie alternative; like most Australians there are aspects of American culture I loathe and aspects I love. My point is that while American products are highly entertaining and accessible for many people, these products often have unrivalled distribution and marketing advantages in our society. That said, and given that the commercial power of the American cultural industry is likely to continue well into the future, a sense of local pride and government support of Australian talent is undoubtedly needed to maintain our own distinct, and evolving, culture.

Questions for Discussion and Writing

1. Brendon O'Connor seems concerned with the idea that American cultural influence will lead to a homogenized world culture where everything will look the same and local differences will be less apparent. Do you have the same concerns as he does? Explain.

2. What would be the advantages to America and Australia if culture did erase cultural difference, as O'Connor discusses here? What would be the disadvantages?

3. O'Connor says that his students learn about what education should look like and how the law works from television shows. Is the same true for you? How does American culture affect the way you see institutions and social procedure? List shows that deal with the law, medicine, and politics. How do you account for their popularity and influence?

In 2,000 Years, Will the World Remember Disney or Plato?

MARK RICE-OXLEY

Mark Rice-Oxley is a correspondent for the Christian Science Monitor, *where this article appeared on January 15, 2004. He reports from his home in London, United Kingdom. In his article he discusses the spread of American culture around the world and the various forms it takes. He notes that some nations are rebelling against such cultural imperialism as they fear their own sense of national culture and identity is at risk of being lost. The other issue at the center of this article is the question of how durable American influence will be in the future.*

◆

Down in the mall, between the fast-food joint and the bagel shop, a group of young people huddles in a flurry of baggy combat pants, skateboards, and slang. They size up a woman teetering past wearing DKNY, carrying *Time* magazine in one hand and a latte in the other. She brushes past a guy in a Yankees' baseball cap who is talking on his Motorola cellphone about the Martin Scorsese film he saw last night. It's a standard American scene—only this isn't America, it's Britain. U.S. culture is so pervasive, the scene could be played out in any one of dozens of cities. Budapest or Berlin, if not Bogota or Bordeaux. Even Manila or Moscow.

As the unrivaled global superpower, America exports its culture on an unprecedented scale. From music to media, film to fast food, language to literature and sport, the American idea is spreading inexorably, not unlike the influence of empires that preceded it. The difference is that today's technology flings culture to every corner of the globe with blinding speed. If it took two millenniums for Plato's *Republic* to reach North America, the latest hit from Justin Timberlake can be found in Greek (and Japanese) stores within days. Sometimes, U.S. ideals get transmitted—such as individual rights, freedom of speech, and respect for women—and local cultures are enriched. At other times, materialism or worse becomes the message and local traditions get crushed. "The U.S. has become the most powerful, significant world force in terms of cultural imperialism [and] expansion," says Ian Ralston, American studies director at Liverpool John Moores University. "The areas that particularly spring to mind are Hollywood, popular music, and even literature." But what some call "McDomination" has created a backlash in certain cultures. And it's not clear whether fast food, Disney, or rock 'n' roll will change the world the way Homer or Shakespeare has.

CRICKET OR BASKETBALL?

Stick a pin in a map and there you'll find an example of U.S. influence. Hollywood rules the global movie market, with up to 90 percent of audiences in some European countries. Even in Africa, 2 of 3 films shown are American. Few countries have yet to be touched by McDonald's and Coca-Cola. Starbucks recently opened up a new front in South America, and everyone's got a Hard Rock Café T-shirt from somewhere exotic. West Indian sports enthusiasts increasingly watch basketball, not cricket. Baseball has long since taken root in Asia and Cuba. And Chinese young people are becoming more captivated by American football and basketball, some even daubing the names of NBA stars on their school sweatsuits. The NFL plans to roll out a Chinese version of its website this month. Rupert Murdoch's satellites, with their heavy traffic of U.S. audiovisual content, saturate the Asian subcontinent. American English is the language of choice for would-be pop stars in Europe, software programmers in India, and Internet surfers everywhere.

America's preeminence is hardly surprising. Superpowers have throughout the ages sought to perpetuate their way of life: from the philosophy and mythology of the ancient Greeks to the law and language of the Romans; from the art and architecture of the Tang Dynasty and Renaissance Italy to the sports and systems of government of the British. "Most empires think their own point of view is the only correct point of view," says Robert Young, an expert in postcolonial cultural theory at Oxford University. "It's the certainty they get because of the power they have, and they expect to impose it on everyone else."

Detractors of cultural imperialism argue, however, that cultural domination poses a totalitarian threat to diversity. In the American case, "McDomination" poses several dangers.

First, local industries are truly at risk of extinction because of U.S. oligopolies, such as Hollywood. For instance in 2000, the European Union handed out 1 billion euros to subsidize Europe's film industry. Even the relatively successful British movie industry has no control over distribution, which is almost entirely in the hands of the Hollywood majors.

Second, political cultures are being transformed by the personality-driven American model in countries as far-reaching as Japan and the Philippines.

Finally, U.S. domination of technologies such as the Internet and satellite TV means that, increasingly, America monopolizes the view people get of the world. According to a recent report for the UN Conference on Trade and Development, 13 of the top 14 Internet firms are American. No. 14 is British. "You have to know English if you want to use the Internet," says Andre Kaspi, a professor at the Sorbonne in Paris.

A main problem is that culture is no longer a protected species, but subject to the inexorable drive for free trade, says Joost Smiers, a political science professor at the Utrecht School of the Arts. This means that it is increasingly difficult for countries to protect their own industries. France tries to do so with subsidies, while South Korea has tried quotas. Such "protectionist" tactics meet with considerable U.S. muscle, Dr. Smiers says. "America's aggressive cultural policy . . . hinders national states from regulating their own cultural markets," he says. "We should take culture out of the WTO."

Another danger, detractors say, is the consolidation of the communications industry into a few conglomerates such as AOL-TimeWarner, Disney, and News Corporation, which means that the "infotainment" generated for global consumption nearly always comes from an Anglophone perspective. "You can't go on with just three music companies organizing and distributing 85 percent of the music in the world," says Smiers. "It's against all principles of democracy. Every emotion, every feeling, every image can be copyrighted into the hands of a few owners."

AMERICAN, WITH A TWIST

A backlash is being felt in certain places. In Japan, locals have taken U.S. ideas like hip-hop and fast food, and given them a Japanese twist, says Dominic al-Badri, editor of *Kansai Time Out*. In Germany, there is still strong resistance to aspects of U.S. pop culture, though there is an appetite for its intellectual culture, says Gary Smith, director of the American Academy in Berlin. In France, resistance is growing partly because of frustrations over the Iraq war—but partly because Americanization is already so advanced in the country, says Mr. Kaspi.

He notes one interesting anecdotal sign of U.S. influence—and the futility of resistance. France has repeatedly tried to mandate the use of French language in official capacities to check the advance of English. "But most of the time, the law is impossible to apply, because if you want to be understood around the world you have to speak English," Kaspi says.

In the Philippines, even the best U.S. ideals have caused complications. "The pervasive American influence has saddled us with two legacies," notes respected local commentator Antonio C. Abaya. "American-style elections, which require the commitment of massive financial resources, which have to be recouped and rolled over many times, which is the main source of corruption in government; and American-style free press in which media feel free to attack and criticize everything that the government does or says, which adds to disunity and loss of confidence in government."

Meanwhile, for all the strength of the U.S. movie industry, sometimes a foreign film resonates more with a local audience than a Hollywood production—and outperforms it. For instance, Japan's *Spirited Away* (2001) remains the top-grossing film in that country, surpassing global Hollywood hits like *Titanic*. In addition, British TV has influenced and served up competition to U.S. shows, spawning such hits as *Who Wants to Be a Millionaire?*, *The Weakest Link*, and *American Idol* [called *Pop Idol* in the UK].

1,000 YEARS FROM NOW

So how much good does American culture bring to the world? And how long will it last? Ian Ralston cautions against sweeping dismissals of U.S. pop culture. British television may be saturated with American sitcoms and movies, but while some are poor, others are quite good, he says. "British culture has always been enriched by foreign influences. In some ways American culture and media have added to that enrichment." Others note that it is not all one-way traffic. America may feast largely on a diet of homegrown culture, but it imports modestly as well: soccer, international cuisine, Italian fashion, and, increasingly, British television.

As to the question of durability, some experts believe U.S. domination of communication channels makes it inevitable that its messages will become far more entrenched than those of previous empires. "The main difference now in favor of American culture is the importance of technology—telephone, Internet, films, all that did not exist in ancient Greece or the Mongol empire," Kaspi says. "American influence is growing, it's so easy to get access to U.S. culture; there are no barriers. "Disney is known worldwide now," he adds. "Plato is more and more unknown, even in Greece."

But not everyone thinks American culture will stand the test of time. "It remains to be seen whether the Monkees and Bee Gees are as durable as Plato," says Professor Young, with a dab of irony. "Let's have another look in 4,000 years' time."

Questions for Discussion and Writing

1. What problems or losses might the world at large be facing if it is prone to American cultural hegemony? Do you want to see a world that shares a single popular culture, style, or set of artistic ideas? How do Rice-Oxley's ideas differ from those of Brendon O'Connor in an earlier article?
2. The writer mentions a problem being that other political systems might become personality driven, as (he says) they are in the United States. What does he mean? Is this an element of politics that should be avoided? Why or why not?
3. What are some of the reasons why the cultural empire of the United States might last as long (or longer) than the culture of previous "empires"?
4. Why do you think that Mark Rice-Oxley uses the term "McDomination"? What does he mean by this and where does the term come from? How do you feel about his use of the term and the context in which he uses it?

Is the World Falling Out of Love with U.S. Brands?

DAN ROBERTS

Dan Roberts is the U.S. Business Editor for The Financial Times *(UK). This article appeared in that newspaper on December 29, 2004. Mr. Roberts was recipient of The World Leadership Forum Award for the Best Communications Submission at the 2002 Business Journalist of the Year Awards. In this article he investigates how*

American military actions and political decisions affect the perceptions of American brands around the world—brands that are synonymous with American culture.

──────────── ✦ ────────────

J oseph Nye, the Harvard academic who coined the phrase "soft power" to describe indirect U.S. influence in the world, likes to recall the dining deliberations of a family in India to explain what he means. Asked what attracts them to McDonald's, the middle-class parents he cites suggest something more seductive than a Chicken Maharaja Mac and fries cooked in vegetable fat. They say they want to take the children out "for a slice of America."

When burgers can stir such emotional aspirations, it is no accident that 64 of the most valuable 100 global brands, as measured by Interbrand, are owned by U.S. companies. For more than half a century, the U.S. and its products have stood for progress, glamour and freedom in the minds of consumers around the world. But Mr Nye sees a growing challenge for U.S. companies in the attitudes of people such as John McInally, a Scottish management consultant living in Brussels, whose boycott of U.S. products goes as far as asking that his four-year-old son not be given Coca-Cola at birthday parties.

"I used to have a lot of respect for America; now there is mostly fear," says Mr McInally. "You feel pretty powerless, but the one thing you can do is stop buying American products."

There is little doubt that there are more Mr McInallys in the world today than there were before Abu Ghraib and Guantanamo Bay became household names. Poll after poll has shown that allegations of human rights abuses and the failure to find weapons of mass destruction in Iraq have tarnished the international reputation of the U.S. But geopolitics is easily left behind when shoppers get to the till. Those activists who express their anger at the U.S. through conscious boycotts of its companies remain a small minority.

The bigger question worrying the business world is whether the opinion poll data point to a more subtle tarnishing of U.S. brands in the minds of millions of ordinary consumers. If the American dream played such an important role in the growth of iconic U.S. brands, what happens if significant numbers of consumers begin to think of the U.S. as a bit of a nightmare?

Mr Nye, a former dean of Harvard's Kennedy School of Government and assistant secretary of defence in the Clinton administration, is one of many who are certain of the connection.

"U.S. brands have benefited from a sense that it is fashionable, chic and modern to be American," he says. "The other side of that coin is when U.S. policies become unpopular, there is a cost."

This kind of unconscious brand association is the lifeblood of the marketing industry, and those taking the threat most seriously tend to reside on Madison Avenue, home of New York advertising. Keith Reinhard, chairman of DDB Worldwide, an agency that counts McDonald's and Budweiser as clients, is leading Business for Diplomatic Action, a coalition of advertising executives and public relations consultants who want to fix "Brand America's" problem.

"That slice [of America] no longer looks so attractive," says Mr Reinhard. "Foreigners are transferring anger at the U.S. government to anger at the U.S. and anger at U.S. business."

Others question whether politics is affecting consumer behaviour. Why, they ask, are more companies not reporting it? Could it be the era of one-size-fits-all global brands, rather than U.S. dominance of consumer markets, that is coming to an end? Earl Taylor, chief marketing officer of the Marketing Science Institute, a U.S. think-tank, is typical of the sceptics. "Consumers are able to compartmentalise the brands of a country from its foreign policy," he says. "If there was a simple relationship between U.S. brands and foreign policy we would have seen it decades ago."

Until recently, U.S. companies have either tended to agree or stayed out of the argument. But there is growing evidence that this is a problem they cannot afford to ignore. In European markets such as Germany and France many iconic U.S. names—Coca-Cola, Marlboro, McDonald's, Wal-Mart, Disney, Gap—have reported weak or falling sales, though each blames other local factors.

Corporate America is not admitting to an image problem just yet, but some companies are at least beginning to talk about it. McDonald's, for example, recently agreed to join the board of Business for Diplomatic Action. It is also expected to co-host a seminar in March at Hamburger University, its management training centre, to discuss how U.S. companies can be better "world citizens." John McNeel, an advertising executive at TBWA Worldwide, says the restaurant group's concern comes as no surprise: "McDonald's is a very vulnerable brand in this context—not only is it closely associated with America but they have fixed assets all over the world." PepsiCo, the soft drinks group, also recently joined Business for Diplomatic Action in sponsoring a travel guide for U.S. college students, which aims to help curb the image of the "ugly American" abroad.

One reason for the growing business interest in this kind of project is that market research increasingly proves the link between politics and brands. Early signs of trouble appeared in a 2003 study of "power brands" by Roper, the market researcher, which showed popularity scores for leading U.S. companies had slipped. NOP World found similar evidence suggesting that U.S. companies were seen as less trustworthy and honest after the Iraq war.

The strongest evidence yet of a link between politics and consumer behaviour was supplied by Global Market Insite (GMI), an independent Seattle polling group, which surveyed 8,000 consumers in eight countries over several months in 2004. In December, one-fifth of the Europeans and Canadians in its sample said their anger over U.S. foreign policy would deter them from buying U.S. brands. Of course, what people tell pollsters and what people do in the privacy of the shopping mall can be two entirely different things. But if even a fraction of these people act out their frustration, a significant potential market is lost.

Most interesting is work carried out by Research International, part of British media group WPP. Its study of Latin American consumers in 2003 supported the idea that you could hate the U.S. but still support its brands. But a repeat of the study carried out this year had gloomier findings, particularly in Chile, Argentina, Brazil and Mexico.

"The news is not all bad for U.S. brands but we have demonstrated that younger people in particular react to [U.S. brands] more negatively," it said. Tom Miller, formerly a pollster with NOP World, is one of many in the profession who feel it is only a matter of time before such attitudes begin to make a serious dent in business performance. "Sales can be a lagging indicator, but no matter how you look at this, it's not good news," he says.

Not all brands are treated the same, of course. GMI's data show that companies such as Kodak, Kleenex, Visa and Gillette are simply not perceived as American. Users of Microsoft software might know its heritage but have few alternatives.

Technology companies also seem immune—as the worldwide success of Apple's iPod and the Chinese purchase of IBM's consumer PC business demonstrate. But among those consumer companies perceived as American, and vulnerable to boycotts there is a remarkably consistent set of problems in the countries that have seen the biggest swing in public opinion. Coca-Cola, which makes 80 per cent of its profits outside North America, sold

16 per cent less beverages to Germans in the third quarter of 2004 than a year previously. McDonald's blamed falling German sales for virtually eliminating growth across Europe. And Altria sold 24.5 per cent fewer Marlboro cigarettes in France and 18.7 per cent fewer in Germany during the third quarter.

In each instance other factors play a role. The falling dollar will also mask problems by inflating repatriated profits and lowering the cost of exports. Marlboro, for example, blames tax changes that encourage customers to trade down to cheaper brands. Coke says German bottling laws have a similar effect. But neither seems able to overcome such obstacles as well as it used to.

Some companies say they do not lose much sleep over political factors that are outside their control. "What could we do anyway?," asks one Altria executive. "Fly the French flag? Tell them it wasn't us that boycotted their wine?" Most importantly, some European companies such as Unilever and Neste have experienced their own problems with weak consumer spending.

"It's too simplistic to say [that] what's happened in Europe is just a function of anti-Americanism," says John Quelch, a professor at Harvard Business School and a leading sceptic about the link between politics and consumer behaviour. "The economic downturn is particularly important in the case of global brands because consumers do not want to pay a premium price and will switch to local brands and private labels."

Yet it is not just discount brands that have been gaining at the expense of American rivals. Swiss private banks claim to be winning savings business from U.S. competitors such as Citigroup in the Middle East, France and Germany. Some rich individuals are said to be concerned at the unpredictability of U.S. foreign policy and risk of asset seizures—a direct threat to the reputation of the U.S. financial system for fairness.

Foreign airlines benefit from the fear of terrorist attacks on carriers with strong U.S. associations. Air Canada says it has seen an upsurge in business passengers opting to fly via Canada rather than brave the notorious U.S. visa system. Similar obstacles for overseas students erode U.S. soft power by encouraging them to enrol at British or Canadian universities.

Even U.S. hotels abroad now fear being seen as terrorist targets. Barry Sternlicht, executive chairman of Starwood—which owns Sheraton—was one of the first business leaders to speak out on anti-Americanism this year: "Our politicians must remember that our businesses are global and we rely heavily on trade and tourism."

For many multinationals, the answer increasingly seems to be to downplay any U.S. heritage or even a single global identity. Neville Isdell, new chief executive of Coca-Cola, is typical of many business leaders who work hard to stress local credentials with sports sponsorship and customised advertising. "We are not an American brand," he says.

Starbucks, the coffee chain, has thrived by making more of its products' associations with the developing world than of its own Seattle heritage. But Doug Holt, professor of marketing at the Said School of Business in Oxford, cautions against running away from historic roots entirely. "Local is not always better," he warns. "People assign value to brands that have succeeded globally; that's why multinational companies do so well."

If nothing else, the trend reveals a declining confidence in the aspirational pull of the U.S. Simon Anholt, author of *Brand America*, sums up how far the U.S. has slipped from its pedestal: "The world's love affair with America isn't exactly over, but it has stopped being a blind and unquestioning kind of love."

Questions for Discussion and Writing

1. This article suggests that there are certain products that "mean" America for people in other countries. Make a list of the ones mentioned in this essay and then write down what elements of American life you feel they represent.
2. Are there products and foods from other countries that you feel represent those nations? What kinds of things are you thinking of and what ideas do they give you about other cultures?
3. Imagine that you are a salesperson and what you are selling is an image of America. What elements of America would you want to emphasize and what kinds of products and images might you use to present your sales pitch?

Exporting the Wrong Picture
MARTHA BAYLES

Martha Bayles is the author of Hole in Our Soul: The Loss of Beauty and Meaning in American Popular Music *(Chicago), teaches humanities at Boston College, and is working on a book about U.S. cultural diplomacy. She has written widely about the role of music in popular culture. Dr. Bayles has also written articles on Miles*

Davis for The New York Times *and is a contributor to the* Wall Street Journal. *In this article, published in* The Washington Post *on August 28, 2005, the writer discusses how the elements of popular culture that are exported from the United States influence the views of those overseas, and how they directly impact other cultures.*

———————— ✦ ————————

When Benjamin Franklin went to France in 1776, his assignment was to manipulate the French into supporting the American war for independence. This he accomplished with two stratagems: First, he played the balance-of-power game as deftly as any European diplomat; and second, he waged a subtle but effective campaign of what we now call public diplomacy, or the use of information and culture to foster goodwill toward the nation. For Franklin, this meant turning his dumpy self into a symbol. "He knew that America had a unique and powerful meaning for the enlightened reformers of France," writes historian Bernard Bailyn, "and that he himself . . . was the embodiment, the palpable expression, of that meaning." Hence the fur cap and rustic manner that made Franklin a celebrity among the powdered wigs and gilded ornaments of the court of Louis XVI.

Today, as we witness the decline of America's reputation around the world, we're paying far more attention to Franklin's first stratagem than to his second. Indeed, despite a mounting stack of reports recommending drastic changes in the organization and funding of public diplomacy, very little of substance has been done. And most Americans, including many who make it their business to analyze public diplomacy, seem unmindful of the negative impression that America has recently been making on the rest of humanity—via our popular culture.

A striking pattern has emerged since the end of the Cold War. On the one hand, funding for public diplomacy has been cut by more than 30 percent since 1989, the National Science Board reported last year. On the other hand, while Washington was shrinking its funding for cultural diplomacy, Hollywood was aggressively expanding its exports. The Yale Center for the Study of Globalization reports that between 1986 and 2000 the fees generated by the export of filmed and taped entertainment went from $1.68 billion to $8.85 billion—an increase of 427 percent. Foreign box-office revenue has grown faster than domestic, and now approaches a 2-to-1 ratio. The pattern is similar for music, TV and video games.

This massive export of popular culture has been accompanied by domestic worries about its increasingly coarse and violent tone—worries that now go beyond the polarized debates of the pre-9/11 culture war. For example, a number of prominent African Americans, such as Bill Stephney, co-founder of the rap group Public Enemy, have raised concerns about the normalization of crime and prostitution in gangsta and "crunk" rap. And in April 2005, the Pew Research Center reported that "roughly six-in-ten [Americans] say they are very concerned over what children see or hear on TV (61%), in music lyrics (61%), video games (60%) and movies (56%)."

These worries now have a global dimension. The 2003 report of the U.S. House of Representatives Advisory Group on Public Diplomacy for the Arab and Muslim World stated that "Arabs and Muslims are . . . bombarded with American sitcoms, violent films, and other entertainment, much of which distorts the perceptions of viewers." The report made clear that what seems innocuous to Americans can cause problems abroad: "A Syrian teacher of English asked us plaintively for help in explaining American family life to her students. She asked, 'Does *Friends* show a typical family?'"

One of the few efforts to measure the impact of popular culture abroad was made by Louisiana State University researchers Melvin and Margaret DeFleur, who in 2003 polled teenagers in 12 countries: Saudi Arabia, Bahrain, South Korea, Mexico, China, Spain, Taiwan, Lebanon, Pakistan, Nigeria, Italy and Argentina. Their conclusion, while tentative, is nonetheless suggestive: "The depiction of Americans in media content as violent, of American women as sexually immoral and of many Americans engaging in criminal acts has brought many of these 1,313 youthful subjects to hold generally negative attitudes toward people who live in the United States."

Popular culture is not a monolith, of course. Along with a lot of junk, the entertainment industry still produces films, musical recordings, even television shows that rise to the level of genuine art. The good (and bad) news is that censorship is a thing of the past, on both the producing and the consuming end of popular culture. Despite attempts by radical clerics in Iraq to clamp down on Western influences, pirated copies of American movies still make it onto the market there. If we go by box office figures, the most popular films in the world are blockbusters like *Harry Potter*. But America is also exporting more than enough depictions of profanity, nudity, violence and criminal activity to violate norms of propriety still honored in much of the world.

But instead of questioning whether Americans should be super-sizing to others the same cultural diet that is giving us indigestion at home, we still seem to congratulate ourselves that our popular culture now pervades just about every society on Earth, including many that would rather keep it out. Why this disconnect? Partly it is due to an ingrained belief that what's good for show business is good for America's image. During both world wars, the movie studios produced propaganda for the government, in exchange for government aid in opening resistant foreign markets. Beginning in 1939, the recording industry cooperated with the Armed Forces Network to beam jazz to American soldiers overseas, and during the Cold War it helped the Voice of America (VOA) do the same for 30 million listeners behind the Iron Curtain.

In his book, *Cultural Exchange & the Cold War*, veteran foreign service officer Yale Richmond quotes the Russian novelist Vasily Aksyonov, for whom those VOA jazz broadcasts were "America's secret weapon number one." Aksyonov said that "the snatches of music and bits of information made for a kind of golden glow over the horizon . . . the West, the inaccessible but oh so desirable West."

To my knowledge, this passage has not been quoted in defense of Radio Sawa, the flagship of the U.S. government's new fleet of broadcast channels aimed at reaching young, largely Arab audiences. But even if it were, who could imagine such a reverent, yearning listener in the Middle East, South Asia or anywhere else today? The difference is not just between short-wave radio and unlimited broadband, it is also between Duke Ellington and 50 Cent.

During the Cold War, Washington also boosted the commercial export of popular culture, adhering to the view set forth in a 1948 State Department memo: "American motion pictures, as ambassadors of good will—at no cost to the American tax-payers—interpret the American way of life to all the nations of the world, which may be invaluable from a political, cultural, and commercial point of view."

And this boosterism continued through the 1960s and '70s, even as movies and rock music became not just unruly but down-right adversarial. During the 1970s, the government worked so hard to pry open world markets to American entertainment that UNESCO and the Soviet Union led a backlash against "U.S. cultural imperialism." In 1967, the VOA began to broadcast rock and soul. And while a provocative figure like Frank Zappa was hardly a favorite at diplomatic receptions, many in the foreign service understood his symbolic importance to dissidents, including Czech playwright (and later president) Vaclev Havel. In general, the U.S. political establishment was content to let America's homegrown counterculture do its subversive thing in Eastern Europe and Russia.

In the 1980s, the mood changed. Under Ronald Reagan appointee Charles Z. Wick, the United States Information Agency (USIA), the autonomous agency set up in 1953 to disseminate information and handle cultural exchange, was more generously funded and invited to play a larger role in policymaking—but at the price of having its autonomy curbed and the firewall between cultural outreach and policy advocacy thinned. It is noteworthy that these changes occurred amid the acrimony of the culture wars. Like the National Endowment for the Arts and public broadcasting, the USIA eventually found itself on Sen. Jesse Helms's list of artsy agencies deserving of the budgetary tax. And while the others managed to survive, the USIA did not. In 1999 it was absorbed into the very different bureaucratic culture of the State Department.

Today we witness the outcome: an unwarranted dismissal of elite-oriented cultural diplomacy, combined with an unquestioned faith in the export of popular culture. These converge in the decision to devote the bulk of post-9/11 funding to Radio Sawa and the other commercial-style broadcast entities, such as al-Hurra (a U.S.-based satellite TV network aimed at Arab listeners) and Radio Farda (which is broadcast in Farsi to Iran). Because the establishment of these new channels has been accompanied by the termination of the VOA's Arabic service, critics have focused largely on their news components. But what benefit is there in Radio Sawa's heavy rotation of songs by sex kitten Britney Spears and foul-mouthed rapper Eminem?

To the charge that the Bush administration is peddling smut and profanity to Arab teens, Radio Sawa's music director, Usama Farag, has stated that all the offensive lyrics are carefully edited out. Yet there is something quaint about the U.S. government's censoring song lyrics in a world where most people have ready access to every product of the American entertainment industry, including the dregs.

American popular culture is no longer a beacon of freedom to huddled masses in closed societies. Instead, it's a glut on the market and, absent any countervailing cultural diplomacy, our de facto ambassador to the world. The solution to this problem is far from clear. Censorship is not the answer, because even if it were technologically possible to censor our cultural exports, it would not be politic. The United States must affirm the crucial importance of free speech in a world that has serious doubts about it, and the best way to do this is to show that freedom is self-correcting—that Americans have not only liberty but also a civilization worthy of liberty.

From Franklin's days, U.S. cultural diplomacy has had both an elite and a popular dimension. Needless to say, it has rarely been easy to achieve a perfect balance between the two. What we could do is try harder to convey what the USIA mandate used to call "a full and fair picture of the United States." But to succeed even a little, our new efforts must counter the negative self-portrait we are now exporting. Along with worrying about what popular culture is teaching our children about life, we need also to worry about what it is teaching the world about America.

Questions for Discussion and Writing

1. In this article it is reported that in a survey of youths overseas "the depiction of Americans in media content as violent, of American women as sexually immoral and of many Americans engaging in criminal acts has brought many of these 1,313 youthful subjects to hold generally negative attitudes toward people who live in the United States." Is this due to the media depiction of America or does it have to do with the attitudes and understanding of the viewers in other countries? How responsible should the media outlets be about the ways in which the United States is represented in entertainment?

2. Martha Bayles seems to suggest that the concepts of diplomacy and popular culture are at odds with each other and that the desired impact of diplomacy is undercut by the violence, profanity, and nudity in popular culture. Do you think that she is right or is she underestimating the ability of foreign viewers and listeners to tell the difference?

3. The writer states that "The United States must affirm the crucial importance of free speech in a world that has serious doubts about it, and the best way to do this is to show that freedom is self-correcting—that Americans have not only liberty but also a civilization worthy of liberty." What do you take to mean by "self-correcting"? What would be the advantages of this approach and what could be the possible problems?

4. The U.S. State Department produces documents to promote U.S. cultural issues to the rest of the world. You can access these through the following URL: http://usinfo.state.gov/journals/journals.htm. One of the areas covered here is that of U.S. society and values. Read some of the articles and write an explanation for someone overseas to explain how these depictions of U.S. life compare to your own experiences.

Global Sports, American Sports

MIKE MARQUSEE

Mike Marqusee is a cultural critic who writes regularly for The Guardian *(UK),* The Nation *(USA),* The Hindustan Times *(India), and* The Hindu *(India). He was born in the United States but has lived in London for 30 years where he has been instrumental in organizing the Stop the War Coalition Steering Committee. His books include* Redemption Song: Muhammad Ali and the Spirit of the 60s, Chimes of Freedom: The Politics of Bob Dylan's Art, *and* War Minus the Shooting. *In this article from ColorLines, a journal out of Oakland, California, he discusses the global perspective on U.S. sport and suggests that the influence of sporting culture is not as great as U.S. observers would have readers believe, although the commercial impact is still significant.*

◆

The discourse of sport has always been prone to planetary-scale hyperbole, and in some respects the ideology of globalization when applied to sports has only taken old habits to new extremes. What is curious, and revealing, however, is the way in which global pretensions are so often mingled with parochial North American myopia. And nowhere was this contorted posture, so characteristic of our age, better illustrated than in an issue of *Newsweek* published in October 1999.

As part of its breathless celebration of the achievements of the expiring 20th century, the magazine ran a 34 page feature on sporting heroes, entitled "America's greatest." Here the history of sport in the USA was presented as a mostly triumphal progress in which barriers of color and gender prejudice were toppled, along with sporting records, by the exemplary efforts of a succession of extraordinary individuals.

Amid the predictable exaggerations and omissions, there was one claim in particular that strayed most egregiously from reality. "Sports may be America's most successful export to the world," the editors wrote. "Whatever the world thinks of us, it loves our games. Major League Baseball is increasingly dominated by Latin players and there is growing infusion of talent from Japan and

South Korea. Basketball is popular on every continent. And in Europe they now play our football along with their own."

When I shared this last sentence with students in London, they burst out laughing. What is known in the rest of the world as "American football" is a very minor sport indeed in Europe, viewed by many as a testosterone-fuelled freak show. And while it is true that basketball is gaining popularity in parts of Europe, Asia and Africa, it does so overwhelmingly in the shadow of the NBA and everywhere lags well behind more established team sports—mainly soccer—just as soccer does in the USA, despite the advances it has made in recent years. In Soweto [South Africa], you will certainly find far more Manchester United shirts than Bulls caps, and Michael Jordan's fame outside his native land rests more on his financial success and his role as a shill for the world's biggest sports shoe company than his achievements on the basketball court.

WHOSE WORLD SERIES?

Contrary to the *Newsweek* dictum, sports are actually one of America's least successful exports. Other products of American popular culture—Hollywood films, TV sitcoms, rock 'n' roll, rhythm 'n' blues, soul, funk, hip hop, fashion—have all traveled further and penetrated deeper into alien cultures than the games of baseball, American football, or even basketball. Indeed, the salient fact about America's sporting culture is that it is shared with so few others. Overseas, the quaint habit of denominating the finals of the North American baseball competition as a "World Series" is regarded as an example of typical American arrogance—more amusing than bombing third world countries, but cut from the same cloth.

It is not only in preferring their own, home-made sports to genuinely world games such as soccer, rugby, cricket or even field hockey that Americans plough a furrow of their own. The ways in which sport is produced and consumed in America are also distinctive. Despite their preoccupation with the expression of American national identity through sports, the *Newsweek* editors seem largely unaware of those features that actually make America's sporting culture distinctive, indeed, to many foreign observers, downright weird.

Cheerleaders, for example, are a uniquely American pheno-menon and attempts to introduce them abroad have enjoyed little success. Crowds at European or Latin American soccer or south

Asian or Caribbean cricket matches would all find the notion that their response to events on the field should be mediated by a regiment of scantily-clad females bizarre in the extreme. Here the songs, chants, jokes and other means of expressing partisanship or commenting on the course of the action emerge from within the crowd itself, often in accordance with long-established (but continually evolving) popular traditions. Of course, American sporting crowds have their own popular traditions, but the degree of official orchestration (not only through cheerleaders, but through electronic signs and announcements) is undoubtedly much greater in America than abroad.

America also enjoys the dubious honor of being the only country to institutionalize the use of higher education as a nursery for professional sport. When it comes to track and field or swimming, sports in which America does compete with the world, this practice has given the USA a major advantage, and leveled the playing field with the state-sponsored athletes of the old Soviet bloc. However, readers will be only too familiar with the corruption and compromise of both educational and sporting values that this long-established American tradition has entailed.

These days athletes from all over the world seek to avail themselves of the facilities of American higher education. For many Third World sportspersons, a stint at an American university is their only hope of translating raw talent into high-level success and financial reward. In this respect, at least some features of the American sporting culture are now spreading across the globe. While sporting professionalism was a 19th century British innovation, in the exploitation of sport for commercial purposes it is the Americans who have led the way. Once upon a time, the idea that a sporting institution like the Brooklyn Dodgers could pull up stakes and move to another locale at the whim of a private owner would have been regarded as an idiosyncratically American phenomenon. Nowadays, the corporate capitalist model pioneered in the USA is taking hold nearly everywhere, reshaping ancient sporting traditions and transforming spectator expectations and behavior.

CAPITAL'S BATTERING RAM

Although we do not share a single global sporting culture, we do, increasingly, live under the aegis of a single global sporting industry. This industry is dominated by a corporate elite whose leading members are only too well known to North American sports fans. Take, for example, cricket in south Asia, a sport with a popular base of many hundreds of millions. The right to exploit this huge audience via television has recently been divided up between Rupert Murdoch's Star TV and Disney's ESPN. The principal sponsors of the Indian and Pakistani cricket teams—whose stars are household names across one fifth of humanity—are Pepsi and Coca Cola.

Murdoch also has major interests—both as broadcaster and franchise owner—in European soccer and Australian and British rugby league. In accordance with his oft-stated belief that sport is a "battering ram" for the penetration of national economies, he has teamed up with both the NBA and Manchester United in long-term projects for the development of basketball and soccer in China, capitalism's favorite emerging market. His partners in these ventures include not only the Chinese government, but also Mark McCormack's International Management Group, which has already played a leading role in reshaping professional golf and tennis. IMG is also the promoter-manager of a series of India-Pakistan cricket clashes held annually in Toronto. Not much of a spectator draw in Canada, but the rights to the telecasts beamed backed to a rapt south Asian audience are worth a fortune.

When the two teams faced each other on neutral ground in Australia earlier this year, Murdoch and ESPN hyped the contest as "Qayamat"—judgment day. With the military dictatorship in Pakistan and the right-wing Hindu communalist government in India exchanging accusations of terrorism and nuclear threats on a daily basis, the cricket confrontation assumed a grotesquely inflated importance, replete with menacing religious and nationalist overtones. That so many of the big players in the global sporting industry (mainly U.S.-based) now have major vested interests in over-promoting the India-Pakistan cricket rivalry speaks volumes about the distorting and dehumanizing impact of globalization on the culture of sport.

Everywhere, the vast concentrations of wealth that this process engenders are transforming long-established competitive patterns and traditional loyalties. Inequalities within and between sports, as well as within and between national sporting cultures, are being exacerbated. In Britain, cricket withers as it finds itself unable to compete for popular attention with soccer; in South Asia, the glamour attached to cricket has marginalized field hockey, once the pride of both India and Pakistan.

WE BRAND THE WORLD

The one claim in *Newsweek's* paean to American sport that has a ring of truth is the assertion that America's "most visible symbol has, over the 20th century, evolved from the Stars and Stripes to Coke to the Swoosh." Note the complacency with which the editors appear to regard this disturbing evolution. The duty of representing a nation state and its culture has been passed from a flag to a mass manufactured consumer product and then to the symbol of a privately owned corporation.

Last year at a cricket match in Sri Lanka, I witnessed the power of the swoosh. A poverty-stricken young boy was hanging around outside the gate, unable to afford the price of a ticket but hoping for a glimpse of his heroes. He had no shoes, scrawny legs and dirty, ill-fitting shorts. His tattered tee shirt was hand-decorated with the letters "NIKE" and a big, black swoosh' drawn painstakingly with a black marker. I wanted to say to him what I always feel like saying to young people in Britain or America who decorate themselves with the swoosh and other corporate logos: they pay Michael Jordan, Andre Agassi or Tiger Woods millions to wear that thing—how much do they pay you? At least the young Sri Lankan hadn't actually paid Nike for the privilege of advertising their product—unlike his contemporaries in the west—but the implication was that he would if he could have afforded to. Since he could not, replicating its corporate symbolism was the next best thing, the nearest he could come to joining the global but exclusive club of the consuming classes.

In adorning himself with the swoosh, this sports enthusiast had become part of a vast web that links sweatshop laborers in south and east Asia, kids in the ghettos of North America, the corporate barons of the clothing and footwear industries, the media moguls and marketing gurus, and not least, sports administrators, sports promoters and professional sports men and women. He had become part of what might be called the media-corporate-sport nexus—a nexus that now links together a substantial portion of the human race, but does so in highly unequal and exploitative fashion.

THE INCREASING SIGNIFICANCE OF SPORT

One of the defining features of an information-based economy is the ever-increasing value attached to what are called "symbolic goods," i.e. images and information. If you break down the components that make up the retail value of a Nike shoe, you find that a mere 10% is accounted for by the costs of physical production; design and marketing account for the remainder. The company spends more on endorsements from star names than it does on the entire army of low-paid workers who actually make the shoes.

Remember that it was Air Jordans—a product entirely dependent on its association with a sports hero—that placed Nike in pole position in the huge global sports footwear market, now worth more than $16 billion annually.

In this type of economy, sport, which is itself a symbolic good as well as a highly effective carrier of symbolic values of all sorts, assumes ever increasing social significance and economic weight. But this development is not necessarily to the benefit of sport, sports fans or society as a whole.

In 1998 global expenditure on sport sponsorship exceeded some $15 billion (a sum that had trebled in a decade and risen by 12% in the previous year alone). But the distribution of this enormous investment neatly illustrates the current imbalances in what the apologists of the IMF and WTO would have us believe is a "global economy." North America accounts for 37.8% of the market; Europe 36.4%; and Asia 20.8%. Africa is left far behind. The recent African soccer championships were followed passionately by a population of nearly one billion, but since it is a population with a meager disposable income, the competition attracted only derisory sponsorship and media interest. The great African players ply their trade in Europe, just as the top Latin American baseball talent seeks the higher rewards available in the USA.

Sports sponsorship in Britain now amounts to some $500 million annually—but two thirds of that sum is consumed by only two sports, soccer and motor racing. Other sports find themselves increasingly disadvantaged in the ever-more furious competition for a slice of the cake, and women's sport is left with only the crumbs. A recent survey revealed that 82% of British companies involved in sports sponsorship indicated they had "no interest" in women's sport; however, 57% of these said they would have an interest if women's sport displayed greater "sex appeal." So, far from busting stereotypes and liberating women's long suppressed sporting potential, the modern marketplace seems to be reproducing the old biases.

Along with television rights and sponsorship, the big money in sport derives today from "licensing." For the 1998 soccer world cup—next to the Olympics, the world's biggest sporting event (in comparison, the Super Bowl is a parochial affair)—FIFA, soccer's governing body, issued 300 licenses to corporations to produce and market more than 400 World Cup-branded products at a total retail value estimated at more than $1.2 billion. The licensing operation was handled for FIFA by the Swiss-based ISL (like IMG, one of a burgeoning number of companies specializing in managing the high-value interface between sport, the media and the corporate sector). A top ISL executive explained the logic driving this super-profitable juggernaut: "Today the marks of international sports events have become extremely valuable properties; the visible expressions of the link between supporters and events are an effective way of giving products added value."

In common with die-hard sports fans in many countries, I continue to believe (perhaps naively) that the "link between supporters and events" ought to be of a different nature. We may occupy diverse national and regional sporting cultures, but we have a common interest in resisting the Murdochs and the ESPNs and the IMGs—and reclaiming our games.

What is happening in global sport reflects a broader crisis in popular culture. Just how popular is it? To what extent are its meanings fashioned among the majority, and reflective of their lived experience, and to what extent are they contrived from above and cynically foist upon a passive public? This crisis isn't something we should regard in a fatalistic manner, bemoaning the loss of a largely mythical sporting innocence from a prone position in front of the boob tube. As events [at the World Trade Organization conference] in Seattle reminded us all, the dominant consensus is a fragile one. The colonization of sport, like the corporate appropriation of the third world gene bank, can be challenged and resisted. But only if sports fans emerge from their nationalist cocoons and begin making links across borders of all kinds.

Questions for Discussion and Writing

1. Mike Marqusee suggests that there is a disconnect between the commercial interests of sports financiers and the fans of sports. He points to the way in which teams move from city to city or how sports teams might invest in short-term success rather than building a solid base for the future. The role of the supporter of a team seems to be diminished in this. Discuss the balance of interests and if it is possible to please both sides in this equation.
2. The writer suggests that there is a problem with using educational institutions as a "nursery" for the professional sports. Make an argument for and

against the current system. Perhaps you do not agree with the writer—how would you dispute his claim?

3. In this article there is a concern about how the "swoosh" and other sports-related symbols and products have influenced the global arena. In the United States we have seen cases of people being killed or assaulted for their sneakers; in the third world workers are paid a pittance to make products that generates millions in revenue for the corporations that sell them. Marqusee also questions the ethics of using people as human billboards for companies like Nike. How aware are you of these issues? Write a document to persuade people to boycott one of the major sports goods producers or write a press release to defend and promote the manufacture of sneakers, t-shirts, or other sporting goods.

American Culture Goes Global, or Does It?

RICHARD PELLS

Richard Pells is a professor of history at the University of Texas at Austin. He writes often for newspapers and magazines, including the International Herald Tribune, *the* Los Angeles Times, *and the* Chronicle of Higher Education. *His books include* The Liberal Mind in a Conservative Age: American Intellectuals in the 1940s and 1950s *(1989),* Not Like Us: How Europeans Have Loved, Hated, and Transformed American Culture Since World War II *(1997), and* Radical Visions and American Dreams: Culture and Social Thought in the Depression Years *(1998). His next book will be* From Modernism to the Movies: The Globalization of American Culture in the 20th Century, *to be published by Yale University Press. Dr. Pells has taught at the universities of Sao Paulo, Amsterdam, Copenhagen, Sydney, Bonn, Berlin, Cologne, and Vienna. This article is from the* Chronicle of Higher Education *and appeared on April 12, 2002.*

———————————— ✦ ————————————

Since September 11, newspaper and magazine columnists and television pundits have told us that it is not only the economic power of the United States or the Bush administration's "unilateralist" foreign policy that breeds global anti-Americanism. Dislike for the United States stems also, they say, from its "cultural imperialism." We have been hearing a good deal about how American mass culture inspires resentment and sometimes-violent reactions, not just in the Middle East but all over the world.

Yet the discomfort with American cultural dominance is not new. In 1901, the British writer William Stead published a book called, ominously, *The Americanization of the World*. The title captured a set of apprehensions—about the disappearance of national languages and traditions, and the obliteration of the unique identities of countries under the weight of American habits and states of mind—that persists today.

More recently, globalization has become the main enemy for academics, journalists, and political activists who loathe what they see as a trend toward cultural uniformity. Still, they usually regard global culture and American culture as synonymous. And they continue to insist that Hollywood, McDonald's, and Disneyland are eradicating regional and local eccentricities—disseminating images and subliminal messages so beguiling as to drown out competing voices in other lands.

Despite those allegations, the cultural relationship between the United States and the rest of the world over the past 100 years has never been one-sided. On the contrary, the United States was, and continues to be, as much a consumer of foreign intellectual and artistic influences as it has been a shaper of the world's entertainment and tastes.

That is not an argument with which many foreigners (or even many Americans) would readily agree. The clichés about America's cultural "hegemony" make it difficult for most people to recognize that modern global culture is hardly a monolithic entity foisted on the world by the American media. Neither is it easy for critics of Microsoft or AOL Time Warner to acknowledge that the conception of a harmonious and distinctively American culture—encircling the globe, implanting its values in foreign minds—is a myth.

In fact, as a nation of immigrants from the 19th to the 21st centuries, and as a haven in the 1930s and '40s for refugee scholars and artists, the United States has been a recipient as much as an exporter of global culture. Indeed, the influence of immigrants and African-Americans on the United States explains why its culture has been so popular for so long in so many places. American culture has spread throughout the world because it has incorporated foreign styles and ideas. What Americans have done more brilliantly than their competitors overseas is repackage the cultural products we receive from abroad and then retransmit them to the rest of the planet. In effect, Americans have specialized in selling the dreams, fears, and folklore of other people back to them. That is why a global mass culture has come to be identified, however simplistically, with the United States.

Americans, after all, did not invent fast food, amusement parks, or the movies. Before the Big Mac, there were fish and chips. Before Disneyland, there was Copenhagen's Tivoli Gardens (which Walt Disney used as a prototype for his first theme park, in Anaheim, a model later re-exported to Tokyo and Paris).

Nor can the origins of today's international entertainment be traced only to P.T. Barnum or Buffalo Bill. The roots of the new global culture lie as well in the European modernist assault, in the early 20th century, on 19th-century literature, music, painting, and architecture—particularly in the modernist refusal to honor the traditional boundaries between high and low culture. Modernism in the arts was improvisational, eclectic, and irreverent. Those traits have also been characteristic of, but not peculiar to, mass culture.

The hallmark of 19th-century culture, in Europe and also in Asia, was its insistence on defending the purity of literature, classical music, and representational painting against the intrusions of folklore and popular amusements. No one confused Tolstoy with dime novels, opera with Wild West shows, the Louvre with Coney Island. High culture was supposed to be educational, contemplative, and uplifting—a way of preserving the best in human civilization.

Such beliefs didn't mean that a Dickens never indulged in melodrama, or that a Brahms disdained the use of popular songs. Nor did Chinese or Japanese authors and painters refuse to draw on oral or folkloric traditions. But the 19th-century barriers between high and low culture were resolutely, if imperfectly, maintained.

The artists of the early 20th century shattered what seemed to them the artificial demarcations between different cultural forms. They also challenged the notion that culture was a means of intellectual or moral improvement. They did so by emphasizing style and craftsmanship at the expense of philosophy, religion, or ideology. They deliberately called attention to language in their novels, to optics in their paintings, to the materials in and function of their architecture, to the structure of music instead of its melodies.

And they wanted to shock their audiences. Which they succeeded in doing. Modern painting and literature—with its emphasis on visually distorted nudes, overt sexuality, and meditations on violence—was attacked for being degrading and obscene, and for appealing to the baser instincts of humanity. In much the same way, critics would later denounce the vulgarity of popular culture.

Although modernism assaulted the conventions of 19th-century high culture in Europe and Asia, it inadvertently accelerated the growth of mass culture in the United States. Indeed, Americans were already receptive to the blurring of cultural boundaries. In the 19th century, symphony orchestras in the United States often included band music in their programs, and opera singers were asked to perform both Mozart and Stephen Foster.

So, for Americans in the 20th century, Surrealism, with its dreamlike associations, easily lent itself to the wordplay and psychological symbolism of advertising, cartoons, and theme parks. Dadaism ridiculed the snobbery of elite cultural institutions and reinforced, instead, an existing appetite (especially among the immigrant audiences in the United States) for low-class, anti-bourgeois nickelodeons and vaudeville shows. Stravinsky's experiments with atonal (and thus unconventional and unmelodic) music validated the rhythmic innovations of American jazz. Writers like Hemingway, detesting the rhetorical embellishments of 19th-century prose, invented a terse, hard-boiled language, devoted to reproducing as authentically as possible the elemental qualities of personal experience. That laconic style became a model for modern journalism, detective fiction, and movie dialogue.

All of those trends provided the foundations for a genuinely new culture. But the new culture turned out to be neither modernist nor European. Instead, the United States trans-formed what was still a parochial culture, appealing largely to the young and the rebellious in Western society, into a global phenomenon.

The propensity of Americans to borrow modernist ideas, and to transform them into a global culture, is clearly visible in the commercial uses of modern architecture. The European Bauhaus movement—intended in the 1920s as a socialist experiment in working-class housing—eventually provided the theories and techniques for the construction of skyscrapers and vacation homes in the United States. But the same architectural ideas were then sent back to Europe after World War II as a model for the reconstruction of bombed-out cities like Rotterdam, Cologne, and Frankfurt. Thus, the United States converted what had once been a distinctive, if localized, rebellion by Dutch and German archi-tects into a generic "international style."

But it is in popular culture that the reciprocal relationship between America and the rest of the world can best be seen. There are many reasons for the ascendancy of American mass culture. Certainly, the ability of American-based media conglomerates to control the production and distribution of their products has been a major stimulus to the worldwide spread of American entertainment. But the power of American capitalism is not the only, or even the most important, explanation for the global popularity of America's movies and television shows.

The effectiveness of English as a language of mass communications has been essential to the acceptance of American culture. Unlike, for example, German, Russian, or Chinese, the simple structure and grammar of English, along with its tendency to use shorter, less-abstract words and more-concise sentences, are all advantageous for the composers of song lyrics, ad slogans, cartoon captions, newspaper headlines, and movie and TV dialogue. English is thus a language exceptionally well-suited to the demands and spread of American mass culture.

Another factor is the size of the American audience. A huge domestic market has made it possible for many American filmmakers and TV executives to retrieve most of their production costs and make a profit within the borders of the United States. That economic cushion has enabled them to spend more money on stars, sets, special effects, location shooting, and merchandising—the very ingredients that attract international audiences as well.

Yet even with such advantages, America's mass culture may not be all that American. The American audience is not only large; because of the influx of immigrants and refugees, it is also international in its complexion. The heterogeneity of America's population—its regional, ethnic, religious, and racial diversity—has forced the media, since the early years of the 20th century, to experiment with messages, images, and story lines that have a broad multicultural appeal. The Hollywood studios, mass-circulation magazines, and television networks have had to learn how to speak to a variety of groups and classes at home. That has given them the techniques to appeal to an equally diverse audience abroad. The American domestic market has, in essence, been a laboratory, a place to develop cultural products that can then be adapted to the world market.

An important way that the American media have succeeded in transcending internal social divisions, national borders, and language barriers is by mixing up cultural styles. American musicians and entertainers have followed the example of modernist artists like Picasso and Braque in drawing on elements from high and low culture, combining the sacred and the profane. Advertisers have adapted the techniques of Surrealism and Abstract Expressionism to make their products more intriguing. Composers like Aaron Copland, George Gershwin, and Leonard Bernstein incorporated folk melodies, religious hymns, blues, gospel songs, and jazz into their symphonies, concertos, operas, and ballets. Indeed, an art form as quintessentially American as jazz evolved during the 20th century into an amalgam of African, Caribbean, Latin American, and modernist European music. That blending of forms in America's mass culture has enhanced its appeal to multiethnic domestic and international audiences by capturing their varied experiences and tastes.

Nowhere are foreign influences more evident than in the American movie industry. For better or worse, Hollywood became, in the 20th century, the cultural capital of the modern world. But it was never an exclusively American capital. Like past cultural centers—Florence, Paris, Vienna—Hollywood has functioned as an international community, built by immigrant entrepreneurs and drawing on the talents of actors, directors, writers, cinematographers, editors, and costume and set designers from all over the world. The first American movie star, after all, was Charlie Chaplin, whose comic skills were honed in British music halls.

Moreover, during much of the 20th century, American moviemakers thought of themselves as acolytes, entranced by the superior works of foreign directors. In the 1920s, few American directors could gain admittance to a European pantheon that included Sergei Eisenstein, F.W. Murnau, G.W. Pabst, Fritz Lang, and Carl Dreyer. The postwar years, from the 1940s to the mid-'60s, were once again a golden age of filmmaking in Britain, Sweden, France, Italy, Japan, and India. An extraordinary generation of foreign directors—Ingmar Bergman, Federico Fellini, Michelangelo Antonioni, François Truffaut, Jean-Luc Godard, Akira Kurosawa, Satyajit Ray—were the world's most celebrated auteurs.

Nevertheless, it is one of the paradoxes of the European and Asian cinemas that their greatest success was in spawning American imitations. After the release, in 1967, of *Bonnie and Clyde* (originally to have been directed by Truffaut or Godard), the newest geniuses—Francis Ford Coppola, Martin Scorsese, Robert Altman, Steven Spielberg, Woody Allen—were American. They may have owed their improvisational methods and autobiographical preoccupations to Italian neo-Realism and the French New Wave. But who, in any country, needed to see another *La Dolce Vita* when you could enjoy *Nashville?* Why try to decipher *Jules and Jim* or *L'Avventura* when you could see *Annie Hall* or *The Godfather?* Wasn't it conceivable that *The Seven Samurai* might not be as powerful or as disturbing a movie as *The Wild Bunch?*

It turned out that foreign filmmakers had been too influential for their own good. They helped revolutionize the American cinema, so that, after the 1960s and '70s, it became hard for any other continent's film industry to match the worldwide popularity of American movies.

Once again, however, we need to remember that Hollywood movies have never been just American. To take another example, American directors, in all eras, have emulated foreign artists and filmmakers by paying close attention to the style and formal qualities of a movie, and to the need to tell a story visually. Early-20th-century European painters wanted viewers to recognize that they were looking at lines and color on a canvas rather than at a reproduction of the natural world. Similarly, many American films—from the multiple narrators in *Citizen Kane*, to the split-screen portrait of how two lovers imagine their relationship in *Annie Hall*, to the flashbacks and flash-forwards in *Pulp Fiction*, to the roses blooming from the navel of Kevin Spacey's fantasy dream girl in *American Beauty*—deliberately remind the audience that it is watching a movie instead of a play or a photographed version of reality. American filmmakers (not only in the movies but also on MTV) have been willing to use the most sophisticated techniques of editing and camera work, much of it inspired by European directors, to create a modernist collage of images that captures the speed and seductiveness of life in the contemporary world.

Hollywood's addiction to modernist visual pyrotechnics is especially evident in the largely nonverbal style of many of its contemporary performers. The tendency to mumble was not always in vogue. In the 1930s and '40s, the sound and meaning of words were important not only in movies but also on records and the radio. Even though some homegrown stars, like John Wayne and Gary Cooper, were famously terse, audiences could at least hear and understand what they were saying. But the centrality of language in the films of the 1930s led, more often, to a dependence in Hollywood on British actors (like Cary Grant), or on Americans who sounded vaguely British (like Katharine Hepburn and Bette Davis). It is illustrative of how important foreign (especially British) talent was to Hollywood in an earlier era that the two most famous Southern belles in American fiction and drama—Scarlett O'Hara and Blanche DuBois—were played in the movies by Vivien Leigh.

The verbal eloquence of pre-World War II acting, in both movies and the theater, disappeared after 1945. After Marlon Brando's revolutionary performance in *A Streetcar Named Desire*, in the 1947 stage version and the 1951 screen version, the model of American acting became inarticulateness—a brooding and halting introspection that one doesn't find in the glib and clever heroes or heroines of the screwball comedies and gangster films of the '30s. Brando was trained in the Method, an acting technique originally developed in Stanislavsky's Moscow Art Theater in prerevolutionary Russia, then imported to New York by members of the Group Theater during the 1930s. Where British actors, trained in Shakespeare, were taught to subordinate their personalities to the role as written, the Method encouraged actors to improvise, to summon up childhood memories, and to explore their inner feelings, often at the expense of what the playwright or screenwriter intended. Norman Mailer once said that Brando, in his pauses and his gazes into the middle distance, always seemed to be searching for a better line than the one the writer had composed. In effect, what Brando did (along with his successors and imitators, from James Dean to Warren Beatty to Robert De Niro) was to lead a revolt against the British school of acting, with its reverence for the script and the written (and spoken) word.

Thus, after World War II, the emotional power of American acting lay more in what was not said, in what could not even be communicated in words. The Method actor's reliance on physical mannerisms and even silence in interpreting a role has been especially appropriate for a cinema that puts a premium on the inexpressible. Indeed, the influence of the Method, not only in the United States but also abroad (where it was reflected in the acting styles of Jean-Paul Belmondo and Marcello Mastroianni), is a classic example of how a foreign idea, originally meant for the stage, was adapted in postwar America to the movies, and then conveyed to the rest of the world as a paradigm for both cinematic and social behavior. More important, the Method's disregard for language permitted global audiences—even those not well-versed in English—to understand and appreciate what they were watching in American films.

Finally, American culture has imitated not only the modernists' visual flamboyance, but also their emphasis on personal expression and their tendency to be apolitical and anti-ideological. The refusal to browbeat an audience with a social message has accounted, more than any other factor, for the worldwide popularity of American entertainment. American movies, in particular, have customarily focused on human relationships and private feelings, not on the problems of a particular time and place. They tell tales about romance, intrigue, success, failure, moral conflicts, and survival. The most memorable movies of the 1930s (with the exception of *The Grapes of Wrath*) were comedies and musicals about mismatched people falling in love, not socially conscious films dealing with issues of poverty and unemployment. Similarly, the finest movies about World War II (like *Casablanca*) or the Vietnam War (like *The Deer Hunter*) linger in the mind long after those conflicts have ended because they explore their characters' intimate emotions rather than dwelling on headline events.

Such intensely personal dilemmas are what people everywhere wrestle with. So Europeans, Asians, and Latin Americans flocked to *Titanic* (as they once did to *Gone With the Wind*) not because it celebrated American values, but because people all over the world could see some part of their own lives reflected in the story of love and loss.

America's mass culture has often been crude and intrusive, as its critics—from American academics like Benjamin Barber to German directors like Wim Wenders—have always complained. In their eyes, American culture is "colonizing" everyone else's subconscious, reducing us all to passive residents of "McWorld."

But American culture has never felt all that foreign to foreigners. And, at its best, it has transformed what it received from others into a culture that everyone, everywhere, can embrace, a culture that is both emotionally and, on occasion, artistically compelling for millions of people throughout the world.

So, despite the current hostility to America's policies and values—in Europe and Latin America as well as in the Middle East and Asia—it is important to recognize how familiar much of American culture seems to people abroad. If anything, our movies, television shows, and theme parks have been less "imperialistic" than cosmopolitan. In the end, American mass culture has not transformed the world into a replica of the United States. Instead, America's dependence on foreign cultures has made the United States a replica of the world.

Questions for Discussion and Writing

1. Dr. Pells talks about the divide between high and low culture. What defines each, and do you agree that there is a particularly global movement to eradicate division between them? How would you respond to the point that each culture might have its own understanding of the high/low cultural divide?

2. Dr. Pells argues that "The effectiveness of English as a language of mass communications has been essential to the acceptance of American culture. Unlike, for example, German, Russian, or Chinese, the simple structure and grammar of English, along with its tendency to use shorter, less-abstract words and more-concise sentences, are all advantageous for the composers of song lyrics, ad slogans, cartoon captions, newspaper headlines, and movie and TV dialogue. English is thus a language exceptionally well-suited to the demands and spread of American mass culture." Do you agree? Perhaps your first language is not English. How do you react to the idea that English has a simple structure and grammar? How would you respond to this argument? What elements do you see informing his claim?

3. Make a list of influential American artists (film-makers, painters, writers, musicians) and a list of influential artists from other countries. Then, think about how you know about each and their work. How do you access the art that these people have produced? What is the difference between work that is presented to you and work that you have to seek out? For example, what access did you have to *Star Wars III: The Revenge of the Sith* compared to *Look At Me* by the French film-maker Agnes Jaoui?

4. How does the relationship between art and commerce work in the United States? Think, for example, of the importance of the television sweeps season. How do the decisions of advertisers influence the choice of programs that Americans get to watch? How might this differ from state-funded systems like, for example, the BBC in the United Kingdon, Sveriges TV in Sweden, or Doordarshan in India?

General Questions for Chapter Four

1. There is a suggestion from many of the writers in this chapter that the cultural influence between the United States and other countries works both ways. This is a subject that we will look at in Chapter Five, but before we move on, make an argument that agrees or disagrees with this claim. What cultural influences from other countries and cultures do you encounter in your everyday life? If you are not living in the United

States, what aspects of U.S. culture are you aware of and what role do they play from day to day?

2. Define these terms using examples from the essays in this chapter: monoculturalism; modernism; infotainment. Also, a term referred to a number of times in the essays included here has been "soft power," a term created by Joseph Nye of Harvard University. What is "soft power" and how does it work?

3. Which cultures are you drawn to? They may be cultures either within the United States or from outside? How would you define the elements of the culture that appeal to you? What signs do you see in the cultures that draw you to them? Are they complimentary or contradictory to the culture from which you come? Are there things within your own experience that you have adopted from other cultures (modes of dress, food, music, language?)

CHAPTER 5

In Its Own Image

So how does a cultural exchange really work? In the previous chapters we may have decided that the relationship between the United States and the rest of the world is adversary by default. This, of course, would be a simplistic view and blatantly untrue. There are many things about the United States, its culture, customs, and influence that are welcomed around the globe. The perfect balance appears to be where there is an effective and equitable give and take. In this final chapter we will be looking at some areas where the United States has borrowed from other countries and cultures to make something very specifically American and specific examples of American cultural influence that have found a foothold in another culture.

The United States is, by definition, a nation of immigrants. While vestiges of Native American culture remain, it has been the influx of people from Europe, Asia, and South America that has shaped the cultural landscape of the United States. This is not to forget, of course, the enormous cultural impact of the millions of people of African descent who have given the United States some of its most identifiably indigenous art forms, such as jazz. The mixture of cultural influences has been linked by one abiding and powerful force: the desire for a connection with a homeland. This desired connection is often to a culture that is older that that offered by the still-relatively-young United States, and it offers a legacy and heritage that are not easily set aside or forgotten. Instead, it becomes adapted and insinuated into an American culture that seems to be in flux much of the time. Thus, we have the phenomenon of the hyphenated nationality. Many people in the United States identify themselves as Italian-American, African-American, Polish-American, or Asian-American (and so forth) even if they were born in the United States and have perhaps never visited the country with which they desire a bond and identification. Immigrants have traditionally found themselves grouping together in enclaves that allow a continued connection with people from their own culture, and a continuation of tradition, festival, and community mores. Where I live in South Philadelphia, for example, is a strongly Italian area. Some of the people on my street were born in Italy and moved to the United States, but others were born here of Italian parents. They fly the Italian and American flags together outside their houses, and many of the young men sport tattoos of the Italian flag. On a summer evening, with my window open, I can hear my neighbors outside, sitting on their steps, taking in the language from the Old Country. I could be in Naples. In other parts of the city there are areas specifically thought of as Korean, Irish, Polish, Russian, and Chinese.

It is no wonder, therefore, that U.S. culture has taken the flavors of many different countries around the world. This continues as more immigrants move to the United States, as communication and technology allows easier access to other cultures of the world, and as new trends and global voices increase in reach and power. In this chapter, for example, we will see how American movie-makers are looking to Asian cinema for ideas and how a popular performer like Gwen Stefani has taken images of Japanese culture to make her look "cool" (though not without protest, as we shall see). On the other hand, cultural ideas from the United States have found a foothold overseas and sometimes in the most unexpected forms—here we will look at rap music in Italy and the global reach of the iconic Elvis.

We will also see how the elements of world culture can be taken and distilled for an American audience. At the EPCOT center in Disney World, Florida, in Las Vegas, and at Busch Gardens' display The Old Country, we get to see what elements of other cultures designers and architects feel most effectively represent international societies. We also get an indication of how Americans who do not travel internationally often, or at all, might be influenced to see the rest of the world through the lens of such simulacra. Why go all the way to Venice, Italy, when one can see the essence of Venice—all we need to know—in Las Vegas or in the representation at EPCOT? Often symbols of other cultures are remade by America into its own image. How many people doubt that the pyramid and sphinx of the Luxor Hotel in Las Vegas are as spectacular as the "real thing" in Egypt? They are certainly in better repair and they have air-conditioning. On the other hand, how do we explain why Africa is not represented at EPCOT? Countries in the World

Showcase have to sponsor their pavilion. Planned pavilions for Russia, Spain, Israel, and Equatorial Africa never made it to existence when it became clear what funding was required. The question is how this skews the worldview of a visitor, while some may argue that the absence of an African presence under these terms reflects a bigger global problem than a mere pavilion at Disney World. In this chapter we will read the thoughts and observations of cultural critic Lawrence Mintz, who will help us to start to make sense of this complex issue.

When the relationship between any country and the rest of the world is at its best, there is a fair and reasonable exchange of culture, respect, interest, commerce, and diplomacy. It is in the area of popular culture that we often see the first and most enduring signs of international exchange and mutual interest. Entertainment travels in ways that other elements of societies do not. Even within the United States we see this—look at, for example, at the popularity of hip-hop and rap among white suburban consumers. It should come as no surprise, therefore, that we see traces of international influence in all walks of American life and that many nations around the world embrace elements of U.S. culture in return. Perhaps it is this common ground and desire to share cultural knowledge and pleasure that give some of us the most hope for a less competitive future.

Simulated Tourism at Busch Gardens: The Old Country and Disney's World Showcase, EPCOT Center

LAWRENCE MINTZ

Lawrence E. Mintz was educated at the University of South Carolina and Michigan State University, and he is now Associate Professor and Director Art Gliner Center for Humor Studies at the University of Maryland. Professor Mintz is especially interested in the role of ethnicity in popular culture and humor. His published articles include "Humor and Ethnic Stereotypes in Vaudeville and Burlesque," "The Standup Comedian as Social and Cultural

*Mediator," and "Unity and Diversity in American Humor." In this
essay Lawrence Mintz examines how two American theme parks
have attempted to re-create a sense of culture and location from elsewhere in the world, focusing on the effect that a recontextualization
of these elements will have. On the other hand, he states that the
pleasure of such parks and recreations is undeniable. This article
has been edited for length.*

◆

The idea of recreating Europe or "the old country" in a
nostalgic, even mythopoetic, construct is profoundly familiar in our culture, from the accidental recreation of ethnic
enclaves in urban ghettoes, Little Italys, China Towns, Little
Polands, and many Irish and the Jewish neighborhoods in virtually all of our large cities, among the more prominent examples,
to more consciously constructed tourist remakes such as
Solvang, California's Danish town and the several Little
Bavarias, Little Hollands, Little Switzerlands et al. dotting the
landscape. We love to use European and other foreign motifs in
our vernacular architecture, adding Spanish or Middle Eastern
motifs to our shopping malls, gas stations, or just about anywhere we can find a place to anchor the iconic clues.
A *Washington Post* writer, John F. Kelly, suggested in a *Weekend*
section special, "The Continent Next Door: Europe on 10 Strolls
a Day," that one might visit Italy, England, France, Germany,
China (stretching Europe, a bit) . . . with a few side trips, all
while staying as close to home as one might (2 Sept. 1988: 6–8).
Such simulations acknowledge the power of our sense of our
immigrant roots, the cultural significance we award to our par-
ent nations, and our taste for the exotic; it co-exists with our
other simulations, of colonial America, of the Old West, and so
forth, as means by which we establish and communicate our
mythic personal, community and national identities.

    Theme parks that simulate tourist experience, most notably
Walt Disney World-EPCOT Center's World Showcase but including such parks as Busch Garden's The Old Country, near
Williamsburg, Virginia, and other, less ambitious recreations of
Europe, Africa, the Old West and just about any other place one
might want to visit, present a special case of tourism. They are
tours within tours, i.e., the tourist travels to the park to travel
within the park. For that matter, in a visit to both World Showcase
and The Old Country, one travels to the park, then travels within

the park by cable car, boat, monorail, etc. to reach specific desti-
nations, and then "rides" each attraction, by transport which is
either entertainment in its own right or means of locomotion
through an exhibit. In World Showcase's Norway attraction, for
instance, a boat ride offers a rather tame version of a North Sea
voyage en route to transportation via film and artifact exhibition
to that country's past as well as present. A particularly amusing
case of the layering of travel within travel is provided by The Old
Country's Marco Polo's journey, a ride with a Turkish motif within
the visit to the Italy sector! Only in America.

   Perhaps the most disorienting thing about Busch
Gardens: The Old Country is its location in Williamsburg,
Virginia, or as their promotional literature puts it, "surrounded
by Colonial Williamsburg and Jamestown." While a visit to
Busch Gardens does not necessarily imply a visit to Colonial
Williamsburg (or vice versa), it is assumed that many if not most
tourists visit both attractions as part of the same trip. The two
attractions were quite nervous about this "odd bedfellows"
phenomenon, when Busch Gardens: The Old Country opened in
1975, since Colonial Williamsburg has so much invested in its
educational and inspirational potential and in the "authenticity"
of its restoration and research programs. However, now they
seem to have a more comfortable, well, let us say less uneasy, relationship, fueled no doubt by the realization that they mutually
benefit one another. There may even be a growing if grudging
acceptance by Colonial Williamsburg that in the areas of entertainment and visitor services at least, its functions are not all that
different from those of its more frankly commercial neighbor.

   Busch Gardens: The Old Country is one of several parks oper-
ated by Anheuser-Busch, brewers of Budweiser, Michelob and
other American mass-market beers. The first Busch Gardens, The
Dark Continent, opened in 1959, in Tampa, Florida, conceived as
a botanical garden and zoo adjunct to the brewery, a private park
built as a public service, community-relations gambit. Success led
to its growth into a theme park, with an African motif largely
submerged into a naturalist-environmentalist theme, and
together with the rides and other entertainments expectable for
the genre. Other Busch Gardens, in Los Angeles and Houston,
failed in the 1970s. The juxtaposition of the parks with active
breweries is another cognitive disruption, or at least it is potentially jarring, joining a family ice cream and coke environment
with a brewery tour and the celebration of beer drinking (promotional literature proudly informs us that 16,000 pounds of fudge,

3 million soft drinks, 40,000 gallons of ice cream—and 31,000 cases of beer—are consumed each season). Visitors to the brewery get a quick, unguided walk through, witnessing the process from distant catwalks and behind glass. At the end of the tour, samples are provided, one to each adult customer (though one of the unofficial amusements at the park for teenagers is to try and get a beer, and for adults to see how many free beers they can obtain).

Busch Gardens: The Old Country covers 360 acres or .58 square miles and it serves some 2 million visitors yearly. The park is divided into sectors: England's Banbury Cross and Hastings, Scotland's Heatherdowns; France's Acquataine; New France which is named so as not to violate the Old Country theme, but actually is Canada; Italy's San Marco and Festa Italia; and Germany's Rheinland and Oktoberfest. Each sector sports clichéd architectural clues and familiar tourist icons to establish its national identity, thus Banbury Cross is cued up by Tudor architecture (sort of) and red London telephone booths, New France has log cabins, San Marcos has statues and fountains, and in a particularly amusing touch, France is falling apart (artificial cracks in the sides of the buildings!). Each sector offers its own selection of Rides and Attractions, including those for small children as well as some rather challenging roller coasters and other thrill rides. The rides are given trappings which are intended to contribute to the theme atmosphere, and names such as The Loch Ness Monster, Drachen Fire, Le Mans Raceway to remind revelers that they are indeed aboard abroad. Food options, most of the fast food variety and not very ambitious even in the sit-down restaurants, include pizza, burgers, barbecue, roast beef sandwiches, fried chicken, french fries and other basic American commercial cuisine, contexted as representing an ethnic dining experience as a part of the visit to the country (i.e., pizza is to be found in Italy, barbecue in New France, etc.). Shopping for souvenirs and rather schlocky imported gifts (kitsch) is likewise contexted by the offering of ordinary products such as cigarette lighters or coin purses which have been decorated, superficially, to make them appear as though they are manufactured in and representative of the crafts of the "countries" in which they were purchased (rather than, more probably, in Taiwan). Ironically, such shopping might be viewed as a realistic modem tourist touch, as genuine native crafts become harder to find and to afford and are replaced by cheaply mass-manufactured junk. One might find, for instance, just the kind of trinkets available in Busch Gardens omnipresent in Paris, for sale near all of the major tourist sites. Rest-amenities such as benches and scenic views, bridges, ponds, lakes, and pleasant park-garden settings are an important feature, and clean, efficient personal services for the comfort of the guests are readily available.

Shows at Busch Gardens: The Old Country have only the vaguest of themes, with the exception of Oktoberfest as discussed below. The Globe Theater, which when the park first opened, offered a fascinating pastiche of Shakespeare's plays, blended into a magic show, light show, extended skit, has more recently degenerated into a variety show distinguished from the shows in the other sectors only by costume, badly rendered accent, and thinly applied motif. The concert and shows division of Busch Gardens: The Old Country is perhaps its weakest, though it is hard to say whether this is a failure on the part of the management or a concession to audience tastes for simple, bland, light variety entertainment. The show in Italy, for another instance, is a set of popular Italian-American classics like "That's Amore" with mercifully brief snatches of Bel Canto. The young performers are clean cut and earnest in the classic American style. They appear to be a little embarrassed at their awkward ethnic charade!

Perhaps the most interesting attraction at Busch Gardens: The Old Country is Oktoberfest, an attraction reproduced from one created for the original Busch Gardens in Tampa, Florida (a simulation of a simulation!), where its connection to the Dark Continent, through German imperialism perhaps, is more of a stretch than its reference to the brewery. Oktoberfest, referring to the German harvest celebration in late September-early October which Americans tend to associate primarily with Munich and Bavaria, is held in Das Festhaus, a very large, barn-like building, nicely decorated with an attractive, gigantic stained glass window above an authentic antique automated organ.

Oktoberfesters file into a cafeteria area where they purchase platters of wurst with kraut and German potato salad or huge corned beef sandwiches, topped off by slices of Black Forest cake that are entirely without flavor and have the texture of Wonder Bread, and washed down by beer or soft drinks served in paper cups. They then take seats at large picnic style tables encircling the stage and dance area. While dining, they are entertained by a rather authentic-looking German elder, dressed in lederhosen, drinking from an authentic beer stein, feebly warbling Edelweiss and other genuine examples of the famed teutonic musical genius. After a few minutes, an oompah-pah band and some young dancers whose visages would have brought tears of joy to

Hitler's face march in. As the band is installed in a circular band-stand which ascends into the heavens, a narrator informs the audience that they are about to experience "gemiitlichkeit," the spirit of joy, abandon, and community spirit. Toward that end, visitors are encouraged to shake hands with everyone at their table within reach. Twelve minutes or so of waltzes and polkas, audience participation encouraged by the dance troupe's selection of suitably cute partners from among the guests, and the experience is over, and on to the next adventure.

Busch Gardens: The Old Country is about a pleasant day of varied amusements in a comfortable environment. As a place for relaxed visual stimulation, it is perhaps not as far from a European experience as it would first seem, in the spirit of Margaret King's observation that "in fact Americans go to Europe largely for the charming cities—for public spaces like the Italian piazza which is human and pedestrian in scale, encouraging the outdoor stroll and public relaxation . . . and the sidewalk cafes which encourage 'people watching'." Busch Gardens: The Old Country offers a safe, clean, comfortable simulation of the cosmopolitan ethos.

The park's diversity encourages family participation. There is something for everyone from a very young child to grandpar-ents, and it is safe to let reasonably young kids wander alone, checking in at designated times and places. Teenagers can travel in groups of peers, young couples can find privacy while sur-rounded by hundreds of others. The Old Country does not overtly claim to be a learning experience or a pilgrimage. Indeed, in that sense it downplays its own theme of European travel. The various theme sectors of the park provide mild visual variety without disturbing the familiar rhythms, the com-fort in formula and familiarity, and the realized expectations on which the genre depends. Visitors know what to expect in each area and from each activity, whether it is the rides or the shop-ping or the dining experience. Yet the park is successful in its suggestion of novelty, of variety rather than redundancy as one moves from England to Italy to France to Germany to Scotland. Though superficial, the environmental changes enhance the sense of adventure, of an escape from the ordinary world into a realm of vacation and recreation. That the same basic formula is repeated in each realm, disguised by the trappings and icons which simulate the local color, is an underlying popular culture verity. The experience is comfortingly familiar, unthreatening, immediately understood and appreciated, yet the illusion of freshness is maintained and apparently accepted. The references to the various ethnic and national identities all confirm universal expectation, that is they are based on familiar clichés and stereotypes. They are clearly intended to be atmosphere, background, more than simulation in any active sense. At Busch Gardens: The Old Country, the trip in-a-sense-abroad is a vacation, an amusement, an opportunity for pleasure.

The World Showcase at Walt Disney World's EPCOT Center is a more ambitious and in a sense more pretentious enterprise. As information provided by the park's educator's center proclaims, "If the look of tomorrow of Future World is the heart of EPCOT Center, then World Showcase with its kaleidoscope of international experience—is surely the soul." The promotional flyer heads into the storm of the simulation controversy with no quarter offered: "Situated around a 40-acre lagoon beyond Future World, the World Showcase nations are re-creations of landmark architectures and historic scenes familiar to world travelers. Built with finite attention to detail, the mini-towns have buildings, streets, gardens and monuments designed to give EPCOT Center guests an *authentic* visual experience of each land" (emphasis added). It could be that World Showcase's location within EPCOT demands a seriousness of purpose greater than if it were located in The Magic Kingdom or a self-contained park, in a relationship analogous to that which Busch Gardens: The Old Country derives from its proximity to Colonial Williamsburg.

In any case, it is truly a more carefully constructed physical simulation than one would expect to find in any other theme park. The Disney organization put an enormous amount of effort—and money—into the materials, the design, and the construction of the World Showcase, and as Ada Louise Huxtable suggested of Colonial Williamsburg, the technological and artistic ("craftistique"?) quality of the recreation might be in fact more significant than its content. The quality extends to the goods and services available. The shopping at World Showcase is of a higher order than at most theme parks, though merely by degree rather than in kind. It is still souvenirs and gifts; they are just better trinkets. The fast food is also of the same order but better than one finds elsewhere. World Showcase's gourmet restaurants, however, issue a challenge comparable to that made by the park itself, as "authentic" tourism. L'Originale Alfredo di Roma Ristorante, the Biergarten, Restaurant Marrakesh, Chefs de France and Bistro de Paris lay claim to originality and top quality. The view of this writer, a well-traveled food lover and amateur chef, is that while they do not quite make it as four-star, come-for the-food attractions, they come amazingly close considering the challenges they face. Any gourmet restaurant would be daunted by having to serve as many seatings with as many meals and by the time-constraints posed by customers with agendas and priorities other than the dining experience. There are also financial limits; while the restaurants are much more expensive than those at any other theme park, they are still considerably less expensive than most first class, gourmet establishments. At the very least, one must acknowledge that as providers of "theme park fare," the restaurants at World Showcase are remarkably admirable.

World Showcase does not rely on exciting rides or participatory games and activities. Rather, it offers tours and exhibitions, in a most interesting way paralleling the definition of tourism which stresses information and inspiration as the paramount goals. The tourist visiting the park's Mexico sector, for instance, is cast in the role of a tourist, given a brief and very superficial survey of that country's history and an equally brief introduction to its tourist attractions, which are dwarfed by the enormous, adjacent Mexican bazaar. This creates the impression that Mexico's primary reason for existence is the revenue which is provided by tourists. The presentation of the dominant national image in the other lands is generally less demeaning than it is in the Mexico sector, to be fair, but the basic theme is that the countries of the world are places which are interesting for us to see, charming diversions for our shopping and dining pleasure.

Whatever lessons about native cultures are to be learned are self-gleaned from reading the annotations on some of the artifact displays (e.g., in Morocco, China, Norway, Japan). The films which are the highlights in several of the sectors are wonderfully done, true visual treats, especially the Circle-Vision 360 presentation "Wonders of China" and the "Impressions of France" sensual audio-visual delight, but they too rely on the spectacular sensory effect rather than any significant social or cultural communication. We see the countryside, some of the landmarks, faces of the people, and we hear music and soothing narration. Germany, England, and Italy are the flimsiest excuses for gawking at the architectural effects and shopping, with casual entertainment which is not much more ambitious than that which one might find at Busch Gardens: The Old Country. Despite the well-publicized fact that World Showcase employs natives of the various lands (who are issued special green cards by The U.S. Immigration Service toward that end), there is no real opportunity to engage in a serious encounter with the people or the culture of any of the simulated lands. Perhaps not surprisingly, the only sector where the visitor learns something about the culture, society, politics, or people to be encountered is the American Adventure! There is much less learning here than in any National Geographic feature, to say nothing of a more extensive stay abroad, but again the case may be made that the experience is closer to the actual package tour experienced by many Americans as the one "trip of a lifetime" to Europe. For all of its quality of detail, World Showcase is neither more informative, more stimulating, more inspiring, nor more fun than Busch Gardens: The Old Country. It may indeed be the quiet respite from the more exciting Magic Kingdom or the newer MGM and Universal Studios parks and from the intellectual appeal made by EPCOT's Future World. Once again, it seems as though tourism emerges as a pleasant, amusing vacation activity rather than anything invested with a higher purpose.

The question is: why should it be anything more than a pleasant, relaxing, entertaining experience? If we make some largely false assumptions about the value of tourism and reason from them that the theme park simulations propose but fail to provide the "proper" tourist experience, and/or if we speculate that the simulations replace the impulse for actual tourism or more extensive travel for their audience, we can come to the conclusion that time spent in-a-sense abroad is not well-spent. If we wonder why trips to these parks, especially to Walt Disney World, seem to be so highly valued, so prominent and even monumental in the lives of American consumers, why we are willing to spend as much money on them as we do, or why our heroes declare a trip to Disney World as their reward for victory, we will not find an answer by uncovering a hidden or over-looked profundity in the theme park formula. Indeed, it is the evaluation of the simulated tourism experience according to a mythic set of standards and assumptions about the meaning of tourism which inevitably misleads. If, however, we focus on what the parks actually deliver, on their mildly stimulating, for-mulaic, predictable, safe, clean amusement, on the opportunity for shopping for worthless but inexpensive goods and for eating convenient and comforting if mediocre food, we can properly understand the nature of simulated tourism. "It's the entertain-ment, stupid."

Questions for Discussion and Writing

1. What is the responsibility (if any) for designers of theme parks like EPCOT's World Showcase or The Old Country to avoid stereotyping or representational simplicity in the depiction of other nations?
2. Discuss and explain the point that Mintz is making about the positioning of The Old Country in relation to Colonial Williamsburg.
3. Do theme parks such as the ones discussed here have any other purpose than to provide entertainment? What does Mintz think? How do you know?
4. Imagine that you are designing a pavilion to represent the United States at a theme park. What elements would you include and why? What would you want the pavilion to look like? How big would it have to be? Who would staff it to represent the United States?

Degas in Vegas

ARTHUR C. DANTO

Arthur C. Danto, born in 1924, was raised in Michigan and studied art and history at Wayne University (now Wayne State University) and then at Columbia University, New York City. He is now the Johnsonian Professor of Philosophy at Columbia. He has been art critic for The Nation *since 1984. His publications include* Encounters and Reflections: Art in the Historical Present *(1990), which won the National Book Critics Circle Award for Criticism;* Playing with the Edge: The Photographic Achievement of Robert Mapplethorpe *(1995); and* The Madonna of the Future: Essays in a Pluralistic Art World *(2000). In this article (published on March 1, 1999), Dr. Danto addresses the subject of simulation in Las Vegas, Nevada. He talks about Steve Wynn's decision to display genuine works by artistic masters within the artificial construct of a Las Vegas skyline that reproduces great architecture from around the world for the pleasure of tourists.*

◆

From various of the Italianate terraces of the Bellagio hotel in Las Vegas, looking over an artificial lake, girdled by balustrades no less Italianate and meant to be emblematic of Como, one may see a half-scale simulacrum of the Eiffel Tower rapidly rising across the Strip. The tower is to be one element in a complex of simulative monuments and buildings, to be called "Paris" when it opens later this year. The Arc de Triomphe is already in place, as well as a fragment of a sixteenth-century chateau; another structure—still screened by its scaffolding—may turn out to be the Madeleine or even the Gare Saint-Lazare. Farther north along the Strip, a similar complex, this time of Venetian landmarks, is under construction, with the Ca' d'Oro nearly completed and the tower of San Marco not far behind. To the south, "New York-New York" has been open to the public since 1997: The Chrysler Building is nearly adjacent to a stunted Empire State Building; Lady Liberty, with two New York Harbor tugboats at her feet, looms over the Brooklyn Bridge; steam plumes up from manhole covers—but one encounters vast ranks of gambling devices upon entering a cavernous Grand Central Station. The sense is irrepressible that before long, Las Vegas will be an architectural theme park, in which every edifice known to popular visual culture—Chartres, the Golden Pavilion (Kinkakuji), the Stone Garden of Kyoto (Ryoanji), the Taj Mahal, the White House, the Houses of Parliament, the Golden Gate Bridge, the Colosseum—will have its simulacrum. That leaves the question of whether any of Las Vegas's own buildings would find a place in that landscape of monumentary knockoffs. Caesars Palace, perhaps, since it itself replicates no known structure of Imperial Rome but stands as a fantasy, inspired partly by the Vittorio Emanuele monument and partly by *Ben-Hur.* Or perhaps one of the rapidly disappearing "decorated shacks" that so stimulated the architects Robert Venturi and Denise Scott Brown when they wrote the classic of postmodernism, *Learning From Las Vegas.*

It would be reasonable to suppose that were some entrepreneur to undertake an art museum in the Las Vegas spirit, it might be called The Museum of Museums, and feature simulacra of all the world's masterpieces—*Mona Lisa, Portrait of the Artist's Mother* (Whistler's Mother), *The Night Watch, The Creation of Adam, Gold Marilyn,* Piero's *Resurrection,* Raphael's *The Transfiguration,* the Bayeux Tapestry, *Les Demoiselles d'Avignon.* Why chase across continents, from museum to museum, when everything one would have gone to see is here in one place, brush stroke by brush stroke, indistinguishable from the prototypes? What difference does it make, visually speaking? One only expects "Reality-Las Vegas" in Las Vegas—like the artificial volcano that rumbles and erupts every fifteen minutes each evening in front of the Mirage, the concrete Trojan Horse at FAO Schwarz or the golden Sphinx, with laser lights for eyes, beaming toward the fabricated pyramid in front of the Luxor Casino and Hotel—and everything is advertised as Magical, Enchanted, Fantastic, Fabulous or Incredible. One does not expect to encounter Reality as such, where things are what they are and not something else they merely look like.

In consequence, visitors are not entirely secure in viewing what it is not hype to describe as the world-class paintings hung in the Bellagio Gallery of Fine Art. Steve Wynn, whose conception the gallery is, asks, "Why, of all things to feature in a new resort hotel in Las Vegas (of all places!) would one select an enormously costly and potentially limited-appeal attraction such as a serious fine-art presentation of paintings and sculptures?" Why indeed, when the possibility of simulacra indiscernible from the originals exists in principle, and visitors only expect "Reality-Las Vegas" to begin with. When it first opened some months ago, an interviewer from a Las Vegas newspaper questioned me on whether I thought it entirely suitable that there should be an art gallery in a site given over mainly to gambling. Well, casinos vie with one another to attract patrons: Approaching the Bellagio, one passes a looming sign: "Now Appearing: van Gogh. Monet. Cézanne. Picasso," just the way other "now appearing" signs announce Cirque du Soleil or Andrew "Dice" Clay. So Wynn has gambled that a significant population would be as attracted by van Gogh, Monet, Cézanne and Picasso as by the magicians, stand-up comics, feminine extravaganzas and impersonators that form the city's standard repertoire of distractions and entertainments. For that population, of course, the art included must be as familiar a part of visual culture as the Eiffel Tower or the Chrysler Building. Those who have taken Art History 101 and traveled a bit are able to tell a Monet from a Cézanne, a Modigliani from a Matisse, a Picasso from a Pissarro, a Degas from anyone else—even if the paintings themselves have not attained the canonical status required by my imagined Museum of Museums. My interviewer asked if I thought the paintings were *real*. That, she said, was what "folks out here really want to know."

I thought it strange that people worry about the reality of the art when reality is required of little else in Las Vegas. "The popular question that seems to have overshadowed the lively speculation about the Bellagio Gallery itself," Wynn writes, "seems to be 'Why?'" I don't think the overwhelming question is "Why paintings?" so much as "Why real paintings?" when "Reality-Las

Vegas" suffices for Paris and Venice. What business does real art have in Las Vegas when we can imagine the Museum of Museums on an ontological footing with "New York-New York"? It struck me that the anxiety the question of reality implies could almost only have been provoked by Las Vegas: In a lifetime of visiting museums and galleries, I have never once wondered if what I was about to see was real. So what is at stake in the Bellagio? And what does it tell us about viewing art? At the very least, real paintings constitute a critique of Las Vegas through the fact that they *are* real. To have installed a collection of real masters is already to have taken a step toward the transformation of Las Vegas from a theme park to something that addresses the "higher sensibilities" of people "who would not easily be fooled by advertising or hype." One outcome of such a transformation would be that the question of whether what one was looking at was real would be as taken for granted as it is everywhere else.

Wynn is impressed by the fact that "attendance at museums in the past few years has exceeded attendance at professional sporting events throughout the U.S.A." So presumably there are enough aesthetic pilgrims in the country (and elsewhere in the world—one hears dozens of different languages in Bellagio's lobby) to put Las Vegas on their map if there were a superlative collection of art to draw them there. But would enough of them come to Las Vegas ("of all places!") to justify assembling a collection that cost $300 million, let alone the expense of presenting and maintaining the art, and turning a profit besides? The question is not without substance. Las Vegas not long ago decided that "family values" pointed the way to profit. Thus the theme-park atmosphere, where factitious monuments can be thought of at once as fun and educational, and the inexpensive buffets—Las Vegas's contribution to dining—that make it possible to bring the kids along. It *is* fun, a kind of toyland full of crazy surprises, a Disneyland with slots. But the family-values crowd is not made up of big spenders or high rollers, and the profits have apparently not materialized. Besides, as Wynn observes, "All the old ideas of resort attractions have become, well, just old." Hence the bold idea of a gallery of fine art as an attraction, and hence the possibility of changing the whole concept of Las Vegas. Suppose that "under the circumstances of today's very competitive world leisure market" other Las Vegas resorts add galleries of their own? Already, the Rio has become a venue for "The Treasures of Russia"—real enough but objects of a kind compatible with the fantasized atmosphere of "Reality-Las Vegas," and hardly the classy drawing card the Bellagio Gallery aspires to be. The more such galleries the better, one might think. But can we imagine Las Vegas as a true art center, even if every casino were to follow suit and build a collection?

In a small way, the city already is an art center, consisting of at least a number of exhibiting artists, initially drawn to the graduate fine-arts program at the University of Nevada, Las Vegas, to work with the legendary art critic and theoretician Dave Hickey. There are no real art galleries to speak of in Las Vegas, other than the somewhat awful emporia one encounters when strolling along the various streets of shops attached to the casinos, which display in their windows objects it would be punishing to have to live with if one thirsted to be in the presence of what Wynn calls "singular creative energy." For various reasons, the artists have remained in Las Vegas, traveling to the coasts or to Europe, where their work is exhibited and sold. In a "Top Ten" guest column in the January *Artforum*, Las Vegas artist Jeffrey Vallance begins by praising "the fabulous Bellagio casino": "Right on the Strip you can see Cézanne, Degas, Gauguin, Manet, Monet, van Gogh, Picasso, Pollock, Rauschenberg, and Warhol." (It is striking that Vallance mentions painters and not paintings—nothing in the gallery would be in candidacy for simulation in the Museum of Museums, for the same reason that few of us are likely to have waxen effigies of ourselves in Madame Tussaud's museum of world personalities, however exemplary we are as people. The important thing is that the art is by artists who have also produced masterpieces by Museum of Museums criteria.) I decided to devote an afternoon to local studio visits, guided by the Rev. Ethan Acres, an artist whose work is shown in Los Angeles and New York. The Reverend—a real Southern Baptist minister—aims, as an artist, to "put the fun back in fundamentalism," and once a week he walks the Strip to preach the gospel in the good old Southern way he learned in Alabama, which he regards as no less religious for being performance art. I was impressed with the quality and interest of everything he took me to see, but it is safe to say that none of it would claim a place in the Bellagio Gallery of Fine Art, not least of all because, as with contemporary art in general, it affords very little by way of a glimpse of beauty.

But there is an important connection between the Las Vegas art scene and the Bellagio Gallery. The latter's collection is made up of works, many of which it would be worthwhile to travel some distance to see—the Miró *Dialogue of Insects*, for example, or Modigliani's marvelous portrait of his dealer, Paul Guillaume. There is Willem de Kooning's great *Police Gazette* and a luminous painting of a peasant woman by van Gogh. A Degas of a dancer accepting a bouquet has not been on public view for decades. And everything is deeply authenticated, to settle the question of reality certain to arise in the context. But surely the gallery is not primarily in place to attract specialists and connoisseurs, and one cannot help wondering, whatever the quality, whether by itself it could draw the numbers and kinds of visitors it is intended to do. Those with money enough to stay at the Bellagio have their choice of the world's centers of fine art to visit. So why visit Las Vegas? The answer is obvious. No one, except those professionally involved in the art world, visits distant places for the art alone. They may come for the art primarily, but they are interested in fine restaurants, in shopping, in entertainment. So in an important sense, plain old unreconstructed Las Vegas is in a synergetic relationship with the Gallery of Fine Art, giving tourists the extra incentive to undertake the trip. What I had not figured in until I got there was a phenomenon of contemporary museum culture: the art tour. The mere existence of the Bellagio collection makes Las Vegas a destination for museum tours from Los Angeles, Santa Barbara and elsewhere—and the mere existence of Las Vegas itself gives the added incentive to subscribe to them. Everybody benefits, and there is even a fallout for the Las Vegas artists. Tour groups really are interested in art, and the curators who lead them will typically be interested in the kinds of contemporary expression produced there. So impromptu exhibitions are arranged and, as often as not, tourists return home with examples of Las Vegas art, as well as with whatever they may have found irresistible in such boutiques as Prada, Chanel, Armani, Gucci, Tiffany & Co. and the other *marchands de luxe* on "Via Bellagio."

In 1963 the world's youngest island erupted into being from the ocean floor in Iceland. It is used as a natural laboratory, enabling scientists to study and observe the stages by which life arrives on a stony tabula rasa of mere rocks. I felt that I was observing something like that in Las Vegas—the formation of an art world. Hickey accepted a job at the university, perhaps to liberate himself from the precariousness of running a gallery of contemporary art and writing freelance criticism. Artists who knew his writing came to work in the graduate program and stayed on, as much perhaps for what Las Vegas offered as for the support they gave one another, and for the kinds of day jobs available to them while making their name: Las Vegas employs as many sculptors as papal Rome. I met one who earns his living executing styrofoam and fiberglass statuary for "The Venetian" hotel.

Reverend Acres told me that when he first arrived, at 4 in the morning, he encountered two Elvis impersonators walking along the Strip holding hands, and he knew immediately that Las Vegas was his kind of city. The January/February *Art issues* shows him on the cover, preaching in a white suit in front of the Bellagio, uniting the art scene and the gallery of notable paintings in a single vision that defines Art-Las Vegas. I imagine Wynn would be indifferent to the local art, though its unforeseen existence may ultimately contribute to his gallery's success. So one had better go slow in transforming Las Vegas—man does not live by higher sensibilities alone. I am still uncertain that art alone, even when part of a hotel that exemplifies "the world as it might be if everything were just right," would bring the required numbers of art lovers. The gallery needs Las Vegas-Las Vegas to make a go of it as a high-cultural attraction. The question is whether the gallery's presence will transform the resort into something higher. Las Vegas is a convention city. Perhaps it should think of hosting an annual art fair!

Wynn himself is about as improbable a compound as Las Vegas with a serious art collection—a showman and a businessman, but also an aesthete, passionately responsive to art. (Warhol did a triple portrait of him in 1983, so he has not just jumped onto the bandwagon of art.) I was able to spend about two hours with him and his curator, Libby Lumpkin, talking about the paintings he has acquired and examining transparencies of works Wynn has his eye on. The gallery has lately added two old masters—a stunning painting by Rubens of Salome in a silken gown receiving the gory head of John the Baptist and a Rembrandt portrait of a mustachioed man in a frogged scarlet tunic. Wynn aims to have exemplary works from each century since the Renaissance. Only someone of the greatest energy and means would have been able to put together, in just three years, an art collection of such quality, given the way the market for Impressionism is. But he is a businessman to his toes, and I cannot for a moment imagine him doing that if he could not justify it on the bottom line. He might not have done it except for the money—but it was not for the money alone that he did it. The gallery is intended at once to be a benefit and to make money, oddly parallel to the way Reverend Acres's sermons are meant to be art and to save souls. The art world is hopeful but cynical, and nothing better testifies to Wynn's status as an outsider than the degree of his optimism and the absence of cynicism. Only someone combining a fierce business drive with an extreme passion for and belief in art would have supposed he could do well by doing good, bringing great art to what Vallance calls "the people."

This combination explains many of the incongruities and anomalies of the Bellagio hotel. A pair of marvelous de Koonings hang on either side of the registration desk, for example. An impressive collection of (real) Picassos—paintings and ceramics—enlivens the walls of Bellagio's flagship restaurant, Picasso. Contrary to the rumor, none of the gallery's works are displayed in gambling precincts, though I was told that before its spaces were ready to receive them, paintings were hung where the high rollers—who are known locally as "whales"—gamble in privacy at the Mirage. But the paintings were there because security is understandably tight, not as a way of enhancing the experience of playing poker or shooting dice. Where better to store paintings worth $20 million each? As if to make the distinction vivid between Bellagio's two functions, one can visit the gallery without even having to pass through the gaming area, whereas in every other casino I visited, the urgent electronic chirping of the slots and the exhilarating crash of silver coins greet you the minute you walk through the door. Instead, you approach the gallery at the far end of the opulently planted conservatory, which varies its floral displays to mark the seasons' changes (there are, of course, no such changes in the surrounding desert). During my stay, the Christmas display gave way to a planting that celebrated the Chinese New Year. The paths to the gallery and to the gaming area are at right angles, as if one must decide which path to follow. The complex connection between money and art, meanwhile, is embodied in the curious fact that everything in the gallery is for sale—though, that this policy can endure for very long, given the inherent scarcity of, well, blue-chip art, is hard to imagine.

Before leaving Las Vegas, I wanted a photograph of the "Now Appearing" sign with van Gogh's name on it. A man rushed out of the shadows, heading toward the Strip, shouting over his shoulder, "He only sold one painting in his *whole life!*" I wondered if he were a painter himself, when it struck me that this *triste* truth of van Gogh's life is a moral legend for us all. However outwardly like frogs we are, there is within us a prince or princess whose golden merit will one day be visible to all. That, I thought, was why it was so important that the art be real. It would not be a redemption for van Gogh that a reproduction of one of his paintings, however exact, should hang in Las Vegas, where the only thing real other than art is money. In the game of life, any of us can become big winners. I conclude, brethren, with words by the Reverend Ethan Acres, describing an encounter between Steve Wynn and the Devil. The Devil says, "Hey Steve, hey buddy old pal, c'mon, who's gonna come to this town, *my* town, to look at a bunch of girlie paintings?

Listen, my man, what you need in Bellagio is a roller coaster, or better yet, just ditch the whole Italian crap and go with the Titanic as a theme." . . . Yes, the Devil offered him the easy road, but moved by God, Steven A. Wynn made his highway the hard way. . . . Flesh over paper, substance over style. Hallelluiah!

Questions for Discussion and Writing.

1. Dr. Danto asks, "Why chase across continents, from museum to museum, when everything one would have gone to see is here in one place, brush stroke by brush stroke, indistinguishable from the prototypes"? The same could be asked of the re-creations of Paris and Venice. Write an argument for going to Las Vegas to see the simulacra rather than traveling to see the real cities.
2. Because Las Vegas seems to be so "fake" we immediately question the things there, like Steve Wynn's art collection, that are said to be "real." Is this blending of the real and the fake dangerous or is it instead something that encourages us to value the real even more than the fake?
3. Have you been to Las Vegas or do you know someone who has? Where did they stay? Did the re-creation of a certain country or culture play a role in that decision? If you haven't been to Las Vegas, go online and look at the websites for the Venetian, Paris, New York-New York, and the Luxor. Would the re-creation of any of these world visions attract your attention more than the others? Why?
4. Explain Steve Wynn's intentions in bringing "real" works of great art and displaying them in Las Vegas. What does he hope to achieve by having elements of world culture on show within "false" re-creations of those very cultures that produced the art in the first place?

We Are What We Eat: We Are a Nation of Immigrants!
DAVID ROSENGARTEN

David Rosengarten is an authority on food, wine, and cooking and the author of the cookbook, Taste, *which won the IACP Award for Best International Cookbook. He is a frequent host on the Food Network and producer of the* Rosengarten Report, *a newsletter about food. His articles about food, wine, travel, and restaurants have appeared in* The New York Times,

Gourmet, Food & Wine, *and* Bon Appétit, *among many other publications. He lives in New York City. This article appeared in* eJournal USA: U.S. Society and Values, *produced by the Department of State, in July 2004. In it David Rosengarten examines how different cultural cuisines have been combined and co-opted to produce what we now know as American food.*

✦

Numerous influences have affected the development of cuisine in the United States. Native Americans are credited with making corn a major ingredient in the national diet. Early immigrants from China and Italy, as well as slaves from Africa, all contributed to the development of foods that Americans commonly eat today. The absence of royalty, a motivating force for culinary inventiveness in other countries, coupled with the "stoic, utilitarian sensibility" of the Puritan Ethic, may have hindered development of fine cuisine during the country's early decades, but adoption and adaptation of dishes brought by new waves of immigrants over the decades have sparked a richness and diversity in the fare on America's dinner tables and in its restaurants.

American food has been woefully misunderstood around the world by those who view it from a distance only. "Americans eat hamburgers, no?" would be the typical perspective overseas on what Americans consume—and it wouldn't be wrong! We do love our hamburgers, and our hot dogs, and other simple, emblematic treats. However, we love many other things as well. And with ever-growing good reason. For the vast patchwork of comestibles that is "American" cooking today is one of the most vital cuisines in the world, owing its vitality, in large part, to the same element that built the strength of America in other ways—the arrival on these shores of immigrants from virtually all over the globe, immigrants who were able to combine the talents and perspectives they brought from other countries with the day-to-day realities and logistics of American life. Finally, today, food-savvy people everywhere are recognizing the high quality of what's now being cooked in America—but it took many years for that level of quality, and that recognition, to develop.

Why? Well, truth be told, the deck has historically been stacked against gastronomic America. For starters, the Native Americans, the long-time inhabitants of this continent who established their American civilization well before the first Europeans arrived, were not ideally positioned to begin building a national cuisine. The very size of this country, and the spread-out nature of Native-American culture, militated against culinary progress, which is so dependent on the cross-fertilization of ideas. In old France, for example, a culinary idea could blow into Paris with the weekly mail from Lyon—but the likelihood of culinary ideas from the Seminoles in Florida and the Pueblos in the Rocky Mountains merging into something national was far more remote. The absence of great cities in the landscape of the Native Americans also worked against gastronomic development— because time has proven that the rubbing of shoulders in a large urban environment is beneficial to the rise of great cooking.

Additionally, American cooking always lacked the motivating drive of royalty (which is part of our national charm!). Cuisines in France, in Italy, in Spain, in Persia, in northern India, in Thailand, in Beijing were all heavily inspired by the necessity of creating "national" food for the royal court. This not only unified the cooking in those countries, but also boosted its complexities—as chefs attempted to outdo each other in pursuit of royal approval. Though the masses in 1788 certainly were not eating what Louis XVI ate (as his famous wife acknowledged in her most famous utterance), the cooking ideas and dishes that developed at Versailles and other royal venues over many centuries were later incorporated into what every Frenchman eats everywhere in France.

PERVASIVENESS OF CORN

Lacking such a galvanizing force, before the European arrivals American food never merged into a unified coast-to-coast phenomenon. Of course, the Native Americans made major ingredient contributions to what we eat today, particularly corn. It's fascinating to think that so many things that we do consider part of our national gastronomic life—such as corn on the cob, creamed corn, corn dogs, corn flakes, grits, tortilla chips, even our cheap American beer brewed from corn—are grounded in this ingredient preference of the early Native Americans. But did that preference lead to a "national cuisine?" By looking at neighboring Mexico—where it did lead to one—I think we can see that the answer is "no." The Spaniards who started arriving in Mexico in the 16th century didn't merely grab a good ingredient and do something else with it; they truly blended their ideas with the Native Mexican Indian ideas.

Tacos al carbon? The Spaniards brought the pork; the Indians supplied the tacos. When you eat in Mexico today, you'll find every table laid with modern versions of Indian ingredients, and Indian culinary ideas for those ingredients. You cannot say the same about the modern American table.

Later in America, other factors, deeply grounded in the modern American spirit, further conspired to stall a national culinary growth. When the Europeans first arrived, the battle for sustenance of any kind was the motif that informed the kitchen, not the quest for creativity; you cannot be inventing a grand cuisine when you're worried about which tree bark might be edible so that you can survive another day. Picture the French citizen in 1607 in Paris—grounded, entrenched, ready to inherit a cooking tradition and help it evolve. Now picture the Jamestown inhabitant, starting from scratch, permanently preoccupied with more elemental concerns.

Of course, as American civilization grew, the pioneer spirit played its own role in the delay of culinary refinement. "There's a ridge over there—we've got to see what's beyond it." And, indeed, there were many ridges between Virginia and California. Not all Americans were moving across the country in stage coaches during the 18th and 19th centuries—but the still-extant flavor of American restlessness, of American exploration, of a kind of life at odds with the "our family has been sitting near this hearth for 400 years" mentality of Europeans of the same day, once again cut against the set of values and interests that normally lead to the development of great cuisine.

SOME QUIRKY ASPECTS

It is this spirit, of course—an ethos of "eating to live" rather than "living to eat"—that has led to other quirky aspects of the traditional American food world. We have certainly led the planet in the development of "convenience" foods—both because we have had the technological ingenuity to do so, but also because we have so many citizens who "don't have time to cook." Let's face it—rice that cooks in a minute, or soup that only needs a minute in the microwave, is not going to play a role in the development of American haute cuisine.

Lastly, it has been the poor fortune of gastronomic America to have fallen under the sway, for so many years, of a mainstream American value system—the so-called Puritan Ethic. A great deal of industry and good has arisen from this set of values—but no one can ever accuse the Puritans and their descendants of fomenting the positive development of the arts, particularly the culinary arts. I remember older people in my youth—this breed is mostly gone now—who considered it grossly impolite to talk about food, even at the dinner table. You received your sustenance and you ingested it, so that you could live another day. Why would any right-thinking person discuss the way something tastes, other than for reasons of vanity? And so it played out, for hundreds of years, in New England and elsewhere—a stoic, utilitarian sensibility at the table, hardly conducive to the development of fine cuisine.

Had this nation stalled after the influx of the original Europeans in the 17th and 18th century, our culinary story may have stalled as well. However, shortly after this period, other immigrants began to arrive—and it is to these groups that we owe the rescue of the American palate, as well as the honing of the American palate into one of the finest culinary instruments in the world today.

One of our greatest national disgraces ever was also the source of many of our nation's early gastronomic triumphs: the awful transformation of free African citizens into bound American slaves. From that tragedy, however, arose a strong sensibility that had a powerful influence on the development of American culture—not to mention American cuisine. The Africans brought intriguing ingredients with them to these shores—okra, yams, peanuts (which originated in Peru, then came to North America from Africa). They dined "low on the hog"—with the slave owners taking the best parts of the pig, and the slaves left to their ingenuity to make the leftover parts tasty. And, they had a natural camaraderie with slaves who arrived from the Caribbean—who brought to this country a whole new set of spices that added tremendous zest to American cooking. The slaves and former slaves were on the scene in Charleston, South Carolina, as that city became a major spice-trading port. They were there in New Orleans, aiding in the development of one of America's most distinct regional cuisines. And they manned barbecue—or BBQ—pits all over the South, helping to develop what I surely believe to be America's most significant contribution to world cuisine.

If all of that early gastronomic activity was generated by immigrants coming in through the Southeast, a parallel activity was occurring in the Southwest—where Mexican Indians and Spanish settlers were bringing their flavors up through Mexico to Texas and New Mexico. What we ended up with in our own American Southwest was not very like what the original immigrants ate in

Mexico, or in Spain—but it became a crucial element in our national dining picture, with enchiladas and fajitas as truly American as any other dish eaten every day across America.

CHINESE AND ITALIAN DOMINANCE

By the latter half of the 19th century, the stage was set for the most important period of gastro-immigration in American history—when the Chinese immigrants and the Italian immigrants arrived. I call it supremely important, for if you go to any American city today, and open the phone book to check on the restaurants, you will find that Chinese restaurants and Italian restaurants, despite the rise in popularity of many other ethnic cuisines, still dominate the restaurant culture.

Chinese food in America, of course, has a secondary position behind Italian. It came to this country with the Chinese immigrants who arrived to work on the railroad in the West—or, rather, who came to feed those who were working on the railroad. The cooks didn't have much to work with, but they imaginatively threw together little bits of meat and vegetables in their large pans and gave it a name: chop suey. As this type of cooking hit the big cities, and spread across the country, a whole new cuisine emerged: Chinese-American, replete with Egg Rolls, Wonton Soup, Fried Rice, Chicken Chow Mein, and Spare Ribs. It never had quite the reach of the Italian-American food that was spawned a little bit later—because, though most Americans ate this food, they didn't usually try to cook it at home. However, it did accomplish something extremely significant—it opened up the minds and palates of almost every 20th-century American to the exotic allure of Asian food, paving the way for the absorption of many Asian cuisines into our national eating habits.

A bit later came the big one: Italian-American food. Around 1880, the first wave began—immigrants from Naples, arriving at Ellis Island. Before long, they were living around Mulberry Street in Manhattan, where they desperately tried to reproduce the food of their homeland. They failed, because they could not obtain the ingredients that they used back in the old country. Through sheer ingenuity, however, they made do with what they had. So what if the new dishes used dried herbs instead of fresh, canned tomatoes instead of fresh, more sauce on the pasta than is traditional, and more meat in the diet? The Italian-American cuisine that they created was magnificent—though, if you were born after 1975, you'd never know it, because the best "Italian" chefs in America today eschew Italian-American cuisine, preferring to climb ever-higher mountains of radicchio, anointed with ever-older bottles of balsamic vinegar.

But the real triumph of the cuisine is in the American home—where pizza, lasagna, manicotti, meatballs, veal parmigiana, through frozen food, or delivery food, or home cookin', play a tremendously vital role in the everyday fare of Americans. And, I daresay, what we learned from Italian-American food is extremely important—that food with origins in another country can not only become an interesting diversion here, but solidly part of our mainstream fare.

THE NEW IMMIGRATION

This got proved again and again. The rest of the 20th century saw the arrival of multiple immigrant groups—and, with a national palate "softened up" by the twin triumphs of Chinese-American cuisine and Italian-American cuisine, the gradual acceptance of many ethnic cuisines into our everyday lives. Though the immigration to America of such European groups as Greeks and French and Scandinavians, for example, was not in numbers approaching the Italian immigration, we still find gyro and souvlaki and shish kebab stands on many an urban corner, we still celebrate the French way of approaching food as a cornerstone of our American kitchen, and we still give Danish pastry a solid position in the world of the American breakfast.

Beyond Europe, foods from the rest of the world too have merged into the American menu. Has any restaurant type, after the pizza parlor, conquered our cities as the sushi bar has in recent years? Have you noticed, of late, the rapid rise of South American grilling restaurants, with Brazilian churrascarias and Argentine parrilladas paving the way? And what of the smaller-than-a-movement but bigger-than-a-quirk ethnic eateries of all descriptions that are mushrooming—from Afghan kebab houses to Korean BBQs, from Ethiopian injeera joints to Cuban pork places, from Indian curry parlors to Thai noodle houses?

But that's not all, in gastronomic America. What's especially compelling about all of this gastronomic activity on these shores is the "melting pot" factor. Yes, at the neighborhood ethnic spots, Thai food doesn't fuse with Cuban, Polish cuisine doesn't get hitched to Philippine. But let an American house-wife take home from the Thai restaurant a taste for coconut milk in stews, and before long—helped by the extraordinary boom in grocery availability—she's combining Uncle George's Hungarian paprikash with Thai red curry. And at the higher levels of cooking, this kind of cross-fertilization goes on at an even more furious pace—with high-profile American chefs raiding the culinary stockpiles of scores of ethnic cuisines from around the world, creating, night after night, hybridized gastronomic flings that the world has never seen before.

It is, in America, always a transformative process . . . and what always comes out is always American food.

Questions for Discussion and Writing

1. What characterizes American food for you? What foods do you associate with specific occasions through the year? Write about what food means to you and your family.

2. Rosengarten suggests that the American cuisine is built around eating to live, rather than living to eat. Do you agree? Does this explain American fast food?

3. Think about the American focus on diets and health foods. How have these elements affected the kinds of foods that are available and the desire to eat foods from other nations (for example, Chinese food seems to lead to a lower incidence of heart disease).

4. Design a meal that would fuse all of the elements that define American cuisine to you. Explain how each part of the meal fits within your overall impression of American food.

Can't Help Falling in Love with World's Elvis Impersonators

JOHN FLINN

John Flinn is the editor of The San Francisco Examiner's *travel section, for which he writes a weekly column and feature articles. He is a keen outdoor sporting enthusiast taking the opportunity to go hiking, rock climbing, and cross-country skiing in Northern California whenever he can. In this article for* The Examiner, *Mr. Flinn talks about the continuing global impact of Elvis Presley (who died in 1977) and how, as he has traveled the world, each country offers its own interpretation of "The King." This article was published on February 8, 2004.*

◆

In the town of Gold Coast, in Queensland, Australia, a mayoral candidate named Dean Vegas recently vowed to govern in a white jumpsuit if elected. He's one of Australia's top Elvis impersonators. In Hamburg, Elvis impersonator Shezad "Shelvis" Eikmeier set a world record last month by singing Elvis songs for 40 hours, eight minutes, without letup. The previous record of 26 hours, four minutes had been held by Kjell Henning Bjoernstad, the No. 1 Elvis impersonator in Norway. In northern England, Eddie Vee, "the Yorkshire Elvis," ran for parliament in 2001 on a platform calling for an Elvis memorial garden in York. He lost, but by the time you read this Vee might have broken Eikmeier's record. He was planning to give it a go at the European Elvis impersonator championships in Blackpool at the end of January.

Travel teaches us that, deep down inside, we're all astonishingly similar. And of all human yearnings, it would seem, one of the most universal must be the urge to fling sweaty silk scarves into an audience while croaking an off-key rendition of "Burning Love." The Guinness Book of World Records estimates that around the globe there are more than 35,000 Elvis impersonators—or, as they're known in the trade, "Elvis tribute artists," or simply "ETAs"—in, among other places, Malaysia, Mexico, France, Japan, Ireland, Spain, the Philippines, Israel and China ("the King from Beijing"). This weirdly ubiquitous American cultural export has fascinated me for many years, ever since I spent an evening with Tomaz, the Slovenian Elvis impersonator. This was back in 1990, when the former Yugoslavia was still the present Yugoslavia, and I'm pretty sure Tomaz had the field to himself.

My wife, Jeri, and I were on an evening stroll through the lakeside town of Bled, not far from the Austrian border, when we heard snatches of oddly familiar music tinkling down the cobbled streets. We traced it to a beer garden at the edge of town, where a band was wrapping up a traditional Slovenian folk song, a tune tinged with melancholy and heavy on the accordion. The sparse audience, mostly vacationers from the nearby capital of Ljubljana, put down their beer mugs long enough to applaud politely. Then the singer turned his back to the crowd, slicked his black hair back, hunched his shoulders forward and, in a metamorphosis worthy of Andy Kaufman, became Elvis. This was not the Vegas Elvis, the jumpsuit-and-mutton-chop Elvis, the caricature Elvis. This was the savage young rock 'n' roll Elvis, in tight jeans and black leather jacket. With a curl of the lip and a shake of the hip, he tore into a blistering version of "Jailhouse Rock." When he finished, the crowd once again put down its beer mugs and clapped politely. Then out came the accordion, and the band struck up another mournful Slovenian folk tune. Jeri and I seemed to be the only ones who thought this odd.

When the band took a break, we went over to say hello. The singer, Tomaz, sat by himself and gloomily sipped a beer.

"Tomaz is having—how you say?—girlfriend troubles," said the bass player.

"Tomaz is always having girlfriend troubles," said the drummer.

I went over to Tomaz and asked him how he came to be an Elvis impersonator.

"What does this mean, 'Elvis impersonator?' " he said.

In America, I explained, there seemed to be an ersatz Elvis in every cocktail lounge and shopping mall. They entertained at bar mitzvahs, marched in formation in Fourth of July parades and jumped en masse out of airplanes. It had become kind of national joke.

"Why is this joke?" Tomaz said. "I want to be like Elvis. He is number one. He is king."

Tomaz, it seemed, was unaware of the whole impersonator phenomenon. He just had an overpowering need to give voice to his inner Elvis. He honed his moves, he said, by watching old Elvis movies, like "Viva Las Vegas," on Slovenian TV. His English was marginal at best, and I gathered he learned the lyrics phonetically. "Love Me Tender," for instance, came out "loo me dander."

The owner of the beer garden wanted to hear Slovenian folk music, but the band was determined to slip in some Elvis numbers and a few of their original rock 'n' roll songs, hence the odd set lists. Tomaz told me they currently had the No. 2 song on the charts.

"No. 2 in all of Yugoslavia?" I said. "That's pretty cool."

"Not Yugoslavia," said Tomaz. "No. 2 in Slovenia."

Each of the Yugoslavian states, he explained—Slovenia, Croatia, Serbia, etc.—had its own pop charts. Crossover hits were apparently rare. Tomaz told me Slovenians did not like to listen to

Croatian music, and vice versa. This was not long before Yugoslavia began to break apart, its tortured experiment with multiculturalism giving way to ethnic cleansing and overrun safe zones. It was a small but telling sign, I thought, that the people sitting in the beer garden didn't mind hearing traditional Slovenian folk music juxtaposed with 40-year-old American rock 'n' roll. But they refused to listen to the music of their ostensible countrymen a few miles down the road. In less than a year, Slovenia would declare its independence, and there would briefly be fighting around Ljubljana. When it happened, I thought immediately of Tomaz. I imagined a frightened young man cringing under incoming artillery shells and perhaps quietly humming "loo me dander" to calm himself.

This, I think, is one of the most important benefits of travel. When we read of wars or disasters in far-off lands, the people involved are no longer faceless Slovenians or Palestinians or Kashmiris. They're people we know—real people with lives and dreams of their own. They get yelled at by their bosses and daydream about holidays at the seashore and suffer through girlfriend troubles.

And quite a few of them, I've discovered, want to be Elvis.

Questions for Discussion and Writing

1. Explain the discrepancy between the seriousness of Tomaz and John Flinn's expectation that impersonating Elvis is in some way funny.
2. Discuss why Elvis Presley has inspired so many impersonators. Research elements of the Elvis mythos—for example, Elvis impersonators have appeared in movies, and tabloids still report Elvis sightings all over the world.
3. What is the uniting power of a cultural icon like Elvis? Flinn seems to feel that there is a comfort in the familiarity and universality of such icons in times of strife. How do you feel about that? Can you think of any personal examples?

Italian Rappers Try to Hang On

ELISABETTA POVOLEDO

Elisabetta Povoledo has a Masters degree in Art History from the University of McGill in Montreal and studied art in Rome, Urbino, and Winnipeg, Manitoba, where she grew up. She has been employed as a journalist for the past decade, working for

Italian state radio and several American publications, including
The New York Times *and the* International Herald Tribune
(where this article appeared on May 4, 2004), focusing on Italian
culture. She lives in Rome, Italy. In this article she writes about
rap music in Italy.

———————————— ✦ ————————————

Except for the language, the Italian rapper Frankie Hi-Nrg MC's concert at Milan's Alcatraz club in mid-April didn't seem to differ much from its American counterparts. The music was pounding, the beats syncopated, records were scratched and sampled, words flowed like quicksilver. Still, in his light blue tracksuit and outsize black frame eyeglasses that hid a slightly goofy expression, Frankie—always a politicized rapper—looked more like a ball boy for Italy's national soccer team than a musical public enemy. And his lyrics, though scurrilous, were never outright obscene.

Frankie's song "Rap Lament," off his latest recording, "Ero un autarchico" (I was self-sufficient), which is being plugged with a national tour, used a soccer metaphor to depict the Italian Republic. Parliament was a "crazy stadium," playing a championship with "two teams wearing identical uniforms." Hardly your misogynistic "gangsta rap" anthem. But Frankie, a.k.a. Francesco Di Gesù, got the crowd riled up when he asserted that some TV stations had refused to play his song. "They think it's too disparaging," he said, "and small radios don't play it because they're afraid someone will say something. This is Italy."

Actually, anyone stumbling into the crowded concert hall—a breathing catalogue of popular American sportswear brands—might have thought this was the United States (or Germany or Japan), at least at first. As far as fashion is concerned, hip-hop culture is making acolytes of many young Italians who have shunned made-in-Italy chic to enthusiastically embrace (sloppier) American trends. "There's a lot of interest in fashion," agreed Daniel Marcoccia, managing editor of Groove magazine, Italy's only magazine dedicated to hip-hop, R&B and reggae, whose advertisers are mostly sportswear companies. "Rappers love to show their brands. Hip-hop is tied to gadgets."

These days, mainstream Italian rap is getting a lot of attention. But if hip-hop in the United States has become the voice for many disaffected and angry young men, in Italy it has tended to be less violent and certainly less misogynistic. "Rappers are much nicer here," said Alberto Castelli, who manages the Roman rapper Piotta, the stage name of Tommaso Zanello. That was also true when politicized Italian rappers adopted traditional dialects like Neapolitan or Pugliese to lash out against such problems as the Mafia or southern Italy's high unemployment.

By American standards, where rap is a multimillion-dollar industry, Italy's homegrown edition has a tiny market, falling far short even of other European countries like Germany, and especially France, where hip-hop sales are second only to the United States. But low demand hasn't stopped the nation's aspiring rappers from turning to small independent labels to have their voices heard and hope for at least modest sales.

"Just call me the Puff Daddy of the poor," laughed Castelli, who also manages small record labels. "It's still an underground market, you'll sell a few thousand copies of a record at best." But Castelli says he believes that in the near future Italian rap will benefit both from the increased popularity of American rap and R&B here, as well as the move many rappers are making from the underground into the mainstream. In March, Piotta and Frankie performed at the San Remo Song Festival, a schmaltzy televised pop music competition. "It's a promotional window that lets you reach millions of people," Castelli said. "Your three minutes during San Remo is like months of touring." Piotta, who competed at the festival, came in last. "That's O.K. It's better to come in last and maintain your credibility," Castelli said.

For years now, hip-hop culture has influenced many aspects of American society, including the visual arts. But here, it was only in the past few years that graffiti, for instance, made the jump from illegal street scrawl to popular art. For most of April, Milan's central train station offered the exhibition "Now Underground," which featured the work of 45 graffiti artists from around the world. "This is like a Renaissance, I feel like it's coming," said Plank, one of the featured artists in the show, the third exhibition he had worked on in the past year. The first was sponsored by Dank shoes.

Near Naples, another graffiti-scrawled area, the region's administrators decided to offer painters an official venue to vent their creativity. Since December, crews of artists have been tacking the walls of the train stations along the Circumvesuviana, the railway that links all the towns at the base of Mount Vesuvius. About 40 stations will be decorated. In giving the writers the space and recognizing the "artistic value and the function of the drawings," the Campania regional government and the railway company hoped to "link the stations to their urban context." They also hoped to reduce vandalism.

"They could see that this could develop into a project with a high social value," said Luca Borriello of Evoluzioni, a group that helped coordinate the project and is organizing the Italian hip-hop awards, which Borriello said would take place this summer. He said that Italian hip-hop was now entering its second generation, which saw a greater number of artists "professionalizing their passion" and so making it legitimate.

But some fans miss the days when Italian hip-hop was more interested in being Italian than in being part of a global phenomenon. Joseph Sciorra of Queens College's John D. Calandra Italian American Institute and the creator of www.italianrap.com, said that one of the problems "is that Italian hip-hop lost its focus." "Instead of being concentrated on the social life of everyday Italy," he added, "hip-hop began to copy the corporate American scene, with its focus on gangsta rap, which we know sold more to white kids in Middle America than it did to urban blacks." Frankie Hi-Nrg agreed: "I have the impression that the influence of commercial American rap has dulled our version a lot. Hip-hop is worldwide and, depending on where you are, it brings out the essence of a place. So there's no reason to imitate the flavor and the feelings of another place. That's why I speak about things that I see as our problems. I expose our raw nerves."

Questions for Discussion and Writing

1. Write a description of the key elements of American rap music and compare them with the aspects of Italian rap discussed by Povoledo.
2. Why is Italian rap trying to "hang on"? What characterizes the resistance from Italian culture?

Hollywood Warms to Asian Movies, American-Style

RENEE GRAHAM

Renee Graham is a freelance writer who provided this story for The New York Times *News Service. It was published on February 15, 2005. In the article Graham discusses Hollywood's growing trend of taking Asian movies and remaking them in English—sometimes even using the same directors who helmed the original version. Graham examines the pros and cons of remaking movies from a different culture in an American image.*

——————————— ✦ ———————————

One of the most discussed movies this year is one that won't even be in theaters until 2006. A Boston-based crime thriller, *The Departed*, boasts an A-list cast including Matt Damon, Leonardo DiCaprio, and Mark Wahlberg. Jack Nicholson has reportedly signed on for a crucial supporting role, and Martin Scorsese will direct. Despite all the buzz, what many people won't know is that it's a remake of the taut, stylish Hong Kong drama *Infernal Affairs*, a 2002 film that got a brief run at the Brattle Theatre last November.

If there's a trend to be found in recent cinema, it's the decidedly Eastern persuasion of more than a few American movies. *The Grudge*, *The Ring*, and *Shall We Dance?* were all based on Japanese originals, and together they pulled in nearly $300 million domestically.

And that's just the beginning: Major studios are continuing to snap up the rights to films from South Korea, Japan, and Hong Kong with the intention of remaking them with American actors. By some estimates, at least two-dozen Asian films are slated for remakes, including South Korea's *Old Boy*, *Il Mare*, and *A Tale of Two Sisters*, and *The Eye*, a Hong Kong/Thailand production. And before even a single frame of the *The Departed* has been shot, Scorsese and DiCaprio are already in negotiations to remake yet another Asian movie, Japanese director Akira Kurosawa's 1948 noir *Drunken Angel*.

Mercifully, we aren't likely to have to endure anything as unsightly as, say, Brad Pitt, Renee Zellweger, and Ben Affleck in an American remake of *House of Flying Daggers*, the current arthouse film by acclaimed Chinese filmmaker Zhang Yimou. But high-wire martial arts stories are about the only Asian films that aren't garnering major attention from Hollywood.

For all the effort being dedicated to remaking Asian movies, however, some wonder whether the same vigor and funding would be better spent promoting the original films, which are often more audacious and challenging than the sometimes watered-down remakes that wind up in American multiplexes.

"Personally, I think 'remakes' are a good thing because it provides exposure for the original source material," says David Leong, news editor of Kung Fu Cult Cinema (kfccinema.com), a popular Asian-film website. "But it's also a bad thing, because the remakes are rarely up to the standards of the originals. Some of the themes are denser in the original source, and they— Hollywood studio—tend to dumb them down. Character development is taken out or plot points are roughed over, and that's a sore point for a lot of fans who like Asian films."

While Hollywood's burst of interest in Asian films might be new, for decades savvy Western filmmakers have taken inspiration from their counterparts in the East. John Sturges's 1960 Western *The Magnificent Seven* was a remake of Kurosawa's 1954 classic *Seven Samurai*. Kurosawa's *Yojimbo* provided the blueprint for Sergio Leone's *A Fistful of Dollars* (as did actor Toshiro Mifune's droll ronin for Clint Eastwood's iconic Man with No Name), as well as Walter Hill's *Last Man Standing*, a lousy 1996 film starring Bruce Willis. And a prime influence for George Lucas's *Star Wars* was *The Hidden Fortress*, also by Kurosawa.

Yet, except for cinephiles, most folks are more familiar with the American remakes. These days, Roy Lee, a partner in the independent production company Vertigo Entertainment, is Hollywood's point man for Asian remakes. Lee finds what he considers the best Asian films, negotiates the remake rights, and sells them to Hollywood studios. He facilitated the remakes of *Ringu*, *Ju-on*, and *Infernal Affairs*, as well as upcoming Americanized versions of the South Korean comedies *My Sassy Girl* and *My Wife Is a Gangster*.

"These are films people here were never exposed to in a way that would make them adaptable to the U.S. market," Lee says. "We take the projects, match them up with actors, writers, and directors, and pitch the studios as to exactly how we would do it in the United States. Before that, Asian films were watched by the acquisitions side of the studios, looking at them only for release purposes."

And remakes, with recognizable actors and no subtitles, tend to be far more profitable than foreign films.

"There's still tremendous resistance to subtitles" among American filmgoers, says Martin Grove, an online columnist for *The Hollywood Reporter*. "People aren't used to reading subtitles, and they don't like doing it." (One of the few exceptions to this rule is Yimou's *Hero*, which pulled in more than $53 million last year. It was greatly helped by action star Jet Li's above-the-title billing and a hearty endorsement from devoted Asian film fan Quentin Tarantino.)

Still, in opting for a remake, American audiences are sometimes cheated of an original film's singular charm and viewpoint. Such was the case with last year's *Shall We Dance?* based on a Japanese film of the same name released here in 1997. That film's cultural component didn't have the same resonance in the American version. In Masayuki Suo's movie, a businessman, stifled by his country's restrictive cultural order, achieves emotional freedom when he enrolls in a dance school. In the American version, Gere's workaholic lawyer seeks a refuge from life's demands, yet the remake lacks the original's poignancy and subtle social critique.

"Certain things just don't translate on a one-to-one basis," Leong says. "The whole idea of being a bottled-up, repressed worker and finding release in dancing just didn't work as well because America is a totally different society. I believe if you treat your audience with respect, you'll get the payoff," he maintains. "Unfortunately, the studios don't think American audiences are intelligent enough to follow a movie plot that's not American. There's a lack of respect by Hollywood studios that, in the end, irritates people. They change the flow of a movie, the intent of a scene; you change the original director's vision, and you end up with trash."

In acquiring the rights to Asian films, Lee has developed a sense for which films probably won't work as remakes. He likes comedies, thrillers, and horror films, but tends to steer clear of "dramas rooted into the culture with family and relationships. They're just harder to translate."

Still, as Leong asserts, Hollywood's interest in Asia has also created a small but burgeoning market for original Asian films. Last year, Kino Video released *The Wong Kar-Wai Collection*, featuring five films from the Hong Kong auteur, as well as prolific Japanese filmmaker Takashi Miike's outrageously graphic *Dead or Alive* trilogy. Home Vision Entertainment put out *The Yakuza Papers: Battles Without Honor & Humanity*, Kinji Fukasaku's tremendously compelling five-part gangster epic, which has often been compared to the *Godfather* films.

And films such as *Ringu*, *Ju-on*, *Shall We Dance?* and *Infernal Affairs*, once only available as expensive imports or dodgy bootlegs, are now regularly stocked in stores selling or renting DVDs.

"I had these awful copies of *Ringu* from the UK and Hong Kong—the subtitles were bad, the picture quality was terrible.

Now the best copy out there is the Region 1 DVDs playable in North America," says Jimmy Nguyen, a Kung Fu Cult Cinema film critic. "With all the remakes and attention toward Asian cinema, even films that aren't being remade are being released on video. That's a great thing. You'd go to Blockbuster, and you were really limited in the foreign section, but now there's all these Korean and Japanese films. It's cool."

The trend has also presented opportunities for Asian film-makers. *The Grudge* was remade by its original director, Takashi Shimizu. And Hideo Nakata, who helmed *Ringu* and its sequel, was tapped for *The Ring 2* . . . Others such as Hong Kong's Johnnie To are also being courted, much as American studios enticed Ang Lee and John Woo in the 1990s.

. . . *The Departed* is scheduled to begin shooting in Boston, and expectations for the film's success are high. Some also hope this remake will respect the integrity of its Hong Kong inspiration, *Infernal Affairs*, which might have found an American audience if it had been given a real chance.

"I'm looking forward to it because Scorsese is a great film-maker, and it'll be interesting to see how he vamps off the originals," Leong says. "But I also dread it because if they pretty it up, it could be a totally different movie."

Questions for Discussion and Writing

1. Rent and watch the original version of *Ringu* or *Ju-on* and then watch the American remake (*The Ring* or *The Grudge*). What differences do you notice in the two versions? Why do you think certain changes were made? Were the films remade to make them palatable to the American audience?

2. Graham covers the subject of subtitled films. What is your experience of watching a film with subtitles? Do you find it distracting? Why? Do you feel alienated from the film by not being able to understand the language? Is it a barrier to you wanting to see films from overseas?

3. If you were an Asian film director and you heard that your film was going to be remade in America, how would you react? What would be your major concerns about a remake? What, for example, does David Leong mean when he is worried about Hollywood deciding to "pretty up" *Infernal Affairs*?

4. Is this culture of remaking foreign films a new phenomenon? For example, investigate and write about the films remade by Josef von Sternberg and Greta Garbo in the early days of Hollywood.

Gwenihana

MiHi Ahn

MiHi Ahn is a writer from San Francisco, California. This article appeared on the Salon.com *website on April 9, 2005, and has proved to be contentious inside and outside the Asian-American community. In the article Ahn takes issue with the stereotyping of Asian women that she sees in the use of the Harajuku Girls by singer Gwen Stefani. As well as being a contributor and reviewer for* Salon, *MiHi Ahn has also written for* Mother Jones, *the* Columbia News Service, *and the* South Asian Women's Forum.

◆

Back when I worked for a political magazine, a big cowboy-hat-wearing Texan who was some sort of DNC muck-a-muck would occasionally come by the office. While most good liberals take pains to say my name correctly, sometimes overly exoticizing the pronunciation with bizarre emphasis and guttural stops that my own mother couldn't replicate, this particular fellow would just fill in the blank with any name that sounded vaguely Asian-y. Never tentative, he would bellow across the room, "Hey there, Michiko" or "How you doing, Ming Na?" I braced for the day I would hear "How's it hanging, Mulan?" or "What's going down, Madame Butterfly?" "Can I get a whoop-whoop, Kikkoman?" Or maybe simply: "Hello, Kitty."

These days, names like Hayao Miyazaki, animation grand-daddy, or Takashi Murakami, the man whose colorful rendition of the Louis Vuitton print sold purses like crazy and who just appeared on a recent cover of *New York Times Magazine*, roll off the tongues of urban hipsters and the fashion forward. *The Cartoon Network*'s programming is anime heavy, movies like *The Ring* and *The Grudge* demonstrate that Hollywood increasingly looks East for inspiration, and along the way, the public is becoming enlightened. Even Norelle, last season's resident bird brain on *America's Next Top Model*, seemed appropriately embarrassed that Panda Express is, like, Chinese and not Japanese. And then there's Gwen Stefani.

Stefani, the platinum-blond No Doubt front woman with the undulating midriff, recently released her first solo album, *Love, Angel, Music, Baby*, a riotous jumble of everything from '80s bubble-gum pop to hip-hop to *Fiddler on the Roof* gone mad on

a pirate ship. And tying all these influences together in one baf-
fling mélange of semiotic ambiguity is her ever-present entourage:
Four harajuku girls, or rather, Stefani's interpretation of Tokyo
street fashion in the Harajuku district. They shadow her wherever
she goes. They're on the cover of the album, they appear behind
her on the red carpet, she even dedicates a track, *Harajuku Girls*,
to them. In interviews, they silently vogue in the background like
living props; she, meanwhile, likes to pretend that they're not real
but only a figment of her imagination. They're ever present in her
videos and performances—swabbing the deck aboard the pirate
ship, squatting gangsta style in a high school gym while pumping
their butts up and down, simpering behind fluttering hands or
bowing to Stefani. That's right, bowing. Not even from the waist,
but on the ground in a "we're not worthy, we're not worthy" pose.
She's taken Tokyo hipsters, sucked them dry of all their street
cred, and turned them into China dolls.

Real harajuku girls are just the funky dressers who hang out
in the Japanese shopping district of Harajuku. To the uniniti-
ated, harajuku style can look like what might happen if a 5-year-
old girl jacked up on liquor and goofballs decided to become a
stylist. Layering is important, as is the mix of seemingly dis-
parate styles and colors. Vintage couture can be mixed with traditional Japanese costumes, thrift-store classics, Lolita-esque
flourishes and cyber-punk accessories. In a culture where the
dreaded "salary man/woman" office worker is a fate to be
avoided for this never-wanna-grow-up generation, harajuku
style can look as radical as punk rockers first looked on
London's King Road or how pale-faced Goths silently sweating
in their widows weeds look in cheerful sunny suburbs. Stefani
has taken the idea of Japanese street fashion and turned these
women into modern-day geisha, contractually obligated to
speak only Japanese in public, even though it's rumored they're
just plain old Americans and their English is just fine. She's
even named them "Love," "Angel," "Music" and "Baby" after her
album and new clothing line l.a.m.b. (perhaps a mutton-themed
restaurant will follow). The renaming of four adults led one
poster on a message board to muse, "I didn't think it was legal
to own human pets. But I guess so if you have the money for it."
Stefani fawns over harajuku style in her lyrics, but her appropriation of this subculture makes about as much sense as the
Gap selling Anarchy T-shirts; she's swallowed a subversive
youth culture in Japan and barfed up another image of submissive giggling Asian women. While aping a style that's suppose to

be about individuality and personal expression, Stefani ends up being the only one who stands out.

It's not only Stefani whose big kiss to the East ends up feeling more like a big Pacific Rim job. Author Peter Carey's own recent foray into Japanophila, the book *Wrong About Japan*, was a semi-autobiographical account of one clueless father's attempt to bond with his son over manga on a trip to Japan, and his futile attempts to understand Japanese culture through a Western filter. Why devote an entire book to being *Wrong About Japan*, when you can just send out a one-page fax that reads, "They *Are* Inscrutable." Even some of the movies that consciously play with Japanese stereotypes can seem puerile no matter how fast the postmodern hipster spin, whether it's Lucy Liu's blood-lusting geisha in *Kill Bill*, or Devon Aoki's killer Miho in the new *Sin City*, who slays a multitude but is never allowed to utter a single word.

In the same *New York Times Magazine* story that featured Murakami on the cover, the Dutch photographer Hellen van Meene was commissioned to photograph portraits of prepubescent girls and teens. The girls all look limp and innocent. Big, fat, unsmiling red lips like two slabs of raw ahi positioned on baby faces. It has that creepy porn feeling that I suppose is meant to reflect the Japanese predilection for "kawaii," or cute, and the sexualized image of schoolgirls. But this is not the way these girls really are. The accompanying text says that "while [van Meene] does not exactly 'stage' her subjects, neither does she try to capture their true, underlying personality or state of mind. Instead, she chooses to see her subjects as the raw material of her own fictions." Van Meene elaborates, "This is not just you now. This is a sense of you, created by me." Well, at least she's honest.

Questions for Discussion and Writing

1. MiHi Ahn claims that Gwen Stefani has "swallowed a subversive youth culture in Japan and barfed up another image of submissive giggling Asian women." Do you think that this is true based on the description here? What elements highlight the stereotyping of Asian women for MiHi Ahn? Find some photographs of Stefani and the Harajuku girls. Do you see the same things as Ahn does?

2. One of Ahn's concerns is the stereotyping of Asian women—she gives many examples in this short article. All of the Asian women, however, allowed themselves to be depicted in this way. If you were one of the Harajuku girls or (for example) Lucy Liu, how would contradict the points that MiHi Ahn is making?

General Questions for Chapter Five

1. If the United States both influences world culture and takes other cultures and assimilates them into its own, does this create a cultural hegemony that is positive or negative? Draw on the examples from the chapters in this book and from examples of your own to explain how cultural assimilation works and whether you feel it is of global benefit or simply advances a feeling of Americanization around the world.

2. What is a simulacrum? How does it work and what is its purpose? Look at the examples mentioned in the essays in this chapter and talk about any experiences you have had with such things. Is making a copy or re-creation of something a form of flattery and praise or should it be seen as a belittling and condescending exercise?

3. Many of the writers in this book have equated the intentions and ideologies of the United States as being driven purely by capitalism and profiteering. Given all of the information that you now have, do you agree with this stance? Using the essays in this chapter, does the idea that commerce, architecture, art, and music are all from the same realm in the American system seem true to you? How would you support or oppose this idea?

Ahn, MiHi. "Gwenihana." © 2005 Salon.com. This article first appeared in Salon.com at http://www.salon.com. An online version remains in the Salon archives. Reprinted with permission. **Al-Shaykh, Hanan.** "What We Think of America" (1) From *Granta* 77, 2003. © 2003 Hana al-Shaykh. **Bayles, Martha.** "Exporting the Wrong Picture." From *The Washington Post*, 28 August 2005. © 2005 Martha Bayles. **Bhargava, Rajeev.** "Responses to 9.11: Individual and Collective Dimensions." From the *Social Research Council* website at http://www.ssrc.org. © 2003 Rajeev Bhargava. **Bush, George W.** "America's International Strategy." From the *White House website*. The whole document can be found at: http://www.whitehouse.gov/nsc/nss.html. **Cohen, Roger, David E. Sanger and Steven R Weisman.** "Challenging the Rest of the World with a New Order." Copyright © 2004 by *The New York Times Co.* Reprinted with permission. **Danto, Arthur C.** "Degas in Vegas." Reprinted with permission from the March 1, 1999 issue of *The Nation*. For subscription information, call 1-800-333-8536. Portions of each week's Nation magazine can be accessed at http://www.thenation.com. **De la Gaarde, Roger.** "Americanization." From *Encyclopedia of Television* by The Museum of Broadcast Communications (MBC). Copyright © 1997 by The Museum of Broadcast Communications (MBC). Reprinted by permission. **Flinn, John.** "Can't help falling in love with world's Elvis impersonators." From the *San Francisco Chronicle*, 8 Feb, 2004. © John Flinn. **Friedman, Thomas.** "It's a Flat World After All." "It's a Flat World After All." By Thomas L. Friedman appeared in *The New York Times Magazine*, April 3, 2005 and was adapted by the author from his book, *THE WORLD IS FLAT* by Thomas L. Friedman. Copyright © 2005 by Thomas L. Friedman. Reprinted by permission of Farrar, Straus and Giroux, LLC. **Giddens, Anthony.** "Globalization." Copyright © 2002. From *Runaway World* by Anthony Giddens, pages 6–19. Reproduced by permission of Routledge/Taylor & Francis Group, LLC. **Graham, Renee.** "Hollywood Warms to Asian Movies." From *The Boston Globe*, February 13th, 2005, page N14. © 2005 The Boston Globe. Reprinted with permission. **Hankiss, Elemer.** "Symbols of Destruction." From the *Social Research Council* website at http://www.ssrc.org. © 2003 Elemer Hankiss. **Koh, Harold Hongju.** "Rights to Remember." From *The Economist*, Oct 30, 2003. © 2003 The Economist Newspaper Ltd. All rights reserved. **Kohut, Andrew.** "American Public Diplomacy in the Islamic World." Testimony given to the Senate Foreign Affairs Committee, 2003. © 2003 Andrew Kohut, President of the Pew Research Center. **Lindsay, James M. and Ivo H. Daalder.** "The Globalization of Politics: American Foreign Policy for a New Century." From *The Brookings Review*, Winter 2003, Vol. 21 (1) 12–17. © 2003 The Brookings Institution. **Marqusee, Mike.** "Global Sports, American Sports." From *Colorlines*, March 2000. © 2000 Mike Marqusee. **Miller, Laura.** "America the Ignorant." © 2001 Salon.com. This article first appeared in Salon.com at http://www.salon.com. An online version remains in the Salon archives. Reprinted with permission. **Mintz, Lawrence.** "Simulated Tourism at Busch Gardens: The Old Country, and Walt Disney World Showcase, EPCOT Center." From *Journal of Popular Culture*, 32(3):47–59, 1998. © 1998 Lawrence Mintz. **O'Connor, Brendon.** "Bored with the USA?" From the *Courier Mail* (Australia) Jun 21, 2003. © 2003 Brendon O'Connor. **Parris, Matthew.** "It's time we all signed up for the Rest of the World team." From The Times of London (UK), April 12, 2003. © 2003 News International Limited. **Pells, Richard.** "American Culture Goes Global, or Does It?" From *The Chronicle of Higher Education*, April 12, 2002. © 2002 Richard Pells. **Povoledo, Elisabetta.** "Italian Rappers Try To Hang On." From the *International Herald Tribune*, May 4, 2004. © 2004 by *The New York Times Co.* Reprinted with permission. **Rice-Oxley, Mark.** "In 2000 Years, Will the World Remember Disney or Plato?" By Mark Rice-Oxley. Reproduced with permission from the January 15, 2004 issue of *The Christian Science Monitor* (www.csmonitor.com). © 2004 The Christian Science Monitor. All rights reserved. **Roberts, Dan.** "Is the World Falling Out of Love with US Brands?" From *The Financial Times*, Dec 29, 2004. © 2004